A Queer Way of Feeling

FEMINIST MEDIA HISTORIES

Shelley Stamp, Series Editor

A Queer Way of Feeling

*Girl Fans and Personal Archives
of Early Hollywood*

Diana W. Anselmo

UNIVERSITY OF CALIFORNIA PRESS

University of California Press
Oakland, California

Library of Congress Cataloging-in-Publication Data

Names: Anselmo, Diana W., author.
Title: A queer way of feeling : girl fans and personal
   archives of early Hollywood / Diana W. Anselmo.
Other titles: Feminist media histories (Series) ; 4.
Description: Oakland, California : University of
   California Press, [2023] | Series: Feminist media
   histories; 4 | Includes bibliographical references and
   index.
Identifiers: LCCN 2022022427 (print) | LCCN 2022022428
   (ebook) | ISBN 9780520299641 (cloth) | ISBN
   9780520299658 (paperback) | ISBN 9780520971295
   (ebook)
Subjects: LCSH: Homosexuality and motion pictures. |
   Lesbianism—United States—20th century. | Motion
   pictures and women. | Fans (Persons)—United
   States—20th century. | Young women—United
   States—20th century.
Classification: LCC PN1995.9.L48 A57 2023 (print) |
   LCC PN1995.9.L48 (ebook) | DDC 791.43086/643—
   dc23/eng/20220721
LC record available at https://lccn.loc.gov/2022022427
LC ebook record available at https://lccn.loc
   .gov/2022022428

Manufactured in the United States of America

32 31 30 29 28 27 26 25 24 23
10 9 8 7 6 5 4 3 2 1

The publisher and the University of California Press Foundation gratefully acknowledge the generous support of the Kenneth Turan and Patricia Williams Endowment Fund in American Film.

Contents

Acknowledgments

I often think of writing as conversations with the dead.

Because of the nature of its primary sources, writing this book felt like conducting a séance, a series of mediated communications with the first generation of girls who loved the movies, who loved them through overlapping times of transformation: adolescence, the birth of Hollywood and media fandom, the Great War. It was a long and painstaking process, researching this book, and it was a challenge to write, because its threads, much like spirits, often felt fugitive, connections surfacing as quickly as they dissipated in dead ends: lack of biographical information, incomplete finding aids, illness, self-doubt. I am grateful for the support of a host of institutions, archivists, colleagues, and loved ones, for their kindness and insight kept the lifeblood flowing in a shapeshifting project that spanned almost a decade.

This book would not have come to fruition without the germane support of doctoral-study grants from the Fulbright/FLAD Program in 2006 and the FCT/European Union in 2011. In the visual studies PhD program at the University of California, Irvine, Kristen Hatch, Bliss Cua Lim, Vicky Johnson, and Cécile Whiting provided valuable feedback at the early stages of my research, while Catherine Benamou and Edward Dimmenberg offered professional advice and support. Funds supplied by the California Studies Research Consortium, the University of California, Irvine's Humanities Research Institute, the School of Humanities, and the Institute for Writing and Translation, as well as the

Phi Beta Kappa Alumni International Scholarship Award, enabled me to travel to collections and present preliminary findings. The Media History Digital Library.org, Archive.org, and the Library of Congress-Chronicling America project supplied infinitely helpful resources.

Like ghosts, ideas thrive when people believe in them. There are no words to express my profound gratitude to Miriam Forman-Brunell, who changed the course of my work with her unfailing support, and to the Department of English at the University of Pittsburgh, where I held a Kenneth Dietrich Postdoctoral Fellowship in Film Studies from 2015 to 2017. Thank you to Mark Lynn Anderson and Lynn Arner, who welcomed me into their home and provided continuous encouragement; to Tyler Bickford, Lucy Fischer, Jane Feuer, Randall Halle, Neepa Majumdar, Courtney Weikle-Mills, Dana Och, Alison Patterson, Jules Gill-Peterson, and the collective of vibrant graduate students and administrators peopling the Cathedral of Learning, including the always dynamic Pitt Humanities Center.

Every archivist and librarian who ever guided me through byzantine finding aids and answered far-flung questions with patience and expertise holds a piece of this puzzle. My sincere thanks to the staff of the Library of Congress Motion Picture Research Center in Washington, DC, the Margaret Herrick Library in Los Angeles, the Seaver Centre in Los Angeles, the Bancroft Library at the University of California, Berkeley, the Washington Historical Society in Tacoma, and the Beinecke Library at Yale University. Thank you to Vassar College, Smith College, the Schlesinger Library at Harvard University, and the National Endowment for the Humanities at the Bard Graduate Center for awarding me research grants that facilitated my work.

To the community of scholars, reviewers, and staff at *Screen, Cinema Journal, Camera Obscura, Film History, Feminist Media Histories,* and *Spectator:* your engagement with my work unfailingly made it better. A partial version of chapter 4 first appeared in the journal *Film History.* Aggie Ebrahimi Bazaz, Márcia Gonçalves, Hilary Hallett, Olivia Landy, Ismail Xavier, Caetlin Benson-Allott, John Cahoon, Agatha Frymus, Mia K., Kelly Chung, Richard Abel, Maggie Hennefeld, Elana Lavine, Tamar Jeffers McDonald, and Brooke Wyatt: your support buoyed me at inflection points on this journey. My colleagues at Georgia State University—Jennifer Barker, Phil Lewis, Alessandra Raengo, Angelo Restivo, Jade Petermon, Ethan Tussey, and Greg Smith—as well as Nedda Ahmed, Regina Anderson, Denise Davidson, Maria Gindhart, Jamie Pellerito, Kelly Stout, Wade Weast, the Humanities Centre, and the College of the

Arts are all here acknowledged for their support. At the University of California Press, I am in debt to Raina Polivka, Jeff Anderson, Madison Wetzell, the press staff, and the anonymous reviewers for their patience, compassion, and helpful feedback.

Shelley Stamp, who back in 2012 asked, "What about the girls in the audience?," gently nudging me to think about the larger questions that would develop into this book: working with you and having you as a mentor for nearly a decade has shaped me into the scholar I am today, and saying I am thankful for your support, insight, and every one of our conversations is nothing but a gross understatement.

Kathy Fuller-Seeley, your generosity, wit, and knowledge knows no bounds, and it has spurred me to become a better film historian. Thank you for all the emails, the relentless optimism and cheerleading, the borrowed scrapbooks, the lemon curd crumpets, and the Ella Hall in my wall. If academia had more people like you, we would all flourish tenfold.

Helena Bauernschmitt, we have never met in person, but there are thousands of letters between us stretching over twenty-three years, and no one knows me for that long anymore. In an age of digital immediacy, I constantly marvel at such nugget of magic.

To my mother, Rosa Maria Anselmo, who is tireless in her support, and I suspect will continue to be so in every and any afterlife.

To cats, the kept and stray ones.

To fictional characters, past and present.

To my dead.

And to M. M. Chandler: we hold the red string even when the fabric frays.

Girl, Fan, Queer

Female Film Reception in the 1910s

We see dimly people, the people in whose living blood and
seed we ourselves lay dormant. They are . . . like a chemical
formula exhumed along with the letters from [a] forgotten
chest, carefully, the paper old and faded and falling to pieces,
the writing faded, almost indecipherable, yet meaningful, . . .
the name and presence of volatile and sentient forces.

—William Faulkner

Pasted inside Kitty Baker's movie scrapbook is a grainy Kodak. It was
likely taken in 1916, when the Virginia-born filmgoer was sixteen years
of age. The amateur photograph captures Baker sharing a moment of
intimacy with one of her movie-loving friends: delicately embraced, the
two girls press their mouths together, parted lips breathing each other's
air, the unnamed girl on the left tenderly holding Baker's jaw while
caressing her chin. Their eyes are closed as the shutter seizes their intertwined profiles, the large bows in their hair smeared by the gossamer
motion of leaning in, touching, kissing. A caption is inked under the hazy
candid ("Two, too, to, sweet!") in Baker's block handwriting (figure 1).[1]

This snapshot, the caption informs, was seen as an image of excess—
specifically excess of young female affect, both represented and perceived. Though the final adjective suggests praise, the adverb "too" and
its surrounding homophones convey an unruliness that undermines the
possibility of acceptance or containment. The kiss—between girls, offering pleasure "to" the "two" of them—is found "too sweet," too erotic,
simply "too much" not to be deemed transgressive by the movie scrapbooker. An exclamation mark renders the image and the emotions
punching through it all the more prohibitive. Punctuation appears here

FIGURE I. "Too much": Kodak of Kitty Baker kissing another girl, safekept in the fan's movie scrapbook, ca. 1916.

as a visual qualifier and a legible border, the place where same-sex female attachment, no matter how sweet-tasting, gains momentum, swells up, and rushes headfirst into a nebulous territory of unchecked pleasures. The exclamation mark whispers loudly, "caution, danger ahead." And yet, as hazardous as the kiss and its driving affect might have seemed to Baker at the time, the movie-loving girl still saved their photographic rendition in her personal scrapbook, where the same-sex kiss rests to this day, over a century later, framed by the fan's handwritten warning.

Kitty Baker is one of several girls coming of age in the United States during World War I (WWI) who used motion pictures to articulate feelings not aligned with dominant views on gender, sexuality, propriety, and well-being. This book proposes that by examining personal materials produced by moviegoing girls during the emergence of Hollywood's star system, we recover an unknown history of media reception shaped around homoerotic identification, same-sex desire, and gender nonconformity. I focus on movie scrapbooks, diary entries, fan mail, annotated collages, and amateur photographs authored by the first generation of adolescent girls who harnessed commercial cinema to negotiate proclivities, aspirations, identities, and acts self-described as "queer" or "different from the norm." Interchanging both expressions in their vernacular writings, adolescent girls deployed the protean syntax of film stardom to forge a foundational language of female nonconformity and kinship. In the context of this book, "queer" is thus used alongside "nonnormative" to characterize deviation and/or questioning of traditionalist binaries that primarily policed gender and sexual behavior during the 1910s.

Following girl fans' own employment of the term, "queer" here encompasses gender nonconformity (e.g., using fashion and pronouns different from those attributed at birth), same-sex attraction, disdain for marriage and motherhood, and other unconventional responses negotiated through the consumption of film stars. I argue that the fluidity of girls' fan reactions—their refusal to be readily classified—intersected with attitudes ascribed to "New Women" of the period. "New Woman," feminist anthropologist Elsie Clews Parsons claimed in 1916, "means woman not yet classified, perhaps not classifiable . . . , bent on finding out for herself, unwilling to live longer at second hand, dissatisfied with expressing her own will to power merely through ancient media, through children, servants, and uxorious men. [The New Woman] wants to . . . share in the mastery men arrogate."[2] In her ambition and self-reliance, as in her trading of "ancient media" for new, the New Woman archetype championed by professional women in the 1910s *spoke of* the actresses on the screen as well as *to* the girls in the audience. The interplay between female performers and viewers, as between star texts and fan responses, hence coalesced around changing notions of femininity, independence, and divergence, notions Richard Abel theorizes struck a deep cord with "the young unmarried working women who formed a significant part of . . . an emerging fan culture" during WWI.

In privileging personal fan archives, this book supplies experiential evidence of Abel's speculations, while dilating them to include a slew of identificatory and affective fan responses that went farther afield than treating the athletic "film roles that women played as projective sites of fantasy adventure," or regarding "the stars . . . as successful role models to emulate."[3] Though professional aspiration and escapism drew unmarried girls in their teens and early twenties to the movies, their attraction to female stars performing a "'freedom' [only] assumed as 'natural' for young men" went beyond longing for alternatives to house-wifery and motherhood. The queerness of their spectatorship resided in what Parsons identified as a modern female desire to be "not classifia-ble," to self-perceive as "new not only to men, but to herself."[4]

A historiography of film reception cannot be disarticulated from its historical context. The partitioning of the silent era into discrete points of transition typically foregrounds 1917 as the end of an "early" period of industrial decentralization and the onset of a studio era consolidating distinct business and storytelling practices. Following Jennifer Bean's heed, I find that "contemporary feminism has much to gain by troubling the period break between early cinema and cinematic classicism by refus-ing to toe the 1917 line."[5] Instead of attempting to distinguish "silent" from "early" cinema through technological and commercial transforma-tions, I am more interested in exploring how the overlapping advents of WWI, the influenza pandemic, and an emergent star system influenced sociopolitical reworkings of gender, sexuality, class, and well-being, and how individual moviegoers weathered such historical happenings through affective engagement with a new media marketplace teeming with girl-fronted goods. The years between 1910 and 1920 serve then as loose brackets to a periodization that could be described as the tail end of the Progressive Era—a contentious period feminist historians have described as tugging between social reform and moral crusades, women's suffrage and white supremacy, anti-immigration legislation and welfare expansion, a love for modern advancement matched by horror at increas-ing urban vice and deteriorating tradition.[6] In that period, women also came to dominate domestic movie consumption. In 1918, US film exhib-itors estimated that "women make up 60 per cent of the average audi-ence.... They study our weekly programs, and it is they who generally are the ones who pick the nights [to] attend our theatre."[7]

In the last two decades, the quest for highlighting women's contribu-tions to silent film history has driven a robust body of feminist research to archival sources.[8] This "historical turn," as Jane Gaines dubs it, stems from a feminist desire to broaden women's media histories across the intersectional axes of gender, sexuality, class, ethnicity, nationality, creed, and race.[9] Characterized by "miscellaneous acts of collection and collections of miscellany," recent feminist film scholarship contemplates an archive of commonplace objects, forgotten people, and first-person recollection.[10] Addressing her own turn to silent actresses' cookbooks, marginalia, and scrapbooks, Amelie Hastie argues that women's film histories survive in a state of "disarray," "inevitably dispersed across genres, forms, spaces. . . . The category of 'miscellany' [thus] guides the authorship of women's histories of the silent period, especially as these women reveal themselves as the subjects of their own work."[11] Dispersed through vernacular and institutional spaces, personal film repositories not only pique academic curiosity but promise diversity—that in their motley bowels lie overlooked, misidentified, unseen sources and subjects waiting for their histories to be told. Building upon Hastie's inventive marriage of women's personal archives, self-reflection, and silent film stardom, I propose that historical understandings of US cinema are incomplete without accounting for the modes of reception and identification engendered by regular moviegoing girls at the onset of the star system. Borrowing from prosopography, that "powerful analytical tool which literally reduces history to atoms, . . . [to] the indivisible unit of human existence," this book probes individual fan artifacts and biographies to provide insight into the socioideological underpinnings of an enduring women-driven media culture.[12]

A GIRL IS A GIRL IS A GIRL: INVENTING "THE SCREEN-STRUCK FAN"

Adolescent girlhood played a significant role in instituting a commercial American film culture. Although the phenomenon is apparent in other realms of promotion—including girls-only giveaways, pageants, and advice columns penned by young stars like Anita Stewart and Mary Pickford—movie magazines were among the first to identify female youth as defining a new class of film aficionados: the ardent "screen-struck fans."[13] An early facilitator of interactive fandom, *Motion Picture Magazine*'s Answer Man designated being young and female as a prerequisite for entering his exclusive group of regular correspondents. When in 1915 a moviegoer named "Abe, 99" asked to be included in "a contest among [his] 'public' for the best communication," the Answer Man immediately rebuffed the moviegoer on the grounds that Abe was "too old (99) to compete with the fair Olga 17, the erudite Vyrgynya, the witty Gertie, the profound Grace, all of whom are young and handsome."[14] "Olga 17" and Vyrgynya (two of the most prolific and long-lasting participants in the "Answers Department"), were specifically identified as adolescent girls: Olga's age is listed as seventeen, and she first introduces herself as "a young . . . innocent, unsophisticated, dear mama's girl" who had just begun dating, while Vyrgynya echoes Bernardin de St. Pierre's fictional

Virginie, the maiden heroine from the French children's classic *Paul and Virginie* (1787).[15] An alleged octogenarian, the Answer Man further describes these girls' fan letters as symptomatic of the "follies of youth."[16]

Although female adolescence becomes visibly intertwined with film fandom by the mid-1910s, journalists noticed that girls dominated local nickelodeons as early as 1907. "After 4 o'clock the audiences were largely composed of schoolgirls, who came in with books or music rolls under their arms," the *Chicago Tribune* reported. "Around 6 o'clock . . . the character of the audience . . . shifted again. This time they were largely composed of girls [employed at] the big department stores, who came in with bundles under their arms."[17] Regardless of occupation, adolescence defined reportage of passionate moviegoing. The first wave of spectators is identified as being middle-class "schoolgirls," their status signaled by the leisurely way they carried their "books or music rolls" and strolled in for an after-class screening. As the business day drew to an end, this relaxed group was replaced by homebound wage-earners, a young female audience that, though similarly unhindered by wifely or motherly responsibilities, rushed to the movies to find respite after a long day's work. This example shows that the feminization and juvenation of film fandom performed by the Answer Man rose concomitantly with the star system. Adolescent girls attended the pictures in noticeable numbers from the very inception of commercial moviemaking, but only in the mid-1910s did they come to be addressed by industry officials as a distinct target demographic, classifiable and therefore marketable.

The enhanced visibility columnists, admen, and exhibitors bestowed on moviegoing girls during WWI symptomizes the development of a film-fan press that heralded Hollywood's narrowcasting practices, by which gender and age groups direct programming and marketing. The designations "movie enthusiast" and "picture lover" began circulating in newspapers around 1910. However, a gendered definition of affective film consumption only entered periodical vernacular by mid-decade, an effect of the industry's move to a star-fronted economy that prioritized more granular audience distinctions.[18] Kathy Fuller-Seeley explains that before advertisers and editors set their eyes on middle-class female consumers, "the designation *movie fan* was flexible enough to apply to a nationwide audience of enthusiastic men, women, and children, blurring many of the class, ethnic, regional, and gender distinctions that had separated audiences for earlier amusements."[19] In fact, prior to movie publications popularizing the term, "fan" almost exclusively applied to baseball "fanatics," carrying either neutral or masculine connotations.[20]

A glance at a standard issue of *Motion Picture Story Magazine* prior to 1914 substantiates this claim, with most usages of "fan" referring to a genderless sports enthusiast, a lady's fashion accessory, or a mechanical appliance. The term seemed so alien in 1912 that the brand-new Answer Man addressed a self-denominated "Moving Picture Fan" with the quip, "Glad to be informed that you are not an electric fan."[21]

Two years later, however, a gendered differentiation between sport enthusiasts and movie lovers was well underway. In July 1914, *Motion Picture Magazine* ran a cartoon titled "American Favorites," portraying "Motion Picture" as an anthropomorphized young lady holding hands with "Baseball," personified by a hunky male player in full striped uniform.[22] By 1916, the term "movie fan" had become so naturalized in national parlance as a distinct entity that the same publication referred to it as "just a little American slang,"[23] while dozens of audience members called themselves "The Official Fan," "An Ardent Movie Fan," "Cunard-Ford Fan," or "Miss Movie Fan" in private and published correspondence.[24] Value judgments quickly stuck to the compound word, film publications defining "movie fan [as] a person who calls all the players by their first name, criticizes the pictures and is, in general, quite superior to ordinary mortals."[25] By late 1917, emotional volatility characterized the film archetype, reporters returning to the term's pathological roots by warning that "'fan' is short for fanatic."[26] It is at this escalation from expertise to excess, connoisseur to obsessionist, that the "screen-struck fan" came to be culturally engendered as adolescent and female, an extension of magazine editors, admen, and film exhibitors courting middle-class women as "custodians of public mores," hoping their patronage would legitimize motion pictures as wholesome entertainment.[27]

Though emotions triggered by the pictures could produce beneficial results, the press often imagined them as provoking reckless solipsism in girls. A touch of hysteria ran through most commercial coverage of what would become a lasting staple of film fandom: "the screen-struck girl."[28] In 1917, *Motion Picture Magazine* painted the typical movie-loving fan as "a young thing, . . . very romantic [and] very foolish. . . . She read sensational best-sellers and the cheapest magazines, [and] always and ever her brain sought far visions, dreamed and moaned over extravagant lovers—people of gilt in a tinsel world."[29] As if lowbrow tastes and a frail grasp on reality were not dire enough flaws, in their adoration of picture personalities screen-struck girls seemed to take leave of their senses. A dangerously mobile patron, she could not be satisfied with "just go[ing] to the theaters. Far be it from such! She just hops on the car, or the train, or the boat, . . . and goes right to the fountain head" (i.e., the studios), believing herself destined to be transformed from anonymous Jane Doe into renowned Miss Movie if given the chance to audition for a famous director or rub shoulders with an illustrious player.[30]

Despite being much bandied about in the WWI years, girls' infatuation with female stars was not a novel phenomenon. Since the mid-nineteenth century columnists had remonstrated female audiences for fawning over stage actresses.[31] Unlike "matinee girls," who supposedly lusted after male players, "stage-screen girls" tended to devote their favors to the fairer sex, their dreams of footlight fame perilously collapsing hero-worship with homosexual desire and self-harm.[32] Papers described the archetypal stage fan as a "silly young girl,"[33] the "small village would-be Juliet"[34] who could not resist the "unaccountable attraction" of mass entertainment and celebrity.[35] Like the moniker indicates, the press conceived of stage-loving girls as the predecessor of movie-struck fans. In drawing a direct lineage between theater and film fandoms and in feminizing both, journalists laid the groundwork for a perdurable model of media consumption shaped around same-sex worship that depended on the hallmarks of female adolescence: high susceptibility, leisure time, and emotional intensity.[36]

It is thus indispensable to distinguish between girl and woman audiences, because, as various scholars have shown, from its very beginning the US film industry valorized female youth as a distinct transactional commodity.[37] By the second decade of the twentieth century, industry officials shifted from regarding "women" as an undifferentiated class of moviegoers to targeting unmarried girls in their teens and early twenties as a separate consumer demographic. More than habitual patrons, adolescent girls were now addressed as a special league of consumers, a constituency with valuable resources film impresarios spared no efforts to secure.[38]

This newfound visibility was not without ambivalence. Looking at fan magazines from the 1910s, Shelley Stamp discusses the "movie-struck girl" as a derogatory representation of female spectatorship fabricated by the press to ally mounting "anxieties about women's filmgoing." Undisciplined, disruptive, and self-involved, the "movie-struck girl . . . suggest[ed] that women were unsuitable patrons of the cinema and unlikely participants in its visual delights."[39] Though groundbreaking, Stamp's monograph conflates anxieties relating to a wide range of female reception practices under the umbrella figure of the "woman." Stamp pays close attention to how social distinctions influenced screen and print portraits of female spectators during WWI. However, class played a lesser role when US periodicals distinguished between an obsessive movie fan and a casual moviegoer—when figuring female fan investment, pivotal distinctions were made according to age. Case in point: when describing the screen-struck fan, newspapers and movie magazines specifically referred to a white, unmarried, childless female in her teens and early twenties, either gainfully employed or attending school. Both working and moneyed white girls fitted the bill of the "screen-struck girl" type, lest they be perceived as adolescent, which is to say, released from the strictures of wifehood and childrearing. It was that newfangled freedom and immaturity US society ascribed to female adolescence that rendered the screen-struck girl a suitable cypher for affective and insatiable movie consumption.

AN INTERIM PHASE: THE SOCIAL CREATION OF FEMALE ADOLESCENCE

To understand how female adolescence became so relevant to the creation of a commercial movie-fan culture, we must contextualize the valorization and visibility US reformers, lawmakers, reporters, and psychologists attributed to girlhood at the turn of the twentieth century. According to sociologist Viviana Zelizer, the sacralization of childhood emerged in the late 1890s, a time when US culture shifted from seeing pubescent children as "useful wage-earning . . . little work people" to considering them "economically useless but emotionally priceless."[40] A shifting interest in the social value of children brought widespread awareness to issues of sexual maturation, underage exploitation, and peer socialization. By interrogating what differentiated a child from an adult, Western psychologists and Progressive reformers delineated adolescence as a unique developmental stage necessitating extensive guidance, leisure, and introspection, conditions absent from most young lives before the twentieth century.

Unmarried girls in their teens caught the eye of turn-of-the-century legislators, activists, and muckrakers, being repeatedly portrayed by them as the most at-risk urban consumers, workers, and sexual subjects.[41] Examples include federal and state laws on age of consent, marriage, parental oversight, and property ownership barring unmarried girls in their teens from making decisions regarding their bodies, livelihoods, and assets. Though mandatory schooling and labor laws were generally gender-neutral, amendments concerned with preserving minors' sexual purity only addressed adolescent girls.[42] This legislative enshrinement of young female vulnerability helped turn adolescent girlhood into a cultural avatar for excessive impressionability and emotionality, the characteristics defining movie-struck fandom in the 1910s.

Key theories on human development sketched in the first decade of the twentieth century built upon already deep-seated beliefs on women's inherent dependence and inferiority. In 1904, eminent US psychologist and pedagogue Granville Stanley Hall published the magnum opus *Adolescence: Its Psychology and Its Relations to Physiology, Anthropology, Sex, Crime, Religion, and Education.* In his groundbreaking monograph, Hall defined adolescence as a distinct life-stage between fourteen and twenty-four years of age.[43] Drawing from eugenics and biological essentialism, Hall considered educated boys of Anglo-Saxon ancestry the only "candidate[s] for a highly developed humanity."[44] "A boy," Hall observed in 1909, "has some self-knowledge; a girl understands very little of herself or of the motives of her conduct, for her life is more ruled by deep unconscious instincts. . . . She is a more generic being . . . [who] *loves to have her feelings stirred because emotionality is her life.*"[45] Constitutionally inferior and atavistically overemotional, white women and people of color remained stunted at the threshold of adulthood, psychologically trapped in a state historian Crista DeLuzio terms "a quintessential and perpetual adolescence."[46]

Profoundly sentimental and "vulnerable to scores of fads," the "budding girl" outlined by Hall closely resembled the "screen-struck girl" disseminated by moviemakers and reporters.[47] I propose that such likeness is not a coincidence. Psychologists theorized female adolescence at the same time the film industry began shifting to a star system. The scientific taxonomization of female adolescence, in other words, produced a legible scaffolding for gendered immaturity, imagination, and alterity that the periodical press readily appropriated as the blueprint for affect-driven film acting and consumption. Private archives expose the porous traffic of influence between scientific discourse, popular culture, and audiences happening during the 1910s. For example, in 1919, Helen Edna Davis, a white educated immigrant living in New York City, told her diary: "I am dreadfully unhappy! . . . It may be adolescence . . . that makes me so restless." Already twenty-one years old at the time, the moviegoing girl attributed her disordered moods to the Sturm und Drang of adolescence, a self-perception confirming that some audience members internalized Hall's periodization.[48]

Hall's vision of adolescent girlhood as a childlike mind tucked in an erogenous body left an equally deep impression on the renditions of young femininity circulated by motion pictures and film magazines. In the novelization of Thanhouser studio's *Her New York* (1917), *Photoplay* writer Constance Severance describes the adolescent heroine Phoebe Lester (Gladys Hulette) as "nearing seventeen, a pretty miniature woman still redolent of the charm of childhood."[49] The novelization of another Thanhouser two-reeler, *The Speed King* (1915), paints its young female protagonist Muriel Randall (Muriel Ostriche) as an eighteen year old whose body showed signs of "the angularity of girlhood" but whose mind lingered in the pubescent "stage of a tomboy."[50] These literary narrativizations of screen girlhood illustrate the impact psychology had in how the film industry portrayed female youth. Characterized as half-child, half-woman, adolescent protagonists like Phoebe and Muriel embodied onscreen Hall's prototypical "budding girl." "No longer a little girl, but by no means yet a young woman," the adolescent heroine surfaced in 1910s motion pictures as a liminal, lovely vessel, her burgeoning sexuality both delighting and discomfiting audiences.[51] In a way, the "budding girl" of the movies gave shape to Parson's ideal "New Woman"—a being "not to be classifiable."

As female adolescence became social, legal, and clinically construed as a decade-long moratorium between childhood and adulthood, age crystallized as an efficient tool to differentiate youngsters from adults, sexual abuse from lawful consent, and labor exploitation from fair work. Fourteen, Hall proposed, inaugurated the official beginning of female adolescence, while twenty-four marked its end. Statistical studies backed Hall's periodization, forwarding fourteen as the average age white US girls reported experiencing their menarche.[52] Census data similarly indicated that, for college girls, age of matrimony usually coincided with that of graduation: around twenty-three. Average marrying age also worked as a determinant social code for mapping female development, providing a legible benchmark to track a maiden's deterioration into unviable spinsterhood. As a Radcliffe College valedictorian declared, "Some one [*sic*] has said that graduation and marriage are the two principal events in a girl's life. . . . Red-letter days, . . . [both dates] mark the development from the school girl chrysalis into the full-blown young woman."[53] During an era when virginal wedding nights and monogamous reproduction still functioned as the primary vehicle for female subsistence and respectability, age-brackets played a salient cultural role in regulating proper passage from girlhood into adulthood.

Following the dominant parameters codifying female development in early twentieth-century United States, when referring to a "girl," "young fan," or "adolescent girl," I am employing Hall's definition of adolescence as unmarried and childless individuals between fourteen and twenty-four years of age—a life-phase defined as much by age and sexual inexperience as by financial and social dependence. That means I only examine fan objects whose author, including name and age, is known, generally through handwritten inscriptions. When data is incomplete, I draw on ancestry sites, school records, and census reports to flesh out individual biographies as thoroughly as possible. The few times that age is not evident, I attribute adolescence to girls who signed their names with the prefix "miss" and made clear references to their juvenile status through mentions of school-going, young peers, or dependence on family members.

Despite surveying girls from a variety of means, creeds, and localities, the bulk of my research focuses on movie fans who identified as literate and white. In my extensive probe of published and private fan artifacts, I rarely came across girls who identified as anything but white, of US birth, or of European descent. The lack of self-reported diversity likely results from ingrained cultural segregation and xenophobia running rampant in early twentieth-century United States, signified by the rise of neo-Darwinist doctrines such as eugenics, recapitulation theory, and anti-immigration nativism.[54]

The commanding valorization of whiteness affected the content printed in best-selling film magazines as well, which assumed audiences to be universally white and literate. The egalitarian "ask and you shall receive" ethos early fan publications promised to underline the personalized inter-activity between picture personalities and fans was also not all-inclusive but likely operated as a perpetuator of white privilege. Not only was star–fan trading of autographs and missives limited to viewers with the language skills, financial means, and free time to invest in correspondence, but, according to published letters submitted by minority moviegoers, both female stars and magazine editors favored a certain type of (white, educated) fan. Hints of systemic disenfranchisement can be found in *Motion Picture Magazine*'s reply to a patron named Radda, a surname of Italian origin associated at the time with working-class immigrants. Bristly in tone, the Answer Man replies, "Very well. No, I don't agree with you. I don't think we neglect the people you mention," suggesting a certain pique at the fan's accusation of readership discrimination.[55] The defensive reaction indicates that the fan indictment must have hit a nerve.

Another "plea"—mailed privately to actress Bessie Barriscale in 1916 and sampled in the comedic publication *Film Fun*—came "from a little colored correspondent in Columbus, Ohio." The Black girl confessed to "have the same feelings as a little white girl, and it makes me unhappy not to have things other girls enjoy."[56] One of those things were hand-signed photographs of cherished film actresses. Because headshots functioned as a conduit nearing fan to star, deprivation went beyond material lack.[57] In being denied access to customized movie ephemera, the Black girl fan read Barriscale's neglect as a personal perpetration of systemic racial discrimination permeating daily life. In tandem with Radda's, this anonymous fan letter implies that eugenic biases dominant in early twentieth-century Unites States had already trickled into the newfangled star system and could be felt by individual moviegoers. The absence of fans of color from press contests and interactive columns intimates that film magazines worked in league with institutional practices of social disenfranchisement to suppress the public visibility and voices of nonwhite movie fans.

However, it warrants recalling that, as Hester Blum observes of nineteenth-century nautical ephemera, "scarcity is a function of reception, not of their generation."[58] Young people of color, the very poor, foreign-born, or illiterate certainly adored the pictures, even if most surviving fan documents do not belong to them. Money and literacy are required for performing sustained fandom, an activity defined by the purchase, collection, and exchange of trademarked paraphernalia and handmade crafts, which in turn necessitate secondary supplies such as admission tickets, transit fare, stamps, and stationery, among other essentials. I am thus well aware of the audiences still unaccounted for in early Hollywood histories; their absence from this book does not deny their existence or relevance. Reception studies parsing non-English speakers, seniors, and Black children, to name a few underexamined demographics, are left roped-off as significant sites of research, inviting other scholars to start digging.

AFFECTIVE HISTORIOGRAPHY: A METHOD TO RESEARCH PERSONAL FAN ARTIFACTS

My focus on moviegoing girls is quite deliberate. Not only did Progressive debates differentiating deviance from normality frequently deploy adolescent girlhood as the litmus test, but self-identified screen-struck girls composed about 75 percent of all signed fan objects I found in private collections and periodical publications from the 1910s; the remaining 25 percent are left ambiguous (anonymous or initialed) or are authored by self-identified married women and male fans. The number of individual collections consulted in preparation for this book amounts to a little under seventy. Institutional repositories like women's colleges and municipal historical societies house the majority of personal papers; a few of the scrapbooks examined were obtained from eBay auctions. If we accept the estimate that three-quarters of US cinema produced before 1929 is now lost, then the sheer volume of surviving film ephemera gathered by adolescent girls during the 1910s should evince how pervasive their movie consumption was.[59]

Placing unmarried female audiences in their teens and early twenties at the center of Hollywood's transition from "a bucolic backwater . . . [into] an industry and a place that specialized in shaping people's fantasies and fears about modern times" affords an expansion of intersectional feminist histories proposing that an "even cursory inspection of the era's fan culture reveals [that] American silent film was mostly made for women with very different tastes."[60] The plurality of "fantasies and fears" Hollywood inspired spurred modes of female reception that questioned homogenous identifications, experiences, and aspirations. As Hilary Hallett heeds, "an origin story about how Hollywood became Hollywood that marginalizes women cannot hope to explain why its first 'social imaginary' lit up imaginations across the world."[61]

Hollywood's promotional address of democratic inclusion and upward mobility largely spoke to and depended upon working and educated girls, a storied demographic comprised of mobile individuals whose proclivities at times stepped outside normative lines, being through gender nonconformity, same-sex attraction, or a desire for livelihoods removed from marriage and parenthood. Considering these moviegoing girls from an autobiographical perspective allows their affective differentiation and cultural significance to take up space and foreground the rise of a national film industry. Together with a cadre of women directors, producers, screenwriters, journalists, and players, screen-struck girls pumped life into a mass celebrity culture, both shaping and challenging a developing star system that applauded female independence while warning viewers against straying off the beaten path.

Other media scholars have noted the seminal relationship between movie fandom and female youth.[62] Jackie Stacey, in particular, pinpointed adolescence as the formative life-stage when British female spectators formed an affective relation of pleasure and identification with classical Hollywood actresses, observing that "many respondents' memories are of a transitional period: their 'teenage' years, [a time] in which change and self-transformation were central to their desires and aspirations."[63] Stacey innovated feminist film historiography by introducing standardized questionnaires as a means to gain first-hand access to women's spectatorial experiences. Despite considering the possibility of homoerotic fan attachment, she does not disarticulate female longing to be *like* an actress from wanting to be *with* an actress. This distinction disappears in the homogeneity of Stacey's statistical method and the restrictedness of her research questions. Blurry and idiosyncratic as such a distinction may seem, its very existence opens a wealth of possibilities that diversify readings of how early female audiences related to a woman-driven commercial film culture and how the Hollywood star system abetted queer modes of looking and feeling at the moment of its inception.

According to Miriam Hansen, female spectatorship in the silent period was mobilized by "long-term psychic investments, in particular ego ideals and primary object substitutes" that found home or echo in the fictional world of moving pictures.[64] Attending to the queer valences of moviegoing, this book sets to historicize female fan reception as an act of affective expenditure, inherently veined with erotic and identarian investments that resist being hemmed in by social expectations on normative femininity, desire, or propriety. When using the terms "affect" and "affective," I am informed by Deborah Gould's sociological work. Gould explains affects as "inchoate, inarticulable . . . but nevertheless registered experiences of bodily energy and intensity that arise in response to stimuli impinging on the body. . . . Affect, then, is the body's ongoing and relatively amorphous inventory-taking of coming into contact and interacting with the world."[65] Jennifer Bean complements this definition by arguing that "much of what is talked about in affect theory is that which escapes, resists, or exceeds language. . . . [Affect] refers to processes of potentiality and becoming, to vital forces and intensities, to physiological and biological matters that lie outside discursive structures."[66] When researching female-assigned filmgoers at the threshold of adulthood, the idea of affect "as something that we do not quite have the language for but is nevertheless in play" is particularly useful.[67] Private papers reveal that for many early movie-loving girls a difference from the norm was diffusely felt—language faltered to convey experiential sensations of deviation, resulting in a cobbling together of established narrative conventions with new visual technology. Fragmentary artifacts—movie scrapbooks, self-portraits, journal entries, and other first-person writings—capture snapshots of this synaptic otherness: feeling on the verge of action, a jolt against the grain, self-discovery perceived and expressed dispersedly through multimediated engagement with images of film stars troubling heteronormativity through male-coded behavior, temporary cross-dressing, or romancing other women onscreen.

Put plainly, I define affect as a spectatorial voltage: the electricity that attaches fan to star but also impels fans to retrieve special meaning from a picture, a gesture, a plot, a performance—the emanative force spurring the response *"you made me feel something I want to remember."* This intensity of meaning/identification/attraction allows for the extension of spectatorial attachment beyond the fleeting act of movie-watching, activating a form of emotional endurance ingrained in embodied modes of same-sex identification: I want to look at the star, the star looks like me, I want to look like the star, I want to touch the star, I want the star to touch me. Queer fan affect, in the context of this book, is hence *of the body* and felt *in the body,* summoning reception performances characterized by sensations of identarian difference and eroticized sameness.

Fan writing, scrapbooking, dressing up—manual, time-consuming, intrinsically subjective and creative activities—are soaked with affect. In their simultaneous engagement of the heart and the hand, commerce and autobiography, presence and absence, film-fan archives comprised of paper, glue, and marginalia sequester interstitial encounters between self and the world. The notion of fandom I use here expands upon what Rosanna Maule and Catherine Russell identify as early female "cinephilia": an "often obsessive and totallizing, personal relation to film . . . [which is] highly experiential and sensory."[68] Maule and Russell claim that in the first decades of filmmaking, "women saw things differently at the silent movies not only because they were preeminently positioned within social and cinematic structures of seeing, but because the cinematic experience was radically destabilizing, exposing new perspectives and unusual views of everyday life." As a result of their socialized gender difference, early female audiences' "love for cinema involved a kind of *bodily incorporation*" that mirrored the larger-than-life stunts, outfits, and personalities galvanizing early narrative film.[69]

The haptic physicality of silent spectatorship bled into girls' modes of reception, saturating their movie-themed juvenilia. For example, on November 2, 1915, fifteen-year-old Constance Margaret Topping from Berkeley, California, wrote in her diary: "It was San Francisco Day at the [World] Fair. . . . Didn't go to the Fair though. Mommit + I went to see Geraldine Farrar in 'Carmen'—only a movie!" The despondent remark "only a movie!" alludes to the upper-middle-class girl preferring live entertainment. It also expresses a filmgoer's frustrating lack for not having witnessed Farrar perform Bizet's *Carmen* onstage, where the diva's famous voice and figure could have been admired in real time instead of disembodied and silenced on the silver screen.[70] For the next five years, Topping proceeded to scrapbook paper paraphernalia related to her moviegoing exploits (including exhibitors' programs, ticket stubs, and clipped reviews) in an attempt to make the ephemeral movie-watching experience last.

Topping was not alone. When film fandom flourished during the WWI years, followers of the novel medium sourced from a preexisting infrastructure of consumer desire and preservation—the scrapbook. Popular in US households since the nineteenth century, the scrapbook functioned as a rudimentary technology of informational aggregation, directed and subtended by a compiler's needs. Print recipes, receipts, color illustrations, mass-produced Valentines, handwritten invitations, doodles, fabric swatches, dried flowers, family photographs, candy wrappers, and celebrity cabinet cards all congregated in personal scrapbooks, providing a visual chronicle of idiosyncratic landmarks and penchants.[71]

In the mid-1800s, scrapbooks became a technology to convey theatrical fandom, patrons collecting memorabilia of thespians as a means to express lasting admiration and extend the rarefied experience of theatergoing. Through a manually curated repository of star headshots, autographs, ticket stubs, playbills, and press reviews, a stage fan could elongate their short-lived exposure to a star's physical presence; they could also manipulate a star's paper figure in the privacy of their homes. Though male admirers assembled theater scrapbooks, most extant examples not left anonymous were compiled by women.[72]

Encouraged by a participatory film press, movie-loving girls took up the mantle of scrapbooking amidst a culture of war relief and resource conservation that tasked girls and women with the maintenance of an upcycled home and country.[73] A staple of fan reception since Hollywood's emergence, movie scrapbooks and fan mail are thus as infrastructural to the network of intimacies girl fans established amongst themselves and with stars as to the excavation of "how women saw things differently at the silent movies."[74] In describing the practice of scrapbooking and life-writing as critical to female film fandom's "infrastructure of intimacy," I draw from Ara Wilson's view of "infrastructures"— the physical "circuits of pipes and cables" found in computer hardware or power grids—as "embed[ding] intimate relations in unpredictable junctures of material and symbolic power, . . . [and] in many cases shap[ing] the conditions for relational life." Hybrid and tactile, both mass-produced and handcrafted, movie scrapbooks, mixed-media diaries, and illustrated fan mail surface as infrastructural pillars of early film fandom that help track how "the concrete force of abstract fields of power . . . enable or hinder intimacy" (figure 2).[75]

In recent years, historians have called attention to the role ephemera plays in LGBTQ+ archiving, theorizing that infrastructures of queer intimacy cannot be disarticulated from vulnerability and precariousness.[76] Arguing for a centering of negativity when discussing self-produced queer records, Heather Love contextualizes queer history through intermittent testimonies of dissident feeling. Ann Cvetkovich further links lesbian archives to legacies of trauma, positing that accounts of queer hurt found in memoirs, scrapbooks, and personal media-making complicate the registry of nonnormative lived experiences.[77] In treating silent film fans' ephemera collections as an understudied repository of vernacular queer feeling, I build on both scholars, echoing their valorization of the negative, not only as lived struggle but as methodology. "Negative" as in negative space—a recognition of the systemic obscuring imposed on marginalized people—but also "negative" as in embracing the uncertainty and incompleteness of first-person sources, especially early movie scrapbooks, artifacts often retrieved third-hand from online auctions, institutional collections, and thrift stores, in tatters or in fragments, and hence troubling researchers' access to complete provenance details such as time, location, biography, and context.

If "the stock in trade of the gay and lesbian archive is ephemera," then it must be recognized that violence shapes its very existence.[78] The survival of marginal collections, much like their destruction, bears marks of neglect, mishandling, or deaccession perpetrated by private and institutional holders that make little effort to preserve the social biography of personal objects.[79] To add insult to injury, the building blocks of fan-made caches are brittle, fugacious, embattled. Conceived as throwaways or keepsakes, paper-based movie paraphernalia are precarious materials, their value retrieved or augmented according to a beholder's contingent eye. Mary Desjardins sees studio-era memorabilia commercialized on eBay as a type of "detritus" that "signifies the ephemeral nature of the mythic rise and fall from fame in American culture."[80] A regarding of ephemera as "detritus" underpins the long history of institutions dedicated to film preservation not acquiring scrapbooks and other loose

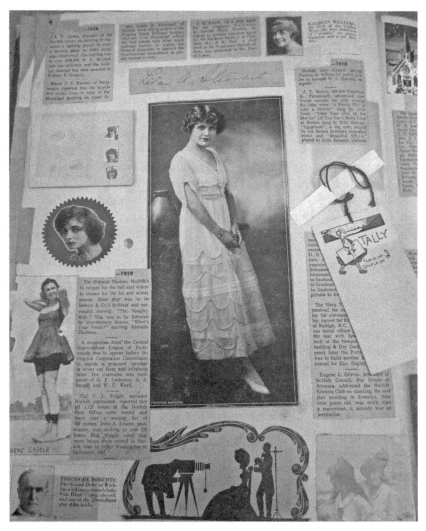

FIGURE 2. A labor of love: Kitty Baker weaves together movie actresses, female fans, and everyday life in her "Norfolk 1916" scrapbook.

movie items considered too miscellaneous to fall under an easy fileable category.[81] Film fans' collections, in particular, have only occasionally found a welcoming home in nonprofit institutional repositories, their inherent merit as historical objects often eclipsed by a star's clout.[82] Writing the history of early female queer reception, in short, forcefully entails to write *about and around loss*—of youth, repute, memory, physical integrity. As such, it demands the adoption of what Hastie terms a "historiography writ not large but in the margins, in objects . . . pulled from the cupboards of feminist curiosity."[83]

Like Hastie and Paula Amad, I spotlight personal film archives whose collaborative custodians may include at turns auctioneers, archivists, scholars, hobbyists, fans, their relatives, and strangers.[84] From that irregular corpus I tease forth an "affective historiography"—a form of researching past film experiences that cannot be disarticulated from autobiography, emotion, and loss and thus must embrace indeterminacy and incompleteness as strengths rather than pitfalls of sociohistorical research. As Cvetkovich points out, "In the archive of lesbian feeling, objects are not inherently meaningful but are made so through their significance to an audience."[85] In taking "the fan as a model for the archivist," queer cultural historiographers decide to privilege the signification of "fetishistic, idiosyncratic, or obsessional" feelings instantiated by fan objects, adjoining their interpretations with biographical and social fact.[86]

To delineate infrastructural intimacies as rarefied as those forged by self-identified queer fans in the 1910s is to beget a balancing act: threading the needle of not overvaluing surviving materials while recognizing that scarcity accumulates cultural significance. Centered around a patchworked feminist archive, this book is not invested in finding definitive answers. Instead, it comments upon the uneasy marriage between the unstable emporium of virtual information that is the internet—with its dead links, timed auctions, nominal finding aids, and ever-expanding grassroot archives—and one-of-a-kind fan artifacts from the 1910s.

Impermanent and incomplete in different ways, the internet, institutional archives, and personal ephemera collections are infrastructural to researching early film reception and to expanding LGBTQ+ histories. My affective historiography seeks to harness the three sources. Movie scrapbooks retrieved from online auctions are contextualized with yearbooks, letters, diaries, and memorabilia stored at women's colleges, university libraries, and sundry nonprofit repositories: from the film-specific Margaret Herrick Library to municipal archives like the Washington State Historical Society and the Natural History Museum of Los Angeles. When read in tandem with contemporaneous legislation, medical literature, magazines, and biographic data culled from censuses, school records, and ancestry databases found online, self-crafted fan archives induce researchers to think of feminist historiography as a living thing, able to continuously incorporate diverse sources, methods, and viewpoints, and as a connective tissue, where the "then" and the "now" of historical research—as the "us" and the "them" Jane Gaines problematizes when discussing feminist research on silent film women—can fluctuate in a state of affective mutuality.[87]

From this perspective, affect approximates the film historian, the eBay bidder, and the queer collector, accounting for their shared attachment to a distant past only brought closer through surviving ephemera. A desire to touch history, to keep history alive through material recollection suffuses them all (collectors, collectibles, collections), much like it propelled early girl fans to assemble personal film records. From keeping moviegoing ledgers, press clippings, and fan mail to journaling and photographing, girl fans' impetus to retain history intersected with the need to chronicle the mutable young self, to pin down evanescent reactions through the infrastructures of intimacy put in place by a nascent commercial film culture.

Beyond preserving queer history, personal ephemera collections are also perversely gregarious, interpellating onlookers to produce their own readings while extending no fixed answers: after all, timelines and intentions are often left ambiguous. We are once again returned to Kitty Baker's Kodak. In her scrapbook, the movie-loving girl saved an image of female intimacy devoid of any biographical data or context, only to eroticize same-sex closeness by scribbling a superlative adverb ("too") next to a coupled numeral ("two") and an affective adjective ("sweet"). Baker's snapshot attests that queerness—as a mode of representation, communication, and identification—factored into girls' silent film reception. Cast as the prototypical screen-struck fan, white adolescent girls may have been portrayed as emotionally unruly in the press, but a side-effect of being so expansively othered is that they also enjoyed unusual leeway in displaying their attachments to picture stars. Considered socially "acceptable in adolescent females, sexual mobility" and self-questioning afforded white literate girls a freer exercise of their wills and wants when expressed under the cover of movie fandom.[88]

Still, female queerness, like female adolescence, remains largely unexamined in silent film history. Scholarship broaching queerness often focuses on popular films, directors, or players, inadvertently perpetuating a narrative of privilege and exception.[89] Laura Horak, for example, compiles an exceptional rolodex of cross-dressing in silent cinema, but screen representation directs her inquiry on female queerness in early Hollywood, so audiences are ultimately subsumed to film narratives and star texts.[90] I use first-person fan artifacts to argue that female queerness is at the heart of Hollywood's star system and its attendant celebrity culture. The promotion of an industry pronouncedly personified by young capable women emboldened female audiences to devise reception methods that licensed a gamut of same-sex intimacies and identifications not newly desired, but never so openly encouraged. By the mid-1910s, it was widely accepted that when it came to the movies, "Girls Admire Girls." A popularity contest administered in 1916 by Paramount Pictures at a Washington, DC, high school ascertained as much, reporting how "despite the fact that it was a girls' institution and there are such men as Jack Barrymore, Dustin Farnum, Jack Pickford, and a host of other handsome men to choose from, the young ladies" selected Mary Pickford and Marguerite Clark as their film favorites.[91] Despite press depictions of screen-struck girlhood pulsating with sexism, they also granted legitimacy to same-sex female closeness. Thus, in spite of its detractors, early film fandom became a rare arena in which admiration, desire, and pursuit of other women was not automatically met with accusations of perversion.

In *Uninvited*, Patricia White introduces the thesis that "female homoerotic desire is in a sense foundational to the star system" and its fan reception, positing that "the same-sex star crush narrative, with its complex negotiation of identification and desire, idealization and recognition, is particularly revelatory for queer subjects."[92] Innovative in centering queer spectatorship, White's work remains tethered to performances and stars that invite a conjectural homoerotic gaze from female audiences.[93] Grappling with historicizing queer presence in the silent era, both Mark Lynn Anderson and Susan Potter turn to Rudolph Valentino to find possible queer identificatory practices ignited, not by screen displays of same-sex intimacy, but by the discursive sexual mobility and gender nonconformity cohered in Valentino's star text.[94] These three historians present compelling cases of queerness permeating the ether of early Hollywood stardom without providing concrete evidence of the shapes queer spectatorship would have taken in daily life. Testaments of nonnormative audience responsiveness, I propose, can be found in ardent private correspondence propositioning screen actresses, in scrapbook collages depicting moviegoing girls in menswear or caressing one another, in diary entries and poems borrowing a man's voice to make love to female stars. Such autobiographical materials flesh out the postulations forwarded by White, Horak, and Potter: that past female audiences looked at other women with desire, that they yearned for difference in gender performance, and that they recurrently turned to screen players to negotiate unresolved nodes of difference, attraction, longing, and self-inquiry.

A project on queer spectatorship, nonetheless, must acknowledge that dissident reception practices do not exist apart from governing cultural scripts but develop within them. As Sharon Marcus reminds us, until the turn of the century "female homoeroticism did not subvert the dominant codes of femininity because [it] was one of those codes."[95] In the 1910s, scrapbooking and autobiographical writing were accepted as part of literate women's culture of sentimentality, leisure, and kinship, operating as venues for first-person storytelling where homoeroticism could flourish. Rather than attributing current gender and sexual denominations to past girl fans, I propose that their archives confirm what feminist film historians have long speculated: that possibility, idiosyncrasy, and fantasy activated female spectatorship in the silent period and that queerness blossomed in the half-light between presence and absence, masculinity and femininity, convention and transgression, the lived and the imagined.

Lastly, a focus on personal fan materials may seem narrow, an inflated privileging of the innuendo, the ellipsis, the outlier. And yet, current conversations on queer media representation continue to operate within those same parameters: the blink-and-you-will-miss-it lesbian kiss in a major film franchise, the insinuated reference in a television show or talent interview.[96] In Hollywood cinema, female queer desire has been continuously relegated to what Terry Castle terms an "apparitional" existence—flickers of potential visibility lurking on the heteronormative threshold of plausible deniability, haunting the fringes of the mainstream, its surfacing depending on a beholder's knowing eye.[97] Tactile signs of a "serial intimacy" with mass media, fan ephemera collections hold a parallel potentiality: they offer themselves up as fertile ground for interrogating apparitional moments of queer reception as crafted by individual female viewers, while availing access to audience responses whose immanent nonconformity found affinity with the transient, the sentimental, the token.[98]

"A REVERSED MANNER": HISTORICIZING THE DEFINITION OF "QUEER"

Fundamental to my historiographical method, the term "queer" demands further clarification. Like "movie fan" and "adolescent girl," "queer" is a polymorphous vocable that gained currency in early twentieth-century US culture. As both noun and adjective, it held a long lineage in English language, forging an alliance with deviation and curiosity as early as the seventeenth century. According to historian Barbara Benedict, "queers" have long been seen as those who "inquired into forbidden topics, [including] physical generation and sex, . . . social customs and human nature, . . . history and hierarchy." Women and collectors fell under this template, "their ambition to know, to know the hidden, and/or to know more than they were told, condemn[ing] them as traitors to their own species."[99] The thrust to go off the trodden path and question the unknown othered the first generations of culturally appointed "queers." Their self-probing curiosity turned them into curiosities—to others, but more importantly to themselves.

At the turn of the twentieth century, however, "queer" became what Benedict calls "a colloquial intensive," being repeatedly deployed in the US periodical press to characterize deviations from normative expectations, including social, behavioral, and sexual attitudes.[100] Achieving traction as an adjective in the 1900s, "queer" also became gendered in newspapers and women's magazines. Often coupled with "girl," the qualifier signified "peculiar, different from the norm" in an incisive gesture towards gender nonconformity and psychological divergence. "A queer girl," according to countless stories published in dailies, "is not like other girls."[101] "Ever so nice but very quiet, . . . she won't dress like a wax lady in a show window"; she goes about in plain, "loose-fitting, short-skirted linen gowns and tennis shoes," her nose in a book, her thoughts errant and concealed behind a "grave smile." Girls her age tended to find her "plain daffy," because "she won't play cards" or say "more than a dozen words," though "she's on speaking terms with bobolinks, and knows all about the woods."[102] Protagonists in fiction frequently felt attracted to the "queer girl" due to her unconventionality, ambiguity, and secretiveness. "Sometimes I like her, and sometimes I do not," Stella Reeves muses in S. H. James's syndicated story "A Queer Girl." "She is not good company, I am afraid, and yet I want to invite her for that very reason."[103]

Together with her refractory personality and gender-nonconforming behavior, the queer girl's "reversed manner" set her apart from "the other girls cutting up their lives in fashionable patterns."[104] The adjective "reversed" reverberates with "inverted," the dominant term in turn-of-century jargons to define homosexuality and gender nonconformity.[105] Defined as "reversed," adolescent female queerness is connected with contrariness and deviation long before it had become academically reclaimed as a term of heteronormative resistance. Foreshadowing the term's future meaning, early twentieth-century "queer girls" showed no interest in domesticated femininity, nor did they value conventional heterosexual romance. In a 1915 newspaper column, Mollie is introduced as "a queer sort of girl" because "she is in love with her independence and successful ability to turn her brain into money. . . . She is not at all desirous of marrying any man."[106] In fact, a head for business and distaste for male courtship are interpreted as telltale signs of female queerness as early as 1904. Presented with "a little romance with a college fellow . . . who got soaked in a thunderstorm," a shy country maiden is given an ultimatum: "If you don't make the best of it, you're a queer girl." "That Miss Sadie Davis was not a queer girl was proved a year later," when she wooed and wedded the male "tourist with a rich dad."[107] In periodical publications, a girl's "queerness" was thus repeatedly associated with a "reversal" of heteronormative femininity or with a knowingness beyond her years, either seen as unnerving or in need of correction. It is that self-awareness of innate difference that makes a "queer girl" stand out while also alienating her from peers and society at large. At times praised as a mark of strong character, such female noncompliance typically found itself chastised as affectation, orneriness, or pathology.

By the 1910s, physicians diagnosed female sexual inversion by employing heuristics similar to those rendering the "queer girl" legible to literate audiences at the turn of the century. Like Mollie, "the average inverted women will be very independent . . . and very likely will engage in business. Being endowed with the assertive force and characteristics of the masculine, the invert [shuns] the frills and delicate accoutrements so dear to the heart of the normal woman," much like James's "queer girl" heroine did. Like her literary forerunners, the female invert of clinical textbooks also experienced a "peculiar" sense of mental alienation, "believing she is different from everyone else and that she is the only person in the world with similar feelings."[108] In short, the "queer girl" of sentimental fiction shares many characteristics with the female invert of medical literature. Symptomatic of a transitional period when sexologists struggled to create a stable taxonomy of deviance that accounted for myriad manifestations of psychological, social, and sexual nonconformity, the queer girl operated in the same vein as "the screen-struck girl" or the mannish "New Woman": as a cypher for female alterity, an embodiment of diffuse patriarchal anxieties tussling with attachments, desires, and identities that strained heteronormative standards of feeling and being.[109]

Girls growing up in early twentieth-century United States would have been familiar with, and likely internalized, such a pervasive template to spot nonconforming female subjectivities among the human mass. When a tenth-grader from Minnesota wrote a short story about "a queer girl," she introduced female queerness as identifiable through aberrant behavior and public witnessing. "Elsie was a queer girl," the omniscient narrator states. "Everyone said so. She was always thinking hard and saying such strange things."[110] "Over thinking" continually features as a telltale sign of deviance, a skip and a hop away from "over feeling," the hallmark of screen-struck girlhood and feminized pathologies. Excess tethers the three together—female adolescents, film fans, and queer girls—ultimately othering them all. That some movie devotees described themselves as "queer girls" in personal documents indicates, then, a recognition and voluntary alignment with a dominant model of gendered divergence made recognizable by refusal to comply with heteronormative requirements of feminine conduct. Such self-characterization ripens when disclosure is enacted in private letters to female stars, commonly couched in sentimental idioms and eroticized identifications.

In marshaling the early twentieth-century valances of the term "queer," my aim is not to uniform nonnormative spectatorship under a transparent rubric where "all objects" or "all girls" may import same-sex desire or cross-gender identification in a tabular fashion. Rather, I seek to expand histories of silent female audiences that proliferated contiguous to those promoted as "standard" in the periodical press.[111] Throughout the 1910s, film publications tended to homogenize movie-loving girlhood as lustful over male idols and covetous of actresses' wares, columnists declaring that "a woman's idea of a poor picture [hinges on if] he was not good-looking and her dresses were too short."[112] First-person fan objects demonstrate that queerness can function, then and now, as "a horizon of experience shaping film reception for some spectators." Certain stars, performances, and images triggered "a structure of queer feeling," a scaffolding moviegoing girls who felt different from the norm used to pin and drape their sensations of divergence and belonging, pleasure and prejudice, aspiration and anxiety.[113] Although material-studies historians like Susan Pearce recognize that "most collections have an element of gendering" and "collecting obstinately remains embodied in traditional erotic experience," they also claim "there is not much evidence that people collect in order to subvert the gender roles available to them," a conclusion movie ephemera gathered by cross-dressed and male-identified girl fans pointedly challenges.[114]

Invariably, research on queer histories will meet with questions of how to ascertain the queerness of a past object, performer, or creator when self-identification is lacking. My heuristics loop back to the notion of affect previously proffered—the discrete propulsive charge attaching a fan to a specific star, a performance, an image. Their queerness is rendered legible as a combination of subject matter, affective intensity, and social biography, as well as by the kinship stirred in me as a queer researcher. Compilers' insistent penchant for the divergent (the male poetic voice, the cross-dressed actress, the pathologized language) guided me through the process of piecing together the multiplicity of sources comprising this archive of early female fan feeling—a lived and leaky repository where queerness, like paper ephemera, persists as a sort of defiance against expected dissipation and compliance, and whose leakage stimulates beholders to question themselves. In the end, if fan affect is *of the body* and felt *in the body,* so is the affect motivating queer historians. It takes guts and is felt in the gut, the drive to go fondling around the past, fingering for tender spots amongst sharp holes and brittle folds, little more than a hunger and a hunch for what "there-theres" might have been.[115]

AT SIXES AND SEVENS: CHAPTER BREAKDOWN

Building upon research on intimate relations between turn-of-the-century women, lesbian spectatorship, and ephemera as queer historical traces, chapter 1 traces the seminal homoerotic language of female fan mail.[116] I draw on nineteenth-century sentimental conventions and emergent sexology literature to historicize how accepted models of schoolgirl crushes and romantic friendships became the blueprint for mediated engagement between early screen actresses and their girl fans. Chapter 2 focuses on private correspondence girl fans sent to actress Florence Lawrence in the early 1910s, while chapter 3 surveys male-voiced love poems girls dedicated to female stars, most of them found in movie magazines and newspapers.

Throughout these chapters, I argue that the sentimental codes of female relationality and homoeroticism popularized in turn-of-the-century fiction, medicine, and everyday life came to undergird the feminization of Hollywood's star system, saturating its main modes of reception: fan-letter writing, movie scrapbooking, and playing dress-up. Fan mail and poetry, by definition stagings of superlative feeling and selfhood, cultivated the homoerotic and the sentimental; published fan poetry, in particular, provides a vivid snapshot of the rhetorical modes of sentimental self-expression that popular imagination naturalized as "feminine." Reading these artifacts alongside biographical data enables a sussing out of the queer codes and identifications a dawning commercial film culture afforded nonnormative girl spectators, while showing how adolescent female audiences drafted an infrastructural dialect of star-fan intimacy that homoeroticized film consumption.

Chapters 4 through 6 tackle a different material corpus: movie scrapbooks and diaries assembled by girls who used film ephemera to negotiate gender play and nonconformity. A study of personal collages of cross-dressed actresses, male-voiced journal entries, and photographic portraits in male drag reveals an everyday queer experience shaped around movie fandom. Chapter 4 traces the "movie scrap book" fad as it was first advertised in the periodical press at the onset of WWI, contextualizing the fan practice as an austerity measure targeting young female film lovers. Advertised in newspapers and fan magazine as a "useful" mode of female-oriented reception, movie scrapbooking became a privileged site for girls to rehearse divergent affinities under the cover of paper conservation and domestic craftwork. Engendering a visual language of media adoration, extant fan collages register the subcultural presence of a queer spectatorship that clustered around embodied erotics, expressed through the manipulation of stars' paper likenesses. This included gathering images of male stars engaged in physical intimacy with other men or known for their dandyism and sentimentality, like Jack W. Kerrigan. Though queer female spectatorship in the 1910s centered around movie actresses, I propose that the relationship some girl fans forged with "emotional" male players allowed for explorations of gender nonconformity, same-sex attraction, and erotic fluidity in a manner complementary to that instantiated by female stars.

Chapter 5 explores early twentieth-century medical literature, film magazines, and newspaper coverage of gender-nonconforming public figures (including criminals and stars) in order to historicize a spreading discourse associating female cross-dressing with pathology. I claim that as women achieved greater agency onscreen playing resourceful serial queens and flirtatious madcaps, pressmen labored to reinforce traditional femininity among film audiences, extolling actresses' gender-conforming lived behaviors and fashion choices across multiple outlets. Analyzing movie scrapbooks and photo albums from both affluent and working girls, chapter 6 examines the predominance of fan collages featuring actresses in menswear next to photographs of movie-loving girls cross-dressing in their day-to-day. This material juxtaposition discloses an undocumented history of queer life centered around moviegoing and gender performance, while also paving the way for a discussion of juridical, scientific, and cultural conceptions of gender and sexual deviance soaring in the early twentieth century. I propose that prior to the creation of the "woman's picture," a subgenre that permitted an identifiable venue for narratives of female desire and emotionality, moviegoing girls flocked to images of actresses in menswear. Like the woman's picture of the 1930s, female cross-dressing in the silent era both coaxed alternative readings and reinscribed heteronormative binaries. Still, from homoerotic desire to longing for liberties only allowed to men, girl fans' play with gender suggests an implicit understanding of femininity and masculinity as constructed social performances they enjoyed testing. The epilogue looks forward to the 1920s, tracing dis/continuities in both industry address and girl-fan practices, especially as they pertained to handicrafts and movie scrapbooking.

In the end, by exhuming the material archive of the first generation of self-identified screen-struck girls, I reach for what William Faulkner hauntingly described as "the living blood and seed [in which] we ourselves lay dormant"—we the historians, the fans, the female-identified and queer audiences, we the descendants of those "volatile and sentient forces" that, like Kitty Baker, may seem to have "faded to . . . just the words, the symbols, the shapes themselves, shadowy [and] inscrutable against that turgid background of a . . . mischancing of human affairs" but whose affective investment in early filmmaking remains "meaningful" to an understanding of cultural memory and media history.[117] Movie-loving girls of the silent period matter because they helped implement one of the most influential institutions in the world: Hollywood cinema and its enduring offshoot, celebrity culture. By giving them a long-delayed spotlight, this is also a book about queer ghosts—that is, if we regard what is present but unremarked a form of apparitionality, if we consider "queer" that which refuses to be fenced in by societal norms or historical periodization and continues to burst through an imposed negative space into a conjuring of possibilities.

CHAPTER I

It Disquiets, It Delights

Same-Sex Attachments and Early Female Moviegoing

Blessed,
    Each day and night I find such comfort in the thought of you—. . . to know . . . that by some beautiful miracle we belong to each other. . . . You came into my life trailing such clouds of glory from such a shining world . . .—I can remember worshipping you and thinking you quite the most wonderful and adorable person I had ever seen. . . . My heart was so hungry for you then darling—and it still is—and ever will be.
    —Nell Dorr

This personal letter, written by Nell Dorr to her girlhood friend and movie star Lillian Gish, apprehends the complex web of homoerotic desire and longing for intimacy undergirding not only the rapport forged between literate women growing up in the United States in the early twentieth century, but also that which adolescent girls established with the first generation of female film stars. Looking at a slew of letters and poems girl fans created for their favorite actresses, I set to exhume a pervasive thread of homoeroticism underpinning early female film reception—a result, I suggest, of the concurrent feminization of movie fandom and the new star system. When employing the term "homoerotic" I follow Jackie Stacey's interpretation, meaning a female fan identification with movie actresses that was not devoid of erotic desire and pleasure.[1] Homoeroticism, in the context of this book, thus designates a fan culture rooted in woman-loving, in appreciation and affinity with femininity.

Once fan and trade magazines selected adolescent girls as the personification of emotional movie consumption, they endowed girls from all walks of life with a rare authorial agency: the opportunity to delineate foundational practices of film fandom, including an epistolary dialect bursting with female desire and intimacy. Attraction to movie actresses did not exactly clash with the tenets of female sentimentalism and romantic friendship ascribed to women's interiority in the 1910s. But the force of these attachments, their frequency, and their recurrent coupling with vocalizations of gender nonconformity and physical desire do signal something essentially queer about early Hollywood stars and their young female fans.

Scholars have long wrestled with characterizing attachments between past women. Historical research on same-sex desire tends to be clouded by extremes: either female intimacy is reclaimed as unmarked lesbianism or foreclosed as nonerotic friendship.[2] In her pioneer study of relationships between educated women in the long nineteenth century, Martha Vicinus uses personal documents and autobiographical literature to actively position Anglo-American women in what she calls "the lesbian continuum."[3] The search for a white lesbian lineage is pivotal to the feminist project of the 1970s and 1980s, and it drives Vicinus's argument. Drawing on a similar corpus, Sharon Marcus argues for a more discrete classification of female relationships, noting that, though some tipped into sexual intimacy, the spectrum of variability in same-sex bonds was much wider and less subversive than Vicinus speculates.[4] According to Marcus, a good number of nineteenth-century ladies harnessed close ties with other well-to-do women to replicate heterosexist models of cohabitation, courtship, and gender performance, while never engaging in coupled partnerships or sexual affairs.

Equally invested in shedding light on the intimacies forged between nineteenth-century women, both Vicinus and Marcus overplay the determinacy of genital contact, privileging it as a main gauge to trace lines between "carnal lovers" and "just friends." Not to say those cannot be useful working categories for historical studies on family and society—Vicinus and Marcus's areas of intervention—but they become reductive metrics when applied to silent film audiences. Because movie spectatorship, fandom, and stardom are predicated on desire held in abeyance—on autoeroticism, projection, imagination, and distance—using physical contact to validate homoerotic spectatorial investments is moot. As Jean Baudrillard's work on collecting reminds us, the beloved "object attains exceptional value only by virtue of its absence."[5] Fans desired movie stars *in spite and because* physical consummation was a built-in impossibility. When investigating queer fan responses we must thus move away from the archeological overvaluation of "material proof" (i.e., sex acts) as capable of staking stable borders and validating monolithic classifications. Not only does that stance reproduce penal strategies historically used to criminalize same-sex desire (e.g., sodomy laws), but it misses the main point of fandom—that, like desire, it is built on subjectivity, fantasy, and changeability. Protean feeling is fandom's breeding ground, the intimate bonds cultivated between fans, as between celebrities and their followers, constantly shapeshifting and running together, complicating fixed absolutes.

Identities operate in a similarly plastic continuum, particularly those self-ascribed or performed by historically marginalized subjects. "Identity is the story or narrative structure that gives meaning to experience," Lisa Duggan proposes, so that, "stories of identity are never static, monolithic, or politically innocent."[6] Identities are, in other words, permeable to social transformation and pliable to cultural context. If identity is a story people continuously draft to make sense of their individual and collective experiences, both in public and in private, then the writings and images early female spectators self-fashioned become seminal loci for encountering identity manifested, embodied, narrativized. Far from homogenous, silent film fan practices are palimpsestic, borrowing motifs from "old stories"—including medical discourses pathologizing female biology and sentimental conventions regulating feminine intimacy—to quilt "new narrative meanings."[7] Some of those meanings were self-questioning and homoerotic.

I argue that, in the 1910s, movie-loving girls' communal devising of a functional language of affective media reception intersected with individual fans' struggle to give voice to nonnormative subjectivities—subjectivities that made them feel "different from most other women."[8] Feminist scholars from past decades have labeled that vocalized longing for same-sex closeness, commitment, and/or physical contact "lesbianism."[9] In the context of this book, that label is as slippery as it is limiting. Girl fans who harbored some or all of these desires for other women (whether a peer or a star) felt their difference stemming from a subjectivity that could not be contained by sexuality. Some stemmed from a dissidence from gender binaries, a hunger for professional independence, or a penchant for lifelong nonreproductive solitude. Overlaps existed, of course, Venn diagram–like. Yet the affects suffusing female queer reception cannot be uniformly bracketed under the term "lesbianism," even though lesbian subjectivities were becoming more visible in the United States at the time commercial cinema grew into a multimillion-dollar, star-driven industry.

Sex acts furthermore cannot and should not be held as instruments that measure, explain, or summarize one's affective engagements. Caution is especially urged when researching past women, whose sexual drive or lack thereof sustains a history of being pathologized by male physicians.[10] Placing weight on genital contact not only negates the very structural appeal of fandom but also erases the plurality of ways intimacy can be expressed between people, especially people whose identities and desires have endured systemic marginalization. Documents produced by early moviegoing girls thus help illustrate that "the history of sexuality is . . . the history of social relations," consisting of varied "human interactions, . . . not simply 'acts' as if sexuality were the enumeration and typology of an individual's orgasms."[11] When working- and middle-class girls confessed romantic "crushes" on film actresses or imagined themselves as their male beaus, they conveyed *an affinity for difference* that spanned the social, professional, emotional, sexual, aspirational, and aesthetic that may not have been made noticeable in their everyday presentation of self.[12] In other words, I argue that the queerness experienced vis-a-vis cinema reflected a fundamental aspect of viewers' being rather than only an aspect of their behavior.

Fan mail provides a corpus central to the broader project of historicizing the diversity of responses US filmdom induced in early spectators. Positioned at the intersection of fantasy and daily life, fan production is fantasy and emotion *in motion*, often abreast of the erotic and adrift of the mundane. Studying personal fan fragments hence helps in teasing out what Heather Love calls "the false starts [of] . . . the affects that drive [queer] relationality across time."[13] The dialect of call-and-response, courtship, and entrepreneurship girl fans instantiated with silent movie actresses evinces that the erotic "meaning and contents" of individual attachments exist "in a continual process of change," and that the sentimental idiom generations of young women had been raised with—in their schooling and leisure, through required readings and recommended pastimes—found its queer valences amplified by the development of commercial cinema.[14]

GIRLS ARE NOT BUILT THAT WAY: ROMANTIC FRIENDSHIPS AND THE MEDICALIZATION OF FEMALE SEXUAL DESIRE

In 1912, a senior at Vassar College wrote a private letter recounting her encounter with a first-year student: "There was the most adorable baby that I came across the other night trying to find a room. . . . We had a long talk and she seemed quite cheerful but when I went away I kissed her good night and that was too much. Between sobs she said, 'If you only hadn't kissed me!' and I felt guilty about it for hours."[15] In her written recollection, Elizabeth French concludes that kissing an "adorable" freshwoman tipped their rapport into the realm of "too much." Though touch seems essential to this perception of same-sex excess, it is unclear if the nameless girl's reaction stemmed from sisterly, sexual, neurotic, or homesick feelings. Similarly, French's "guilt" has no verifiable rationale, just a source: a kiss between two schoolgirls that ended in tears. The only direct quotation from the anonymous freshwoman is itself ambiguously fragmented to an accusatory exclamation: "If you only hadn't kissed me!" Like the caption underlining Kitty Baker's snapshot, female intimacy is seen as "too much," a self-diagnosis implying that transgression lurked in schoolgirls' physical closeness, as in the recording of said experiences.

Numerous historians have documented that romantic friendships between educated women became "a powerfully idealized social form" in nineteenth-century Anglo-American culture.[16] Though characterized by deep commitment and tenderness—including exchange of love letters, tokens, and caresses—female romantic friendships were generally perceived as sexless and spiritual affairs, harmless symptoms of over-emotive interiority divorced from deviant acts. In a way similar to its stance toward sentimental writing, turn-of-the-century US culture brushed away homoerotic bonds between girls as a fanciful, domesticating practice. To the eyes of patriarchal society, romantic friendships spoke to women's innate connection to "the heart" in lieu of the intellect, the home instead of the office.

Moreover, since the late eighteenth century medical professionals, educators, and etiquette writers had proposed that ladies of proper breeding lacked sexual appetite. Built for motherhood, female bodies supposedly did not require or recognize carnal pleasure. Such inherent asexuality resulted in disinvestment from genital contact, being that with men or other women. Clemence Dane, a celebrated female author who wrote at length about schoolgirl crushes during World War I, summarized these common beliefs by affirming that, for most girls, "the sex feeling is rather indirect and passive, and their active emotions are more maternal and spiritual than passionate."[17] Intimate relationships between women, as ardent as they may have seemed to outsiders, thus remained unthreatening to society at large because they were considered neutered bonds: undesiring of sexual contact and incapable of reproduction, mobilized by sentiment not lust.

Like sentimental culture, the turn-of-the-century idealization of non-sexual female friendship was a carryover from a previous time. A hybrid product of Romanticism and new discoveries about sexually transmitted diseases, the high cachet placed on women's romantic friendships rested on both its exuberant sentimentality and its presumed lack of genital contact. Taking root in youth, romantic friendship also could not be separated from adolescence, by definition a tumultuous period in women's lives. Acting from within a strictly desexualized framework, throughout the nineteenth century family and community members even encouraged unmarried girls to have a female "bosom friend" as a means to sate emotional instincts while staving off premature male congress. According to Carol Lasser and Carroll Smith-Rosenberg, middle-class girls' closeness was thought to replicate the sexless models of solidarity established between sisters, cousins, and mothers and daughters. This spiritualization of women's intimacy as a continuation of familial kinship conspired to confine girls to a homebound world defined by heterosexist submission during a time when the strictures of such gender-coded roles were challenged by a generation of outspoken female activists, many in their teens and twenties.[18]

At the end of the century, when sexologists began examining female sexuality in earnest, they tended to reinforce the longstanding notion that "normal" girls existed rid of lewdness, their infatuations with female peers paving the way for a healthy social development toward heterosexual coupledom. In 1886, pioneer sexologist Richard von Krafft-Ebing famously postulated that, during pubescence, women existed in a "neuter" state where "impressions . . . are stripped of sexual meaning."[19] Two decades later, US sociologist Irving King observed that in high-school "the social side of the girl reveals itself, [spurring] the desire to have . . . deep and ardent [female] friendships. . . . The girl in her teens invariably has a 'dearest friend,' who shares her joys and sorrows and confidences."[20] Because girls' "sexual neutrality" translated into "innocence," medical literature typically dismissed girls' same-sex "crushes," "mashes," or "cases" as quintessential symptoms of women's emotional nature.[21]

Understood as a landmark of female adolescence, romantic friendships roused little distress as long as they were temporary, just "a phase, an education in feelings for the young."[22] Local physicians underscored this point aggressively, considering that what normalized such affective female ties—and thus distinguished them from an "unnatural" affliction—was their "short duration only, being usually terminated by the entrance of some young man into the emotional life of one of the girls."[23] In a graduation speech, the president of Vassar College, Samuel Caldwell, summarized the prevalent trivialization of same-sex adolescent attachments when he described female students' "crazes" as "fleeting" and "unsubstantial" attachments "born of imagination, of young impulse [and] temporary fancy."[24]

The narrative of tolerated female homoeroticism dominates historical research on the long nineteenth century. However, print evidence indicates a more complicated lived reality. In her study of close relationships between affluent women, Vicinus notes that the idea of same-sex female desire unsettled heteronormative power structures so potently that during the late 1800s, Anglo-American pundits worked diligently to demonize or dismiss the complex sensual arrangements settled between women in everyday life. Vicinus astutely points out that "strenuous efforts to define and delimit the bodily nature of female friendship," like those found in Caldwell's speech, implies "that the barrier between admired romantic friends and excoriated Sapphists must have seemed permeable. *Only by constant reminders would women, and men, distinguish between friendship and love.*"[25] In fact, scientific literature produced in the early 1900s shows male psychologists investing exceeding time and energy in determining the boundaries between the "greater familiarity and intimacy [to which] we are accustomed between women . . . and . . . any abnormal passion."[26] European sexologists Havelock Ellis and August Forel, for instance, more than once bemoaned that centuries of cultural tolerance towards women's open displays of physical affection had allowed them to get away with stealing "vague sensual pleasures" from their female peers without those surrounding them being none the wiser.[27]

A Gordian knot of medical, legal, social, and psychological scrutiny, in the 1910s female romantic friendship functioned on the "principle of ignorance," characterized by Eve K. Sedgwick as a deliberate and concerted "ignorance of a knowledge"—in this case that female sexual desire existed and was at times directed at other women. Acting as a mechanism of heteropatriarchal control, such "particular opacities, . . . far from being pieces of the originary dark, are produced by and correspond to particular knowledges and circulate as part of particular regimes of truth."[28] To wit, in the early twentieth century various spheres of knowledge production *decided to ignore* the existence of sexual desire between women, which is vastly different from *being igno-rant* of its existence. This is a critical distinction to an understanding of the tensions animating female fan correspondence during the early silent period.

In spite of being poked at and waived away, infatuation between adolescent girls became an unavoidable topic of conversation within women's reformatories, boarding schools, and colleges. By 1908, one physician observed that same-sex crushes were the province of secluded girlhood, appearing "almost universal among institutions for girls in the adolescent period, [while] there seems to be no exactly comparable phenomenon among boys of a similar age and in similar circumstance."[29] It is no surprise that the cultural ties between young femininity and romantic friendship regained visibility in the early twentieth century, when the proliferation of secondary and tertiary institutions dedicated to training girls had been ongoing long enough to foster a distinct peer culture. The erotic closeness brewing between schoolgirls in the early 1900s did not go unnoticed, nor did it go unspoken on the ground, as personal archives denote. A note swapped in 1905 between two freshwomen at Radcliffe College reads: "Kate [is] enamored of Wanda/Wanda loved the agile Edna/She by her unmoved/Loved only Captain Mary." When nineteen-year-old Mabelle Smith Kent pasted the ripped piece of paper on her scrapbook, she scribbled next to it "one of several such poems on the same theme," confirming that girls' homoerotic bonds were as visible as they were humdrum at an elite women's college like Radcliffe.[30]

By 1914, "the school girl 'crush'" phenomenon grew so prevalent that it leaked out of cloistered school halls, attracting the attention of reporters and clinicians. Papers published in medical journals throughout the 1910s not only explicitly address "the homosexual character" of "one girl's enthusiastic attachment for another," but further "urge some first-hand studies by those dealing with schoolgirls addicted to crushes."[31] One such piece unequivocally recognized that "the phenomenon of the [schoolgirl] crush has undoubtedly *a sexual basis*. . . . Such situations should naturally be guarded against."[32] What these articles evidence is an alteration of scientific outlook on gendered behavior. Sexuality now figured as a major component and concern in male-penned studies mapping women's interiority and sociability. By the mid-1910s, physicians and educators no longer tended to deny the possibility of sexual desire between young women, permanent or passing. Instead, they explained it as a deviation, the result of juvenile foolishness, social contamination or, in more extreme cases, physiological dysfunction.

As a result of the psychiatric shift toward female deviance, same-sex carnality increasingly featured in US research on juvenile delinquency. Margaret Otis's 1913 study of interracial romances between incarcerated girls signals an emergent scientific scrutiny of female intimacy within same-sex institutions. By situating these homosexual relations in the criminalized space of reformatory schools, Otis inherently pathologized their nature.[33] Likewise, in his diligent taxonomy of adolescence, psychologist G. Stanley Hall theorized that girls' genital desire for female chums resulted from aberrant socialization, such as "being segregated from the other sex." Unable to attract the favors of boys, jilted girls presumably sought out a poor-man's substitute of the ideal male suitor, a transference process that accounted for some female adolescents "'mash[ing]' or 'crush[ing]' on some older girl with masculine traits."[34] It bears note that while psychiatry classified homosexuality as an abnormality at the time, the US law regarded it a felony, punishable with jail time.

Most allusions to the manly lesbian or the "female invert" not only identified same-sex attraction as anomalous, but often retrofitted it to uphold conventional gender, sex, and wellness binaries. Struggling to classify female "homosexual tendencies," in 1915 US sexologists revived the figure of the "unscrupulous Lesbian," tracing the "intense emotional relations between women" back to "Sappho, the Greek poetess."[35] Though consensus about the origins of female inversion remained elusive—theories ranged from endogenous to reactive, biological to environmental, inherited to acquired—most researchers agreed that coupled happiness could not be lasting. Conceding that "the love between two [women] is as intense in its passion as that between man and wife," physician Douglas McMurtrie immediately cautioned that "when such *liaisons* are broken [it] *is liable to result in crime—even murder*. It is of singular interest that the annals of such crimes show the United States with an exceptionally large number recorded."[36]

Tracking the press coverage of "lesbian love murders," Duggan observes that, as early as 1892, US newspapers recognized the profitability of depicting women's romantic friendships as hotbeds for "mad infatuation."[37] By the mid-1910s, reports on "a strange attraction" between schoolgirls toppling into murder and suicide peppered US dailies.[38] One of the most infamous cases took place in March 1917, when eighteen-year-old Ethel Stanton and twenty-year-old Peggy Spalding—two "ravishing beauties" who had met in "physical culture class" at Boston's Garland school—sat across from each other in a "curtained booth" of a "fashionable café" in Portsmouth, New Hampshire. After ordering black coffees, both "placed revolvers to their temples and fired instantaneously."[39] Tabloids anchored the double suicide in "morbid" homosexual desire, reporting that "defying every effort of friends to break it up, the uncanny love proceeded to the point when, fearing even short separations, the girls ended their lives."[40] Mentions of the girls' "death note" requesting to "be buried side by side" and reports of their last "night and day" being spent locked together in a hotel room subtly indicated the sexual nature of Stanton and Spalding's "weird love affair," while blaming the unhealthy erotic attachment for the girls' tragic ending.[41]

As sensational as it was reproachful, newspaper coverage of girls' fervent dyadic relations proves that popular imagination continued to be concerned with regulating female sexual desire and same-sex intimacy as the new century progressed. Examination of the concurrent campaigns to classify and pathologize same-sex female attachments is indispensable to an understanding of the sociocultural context in which the first generation of movie-loving girls engineered (linguistic, discursive, aesthetic) strategies to manifest their investments in film actresses. Passion was both a requirement and a pitfall of screen-struck fandom, with the line separating same-sex devotion from deviance growing ever thinner and more treacherous. It is telling that the press discourses on "movie-mad girls" and "mad" girl lovers surface simultaneously around 1916. They are both components of a wider cultural narrative seeking to discredit female autonomy (sexual and otherwise), as well as delegitimize any modes of social, economic, or erotic engagement that did not directly support heteronormative patriarchy. Two figures of same-sex deviance, the mad girl fan and the mad girl lover stem from a conservative backlash against a vibrant woman-centered culture blossoming within single-sex schools and clubs, in which cinema played a salient part. As Monica Witting remarks, desire between women must be seen as "the product of a clandestine culture that has always existed in history" and that found survival by devising "its own codes of language, codes of social relations, codes of dress, its own modes of work," while consigned to the margins of "*the* culture"—that is, a mainstream heterosexual culture early Hollywood cinema reinforced, while concurrently inviting a host of same-sex female intimacies.[42]

Swelling public surveillance, in sum, spurred girls who thrived on closeness with other women to design complex modes of communication. Certain words, touches, and gestures telegraphed an unspoken dialect of adoration, desire, mutuality, and understanding. Steeped in established sentimental and spiritual conventions, these calculated behaviors did not stem exclusively from sexual interest but were pervasively cultivated to find a measure of privacy and agency within a patriarchal society that constantly surveyed the personal affects and public attitudes of proper young ladies. Girls growing up in the 1910s had to learn to express nonnormative inclinations by way of concealment, rendering the homoerotic, the gender nonconforming, the neurologically divergent, and the homosexual legible through subcultural innuendoes, indexes, and ellipses. That same encrypted vernacular would be marshaled by movie-loving girls who sought to communicate queer responses to beloved film actresses.

A COVERT FEELING: HOMOEROTICISM IN FEMALE MOVIEGOING

The fan codes crafted by the first cohort of screen-struck girls resulted from an active dialogue with medical, legal, journalistic, and pedagogical debates ascendant in US popular culture at the turn of the twentieth century, many of which aimed to regulate women's development and sexual behavior. Capturing such an interwoven tapestry of social surveillance and self-policing, the modes of self-documentation prevalent in girls' private papers made during the 1910s privilege the fragmented, the intimated, the unresolved. The negative space between facts invites inference, much like French's letter invites the reader to supply their own connectors: presumed motivations, circumstances, and backstories color the female encounter the Vassar girl so poignantly but sparsely sketched. Contextualizing the traffic of influence between female movie fans and cultural discourse shows that key reception practices practiced by girls in the 1910s stemmed from long-established models of same-sex relationality, specifically women's "romantic friendships."

Though educated filmgoers had an advantage, the creation of a homoerotic female fan language transcended class. Not only did girls from all backgrounds contact screen actresses, but the movies themselves suggested that the language of female affinity bypassed the written word, residing instead in the gestural and the unspoken. For example, in a narrativization of the popular 1912 serial *What Happened to Mary,* published as a tie-in in *Ladies' World,* an exchange between the titular heroine and another female character is described in the following terms: when "the girl's eyes had met Mary's, something subtle had passed between them—the secret unspoken password of maidenhood."[43] Clearly the film industry promoted the belief that girls shared a "subtle" encrypted dialect only legible to their own sex. In framing female interplay in this charged fashion, the new star system also stimulated a permissibility toward the homoeroticization of glances exchanged between women: not just onscreen, but further inviting female spectators to look back and include their gaze in a triangulation of same-sex desire. In a close-circuited act of looking where silence functioned as the means for accessing "the secret password of maidenhood," girl audiences could be simultaneous voyeurs and participants, their gazes at silent film actresses going without answer but not without communication. That particular mode of call and response, contingent not on reciprocation but on identification, will shape female fan mail.

Tapping on the fraught cryptography of homoerotic attachments, Heather Love contends that in the early part of the twentieth century same-sex friendships pulsed with "a desire-in-uneasiness."[44] With homosexual desire denied public expression and heterosexual interactions corseted by social regulation, same-sex friendships came to function as a self-questioning space and a razor's edge, uneasy with undefined potential. Moviegoing, an act of contemplation and immersion in a dark, public, and peopled space—an act that extended into the private and the affective through remembrance, ephemera consumption, and fan communion—facilitated a platform for exploring such "desire-in-uneasiness." Nonnormative girls latched on to that platform, to the liminal space film fandom allowed in their inner and daily lives. There resided a powerful feedback of desire between the highly haptic, emotive actresses and the female spectators sitting in the audience. Case in point: in the late 1910s, a woman in her thirties connected her same-sex arousal and shame with the experience of watching actresses onscreen. When questioned about her sexual habits for a nationwide survey, the anonymous filmgoer stated that "she thinks that sex thoughts should not be encouraged. Usually, she tries to drive them from her mind and is successful . . . *unless a movie is very suggestive. 'Then I feel wrong in being there'* [in the picture house]." She reported having no sexual history, only unconsummated crushes on other girls. In her urgency to distance herself from the sapphic vampire of sordid headlines, the woman quickly clarified that, by crushes, she means "a deep admiration for women." She concluded by adding never to have had such "feelings" or "friendships with men."[45]

Anecdotal as it may seem, this first-person testimony exposes the complicated network of queer responses triggered by US moviegoing in the 1910s. In part, these complications result from unresolved same-sex desire and from linking, albeit unconsciously, moviegoing to troubling female intimacy and arousal. Both reflect female spectators' internalization of discourses pathologizing homosexuality and women's erotic desire. I propose that the specter of homoerotic impossibility and uneasiness bleeding through moviegoing girls' self-reportage very much illustrates this tense blend of female sentimentality, internalized homophobia, suppressed longing, and active self-policing. Many of these psychological states ultimately became externalized through mediated female idolization, vocalized self-reproach, and written dis/identification, a patchwork of contradictory emotions seized in screen-struck girls' personal journals, fan correspondence, and scrapbook collages. An extension of movie-watching, movie fandom afforded some girls a forum for fantasy, introspection, and vulnerability where they could safely contend with such intricate libidinal knots.

Penned between 1914 and 1916, the private diaries of a middle-class schoolgirl exemplify the intersections of moviegoing and sentimental life-writing, revealing how these could be wielded to help an adolescent fan negotiate the unease and exhilaration of same-sex limerence. the oldest daughter of a Washington State senator, Medora "Middy" Espy (b. January 3, 1899) led an eventful social life while boarding at the all-girls Portland Academy in Oregon (figure 3).[46] Cinema featured constantly in her social life. Her collection of personal papers overflows with ticket stubs, handwritten film reviews, lists of pictures watched, and ledgers with moviegoing costs. A considerable amount of Espy's entries are also dedicated to ranking her affects for a coterie of girl-friends with such jovial sobriquets as Marge, Dote, Bunch, and Knicks. An exuberant attachment to one girl in particular not only demanded several nicknames ("my sweetheart, Betty, Bunch and Rosetta are all the same thing"), but could only be appropriately conveyed though the hyperbolic vocabulary assigned to heterosexual courtship: "Bunch is darling and I am crazy about her," Espy gushes in early 1915. "Bunch and I are very intimate—I love her to death."[47]

By March that year, Espy's attachment to Betty had escalated in size, as in burden. One evening, Espy muses, "Betty is my most precious darling, but *caring more would have disturbed me too much.*" This diary entry shows the moviegoing girl conscious of the potential danger of her emotions if they were not kept in check. Though Espy attempts to act accordingly, she is overwhelmed by the depth of her unparsed same-sex feelings:

> I felt so so forlorn while Betty acted like nuts and I was oh! so quiet when *I went to bed and my sweetest little lover come and kissed me, such a loving*

FIGURE 3. Medora Espy at fifteen, dozing off while reading, 1914.

kiss. . . . The fact that she loves others better than I used to make me jealous. . . . I love deeply but *it is a quiet intense love, I don't think I can explain it.* . . . I love Betty and Mary K. so much but they don't understand— *they love me but not as I love them.* . . . Aren't thoughts funny [?] I don't believe I will ever get mine sorted correctly.[48]

Espy's inability to "correctly" "sort" her "thoughts" concerning Betty reveals the kind of suppressive and self-aware discourse regulating girl-to-girl attachments, especially those lived within the semipermanent confinements of a same-sex boarding school. The adolescent moviegoer evidently delighted in being intimate with Betty and is hurt when, later that month, physical touch becomes unrequited: "This evening I would feel morbid if I wanted to because I love Betty a great deal and she does not care for my caresses."[49] Repeatedly Espy commends herself for being able to keep "quiet" through the torment of "loving so deeply." Yet a sense of inappropriateness continues to underline Espy's uneasy connection to Betty as her emotions grow one-sided. This is further emphasized by Espy's use of the adjective "morbid" to characterize her same-sex attachment. Vicinus confirms that "morbidity . . . [was] a familiar code word for homosexuality" in the early twentieth century, while literature of the time notes that "made me morbid" was a common expression employed by young women who regretted having or desiring homosexual experiences.[50]

Such unsettling same-sex desire is only fully grappled when put in the context of moviegoing. For Espy, a date to the pictures actualized the deep bond between the two girls. The public space of the picture house made their attachment something more than a run-of-the-mill "boarding-school crush"—it made it a visible and lived reality. In the honeymoon phase of their relationship, Espy first commented, "Sweetheart and I went to a movie as we are very, very much attached." Weeks later, moviegoing is revisited as the main site of jealousy and jilted discontentment: "Bunch made me awfully mad though I am trying not to show it because she went to a theatre with Miss C. instead of going to a movie with me. I have asked her every Saturday but she never wants to go." Espy considers moviegoing such a vital ritual of her relationship with Betty that she felt as much betrayed by Betty's change of date (Miss C.) as of medium (theater). For Espy, in short, the act of attending a movie with her "sweetheart" was instilled with romantic connotations. In treating moviegoing as a space for courtship and peer recreation, the high schooler enacted a cultural practice historian Kathy Peiss first recorded among working-class urban women in the late 1800s. While Peiss identified the picture house as a new public space that licensed young women's heterosexual autonomy, Espy's personal writings reveal that girls with same-sex attachments also regarded moviegoing as an activity replete with erotic potentialities. [51]

The same year Espy wrestled with filmgoing as a site for female intimacy, the belief that sexual desire in well-bred schoolgirls took the shape of foolish "smashes" reached movie magazines, coloring film fandom's fledgling language. In 1914, *Photoplay* dismissed the fervid feelings of Mary Pickford's girl admirers as "one of those 'boarding-school crushes.'"[52] Four years later, it was actress Mae Murray who promoted the de-eroticization of girls' same-sex fan attachments, declaring that an actress's "perfect lover is a little girl anywhere from six up to sixteen."[53] Murray clarified that, for her, a "perfect lover" was personified not by a virile suitor but by "a primrose ring of young, young girls who send daily letters to their favorite movie actresses." Murray's nonplussed reaction to girls' intense "love letters" reflects that of nineteenth-century pundits who believed civilized girls were more of the spirit than of the flesh. When movie magazines promoted young girls as actresses' "perfect" correspondents, they built upon this idealization of women as ethereal beings, by nature "the sole cherishers of fast-vanishing arts," such as letter-writing, scrapbooking, crafting, and journaling.[54] Simply put, unlike male fans girls were seen as unthreatening pen pals. Devoid of any sexual sub-text, their lovestruck letters were literally romantic duds.

In the 1910s, most modes of affective communication afforded to schoolgirls centered on correspondence and journaling, both occupations associated with a moderate-to-high level of literacy, introspection, and sentiment—all purviews of the mind rather than the body. Society, in the shape of parents, educators, and peers, trained "good girls" to spiritual-ize their physical passions into religious worship, manual work, and care-taking. When a girl felt compelled to "pour all the heart's devotion at the feet of" a female teacher or friend, physicians—some women them-selves—urged her to "wake up to the foolishness of the situation . . . [and] guide [her] feelings into more wholesome channels," including het-erosexual romance. "More susceptible to *morbid emotions* than boys," girls were constantly instructed to be vigilant and ashamed of ardent female ties. "When you go to a concert, even though you have your 'best friend' next to you, don't sit and hold her hand during the performance," a *Ladies' Home Journal* columnist remonstrated. "That does you no good and when you think of it in sober earnest, it is pretty silly isn't it?" Likewise, jealousy and yearning directed at other girls should exact ener-getic sublimation, redirection, and self-chastisement: "When you go skat-ing with the 'dearest girl in the world' don't be miserable because your chum had the privilege of strapping the dear one's skates. . . . Would you want your big brother to know how you felt? You would be ashamed to tell him."[55] By late 1914, Espy struggled to follow suit, since so many of her responses to Betty replicated those being widely upbraided as improper and unhealthy. Taking these indictments to heart, the devout Baptist girl vowed to "make up" her "diary of 1915 more a budget of my thoughts and accomplishments" than a ledger of her crushes and social outings.

Set up as an uneven system of adoration that should find a balance between want and detachment, female film fandom presented a frame-work to work through complex same-sex feelings. To suffer for an unreachable muse particularly appealed to a generation of god-fearing schoolgirls who had been taught to worship "good womanliness" while fearing sexual activity. Homoeroticism thrived in that rife no-man's-land. Youth leaders—schoolteachers, club organizers, and faith counselors—repeatedly observed that girls' excessive attachment to female superiors fed on institutional power differentials and cultivated aloofness. A 1915 training manual addressing "girls in their teens" warned that "a leader who tries to make herself unapproachable for she believes that by making things hard for the girl and holding her at a distance, the [crush] will be overcome" would soon discover that "this method does not cure [but] actually intensifies the girl's morbid emotional condition. Sometimes the more difficult the access, the greater her desire to be near and show her devotion [to] her adored one."[56] The unrequited strand of sentimental writing customarily exchanged between educated girls—where the sender showboated her humble dedication to a deified female addressee— rehearsed these eroticized power asymmetries, while incorporating chivalric codes of conduct prevalent in sororities, upper-under classmate relations, and teacher-student interplay. Such generic continuities rendered female sentimental correspondence the ideal blueprint for same-sex screen-struck language—a relationship predicated in the fan's agreement to remain in awe of the alluring star without a viable possibility for equal reciprocation or consummation.

LETTERS TO THE STARS: THE "SENTIMENTAL IDIOM" IN FEMALE FAN CORRESPONDENCE

It warrants remarking that the act of courting a star harbored subversive valances, even when operating within a heterosexual framework. "Don't Fall in Love with Stars" topped the list of dictates "movie-struck" fans should heed, according to newspapers and film studios. "Don't fall in love with the leading man," the Los Angeles Times admonished in 1917; "he's nearly always married; nor with the leading lady—she's thinking of nothing but her art, her clothes and her salary."[57] To romance a picture personality went against the circulated etiquette of film fandom. Industry officials described fans' erotic desire as a trespassing: of men's marital obligations as of women's personal bounds.

There was, however, an instance where such rules did not hold fast: fan mail by girl spectators. As Motion Picture Magazine's Answer Man reassured Lois F.C. in 1916, "Since you are a girl, it is perfectly proper for you to write to Norma Talmadge telling her you love her."[58] Within the confines of female correspondence, movie-loving girls were given tacit permission to voice proclivities that in any other venue could be seen as inappropriate. Girls who wrote to actresses gushing over their physical attractiveness, who disclosed a longing to kiss them, to mimic their bodies, to place their likeness over their beds, or share in their lives treaded a precarious line. On the one hand, they risked overstepping codes of conduct promoted by the film industry and their press affiliates;

on the other, they took full advantage of cultural exemptions attributed to their neutered gender and age. In this calculated testing of borders, in their written displays of same-sex want and ardor, girl fans—in spite of their sexual or gender identifications—engaged in a queering of film reception.

The few extant collections of early stars' personal fan mail suggest that girls wrote to movie players in much larger numbers than boys. In both the Florence Lawrence and the William S. Hart private archives, female writers make up an average of 85 percent of all correspondence received throughout the 1910s, with a majority self-identifying as white, unmarried, and in their teens and early twenties.[59] This may be because in Anglo-American culture, feminine expression had been linked with sentimental writing since the late 1700s.[60] Having its heyday in the mid-nineteenth century, sentimental fiction primarily sought to trigger strong emotional responses in its readers by privileging highly empathetic language and sensitive topics like love, death, domesticity, kinship, and religion. A genre of the heart and the hearth, sentimental literature expediently became associated with female consumers and disparaged by male critics; like its intended audience, the genre was dismissed as limited, overwrought, and cloying.

Though born half a century later, the first girls who wrote to movie actresses drew heavily on this "sentimental idiom." Their epistolary language is exalted and confessional, their film responses often lingering on intimate grievances, their life-narratives painted with gusto, gush, and pathos. Historian Joanne Dobson argues that in spite of its many detractors, at the turn of the twentieth century "sentimentalism became a written imaginative mode," affording significant agency and belonging to the women who produced and consumed it.[61] Far from alienating, female audiences' "use of the sentimental aesthetic [generated] . . . sympathetic identification and an examination of familial and social relations—the self-in-society and all that entails."[62] As the language of the heart, sentimental writing became an indispensable connective tissue in a still poorly connected but rapidly developing United States. A vehicle for confession, introspectiveness, and closeness, it allowed affective ties to flourish and endure across long geographic distances. Following Dobson's appreciative take on sentimental literature, I propose that the exuberant writing style adopted by girl fans when addressing female stars should be interpreted not as rhetorical parroting but as a cover for parsing noncompliant feelings. "An imaginative orientation characterized by certain themes, stylistic features, and figurative conventions," the sentimental idiom operated as a tried-and-true method to verbalize complex responses called forth by seeing young-looking screen actresses publicly perform rewarding positions of power, entrepreneurism, and pleasure.[63]

By the mid-1910s, film-fan magazines actively prompted readers to correspond with stars, various film historians have shown.[64] Studying Mary Pickford's advice column published in McClure syndicated newspapers from 1915 to early 1917, Anke Brouwers adds that, "working with the familiar and effective tradition" of nineteenth-century advice literature, "Pickford strengthen[ed] her star appeal" by modeling "how to live a 'good' life . . . , exemplified by [her] idealized, almost sanctified embodiment of American womanhood . . . , domesticity, morality [and] fellow-feeling."[65] Early implementation of star-fan interactivity thus derived from sentimental modes of female autobiographical closeness and "moral fabulating" promoted in popular conduct and courtesy books. Presenting them as epistolary call-and-response, Brouwers claims that Pickford's replies to queries by (mostly) young female fans "contain similar rhetorical strategies" relative to those found in these nonfiction genres: "metaphors, anecdotes, and aporia put in the familiar and reassuring voice of the intimate friend [and] mixed with the hortatory of the teacher."[66]

In addition to didacticism, by inviting fans to personalize writings to their idols, early Hollywood worked to humanize picture personalities, by definition remote beings. First-person sharing lubricated that process. Pickford described her daily column as "pages of my diary," where she dialogued with a bevy of movie-struck "girls." The column was also featured in "women's interest" sections, evincing that fan correspondence engaged female moviegoers most directly.[67] Pickford's "Talks" paved the way for other young film actresses to become columnists, including Anita Stewart and Ruth Stonehouse, whose advisory letters interactively addressed so-called "girl" fans.[68] It bears noticing that first-person written disclosure—first in the form of onscreen intertitles and later in magazine interviews and newspaper columns—defined players' "voice" during a period when cinema was silent. Harmonized with screen work, the editorialized autobiographical voice textured the movie star as a relatable three-dimensional entity, complete with life experiences, opinions, and expertise.

In sum, in the pursuit of profit, the film press reinvigorated an epistolary shorthand familiar to generations of literate young women, including the actresses themselves—an idiom grounded on same-sex identification, sharing, and caring. Resultantly, fan-star correspondence emerged as a trusted platform through which moviegoing girls could explore divergent desires that might not have found an outlet in everyday life. This included but was not limited to same-sex attraction, repulsion from matrimony and motherhood, dreams of an unconventional career, antisocial feelings, a nonconforming gender identity, or self-perceived abnormality.

Fan writings from the 1910s further grant historians unparalleled access into the highly subjective and idiosyncratic process of watching and loving cinema at the very moment the notions of "film star" and "movie fan" burgeoned. These first-person documents render reception plural via the individual. Because sentimentalism functions as a relational mode of self-expression that envisions "the self-in-relation" to others at its most vulnerable, to unpack the ways early moviegoing girls employed sentimental conventions in their fan mail admits entrance to a semiprivate stage where dissident desires were performed in an unusually unfettered manner.[69]

Stowed away in the history of female sentimental writing traveled the double-entendres of homoerotic communication substantive to the idiom; when it went on to scaffold movie-fan language, such codes traveled within. Such an absconded aspect of the sentimental dialect is determinant to my reading of personal female fan materials as queer, as symptomatic of ever-present, barely under-the-surface modes of reception historically devised and deployed by people who identified as different from the norm. Historian Susan K. Harris argues that sentimental literature is intrinsically dual, defined by what she coins "the coverplot."[70] Literature scholar Jennifer A. Williamson expands on this notion, claiming that, "sentimental fiction works within the confines of the legal doctrine of the 'femme covert,' also known as coverture, the social and political practice by which women were rendered legally invisible and considered to be under the protection, guidance, and control of their fathers and, eventually, their husbands. *Sentimental fiction reveals the social problems women experience under coverture,* both illustrating the tragic failures that occur when male protection fails and offering potential remedies [through] women's empowerment."[71]

Faye Halpern concludes that sentimental writing is always a layered affair whose "unmasking is a particularly delicious project."[72] Revealing and concealing, coming out and passing undetected, are paramount aspects of queer experience, as are historical modes of queer communication: messages and gestures are encoded to ensure safe passage under hostile scrutiny, their double meanings intelligible only to those audiences in the know. Vicinus makes the connection between lesbian desire and cryptographic communication explicit when she declares that nineteenth-century lesbians "wrote in code."[73]

A dedication left in a Hollywood High School memory book beautifully illustrates the subversiveness ensconced in common girl-to-girl correspondence. In 1919, eighteen-year-old Mary Dinning (aka "Dody the Darlin'") said goodbye to her best friend and moviegoing buddy Margaret Croft with the following lines: "You know Margie, a boys [sic] love is like a pinch of snuff, a little bit and that's enough, but a girl's love is prized like gold—hard to get and hard to hold [.] Here's hoping I may get yours and hold it. I can say no more *nothing* but I have *something* to say that I cannot seem to find words for—but here's best wishes and love to you always."[74]

So much is left unspoken in this message, sheltered by playful references to heterosexual courtship and linguistic ellipsis. Yet so much is revealed by clever turns of phrase and one grammatical error. In seventy words, Dinning tells her friend that one girl's "love" is more valuable than that of all "boys" combined, that her attachment to "Margie" (who, tellingly, everyone else called Peggy) is as rare and enduring as a precious metal, and that for unstated reasons Dinning "hopes" her affection will be perennially "prized" above heterosexual dalliances. Dinning's refusal to commit to paper that last unintelligible "*something*" infuses with haunting power the unspoken love confession: it is there, ghosting every inked word, making even the most trivial commendations ("best wishes and love always") vibrate with the weight of the emotions unstated. Immanent and suppressed, Dinning's attachment to Margie falls in line with what Terry Castle and Judith Butler postulated about lesbian desire: that conscripted to the margins of heteronormative representability, it is forced to exist as an apparitional force, its existence perceived but not openly recognized or named.[75] Evocatively, Teresa de Lauretis correlates the systematic invisibilization of same-sex female desire with cryptographic sentimental writing. In her analysis of Djurna Barnes's fiction, Lauretis argues that the queer author's "highly metaphoric, oblique, and allusive language . . . both thematizes and demonstrates the [systemic] failure to represent, grasp, and convey [lesbian] subjects."[76]

That ability to concurrently disclose and conceal through first-person writing—to trust the unspoken to be perceived by a reader via innuendo, to confess the impermissible or unrequited under the excusable veneer of female sociability and sensibility—is what the sentimental idiom proffered girls coming of age in the 1910s. Those deliriously blurred lines between quotidian life and fantasy, the vernacular and the hyperbole, the homoerotic and the homosocial are at the core of sentimental writing as of female film reception during the silent period. Both also shared an overreliance on charging "every gesture, however frivolous or insignificant . . . with the conflict between light and darkness, salvation and damnation."[77] Drawing on long-held melodramatic conventions, that hyperbolization of gesture and feeling shaped America's emergent narrative cinema and its expressive language, both as performed by stars onscreen and as rehearsed by their followers in everyday life. We find such retooled modes of affective expression distilled in Dorr's letter to Gish: the purposefully fogged distinctions between friend and fan, companion and muse, the ideal and the lived self, the idol and the lived other, exemplify the ethos and lexicon of female film hagiography as it developed in the early twentieth century.

In conclusion, when US schoolgirls fell in love with movie actresses, they brought long-established rhetorical devices and encrypting strategies to their fan writings. The queer poems and letters they dedicated to female players are carryovers of the textured emotional relationships forged among a cohort of girls coming of age at a time when the "femme covert" social doctrine had begun to be exposed by psychologists, suffragists, and Progressive reformers. This affective archive visibilizes the democratic possibilities filmgoing opened for many girls, leveraging movie actresses to become muses/confidantes to a generation of growing citizens and, through an established feminine idiom, help them render "the unimaginable . . . finally the obvious."[78]

Despite seeds of political and social change being sowed during the 1910s, most girls coming of age in that decade remained bound to a heterosexist structure mandating wifehood and motherhood to all respectable maidens regardless of their backgrounds or preferences. In an era built on sex and gender power asymmetries, women often relied on each other to find satisfying companionship and support. As historian Nancy Cott points out, during the long nineteenth century,

> In one sense, the female friendships of this period expressed a new individuality on women's part, a willingness and ability to extract themselves from familial definition and to enter into peer relationships as distinct human beings. In another sense, these attachments documented *women's construction of a sex-group identity.* Women had learned that gender prescribed their talents, needs, outlooks, inclinations; *their best chance to escape their stated inferiority in the world of men was on a raft of gender "difference."* Female

friendships, by upholding such attributes as "heart" as positive qualities, asserted that women were different from but not lesser than—perhaps better than—men.[79]

Carnality, in other words, did not unanimously impel women's bonds with one another: the quest for individuality, respect, valorization, and mutuality did, at times galvanizing the crossing into physical intimacy. The "hunger" burning in Dorr's "heart"—like the hunger in the hearts of many other girls reaching out to silent screen actresses—was a hunger for alternatives to the stock roles ascribed to schoolgirls during the 1910s. It was a hunger that shaped a homoerotic female gaze, a mode of looking that desired difference (of options) through an embrace of sameness (of gender, of age, of interests, of heart).

The sentimental language of female socialization and unconsummated adoration movie lovers like Espy and Dorr applied in their private writings trickled into the vocabulary girls used to articulate affective responses to film actresses of similar age. With the inception of the star system, moviegoing girls strove to formulate a language that accurately conveyed their strong reactions to young actresses who, though still distant, were now named and known. Socially accepted, the confessional and hyperbolic dialect of sentimentality became the matrix of female fan correspondence, while movie fandom became the overarching framework though which marginal identities could find a public "narrative structure [to give] meaning to [their] experience."[80] From this perspective, Dorr's letter to Gish aptly illustrates a typical overlap of female film reception: that of wanting *to know,* wanting *to be,* and wanting *to be with* a beloved actress.

The nineteenth-century feminization of sentimentality and sentimentalization of women's close friendships therefore enabled the acceptability of female homoerotic film reception in the 1910s. The affective lexicon of yearning, hero-worshipping, homoerotic uneasiness and unrequitedness running through female fan writings in the 1910s recycled the conventions of women's sentimental correspondence popularized during the previous century. However, while profiting from female audiences' same-sex devotions, the film industry reinforced popular moralistic scripts stating that a good girl (and consequently a good fan) had to sublimate all erotic passion into sentimental worship. Likewise, male fans should show respect for female stars by refraining from tarnishing their respectability with uncouth advances. Absence of carnal desire hence figured preeminently in what the press advertised as appropriate movie-fan engagement. So, at the same time movie impresarios stoked female fans' intense investment in screen actresses, they reframed same-sex attraction as simulacrum of romantic friendships in order to preserve respectability and revenue.

Positioned at a cultural crossroads regarding views on women's sexuality, public agency, and socialization, girls coming of age during the 1910s inhabited a transitional period where, though female sexuality had begun to elicit the scrutiny of scientists and newspapermen, most general audiences still considered schoolgirls' romantic friendships commonplace and harmless. It is in that liminal space between creeping surveillance and receding freedom that early girl fans rehearse their charged responses to film actresses. In their published poems and private letters, homoerotic spectatorship is passionately—and at times openly—mounted. Protected still by the same gender bias that imagined epistolary exchanges between young women to be natural and neutered, movie-fan girls engaged in amorous declarations, flirtatious requests, and sensual confessions not unlike those found in schoolgirls' personal diaries and correspondence. A rare emporium of the protean tensions between female spectatorial desire, creative license, queer uneasiness, and mediated intimacy can be found in the archived letters screen-struck girls sent directly to Florence Lawrence in the 1910s, the apogee and eclipse of the actress's film career.

CHAPTER 2

"Dear Flo"

Homoerotic Desire and Queer Identification in Private Fan Mail

Oh! these postscripts. How dangerous.

—Dorothy Strachey

It should hardly come as a surprise that homoeroticism permeated female film reception in the 1910s. Founded at the beginning of the decade, the US star system appealed primarily to women and was primarily staffed by them.[1] One of the first female performers to achieve nationwide recognition and be dubbed a "movie star," Canadian-born Florence Lawrence struck a nerve with movie-loving North American girls, especially after March 1910, when film producer Carl Laemmle falsely announced that the twenty-four-year-old actress had been killed in the streets of New York City. The promotional stunt helped usher in the birth of a star-driven film industry, movie players becoming full-fledged personalities, as vulnerable to fatal accidents and mundane misfortunes as any of their anonymous followers.

Resulting from concerted efforts by pressmen, advertisers, and exhibitors, the humanization of shadow players encouraged spectators to regard them as flesh-and-blood individuals and to perceive their screen characterizations—so familiar and so beloved—as reflections of a lived identity.[2] That newfound intimacy with the humanized picture-personality underpins girls' letters to Lawrence. Punctuated with devotion, friendship offers, photo requests, and professional inquiries, this private cache provides remarkable insight into the forging of "queerness in the dream language of fans."[3] First-person testimonies of early film fandom, the following writings render homoerotic desire legible through *the sentimental language of courtship* (the declarations, the promises, the flattery) and *the ecstatic tone of conquest* (the imperatives! the absolutes! the ultimatums!).

"I CAN'T HELP IT": ECSTATIC FEMALE FRIENDSHIPS AND THE HYPERBOLIC LANGUAGE OF FANDOM

Although adolescent girls aided in implementing the star system, most film histories still do not account for their individual contributions, let alone their deviations from normative behavior. To excavate a history of youth agency and queer reception so widely disregarded, I focus on letters girl fans sent directly to Lawrence between 1909 and 1919. A rare archive, Lawrence's private collection amasses dozens of missives, many in their original envelops, which extends direct access to personal information like the senders' full names and home addresses. About 95 percent of all mail is penned by self-identified white girls from all walks of life, many disclosing being in their teens and twenties. Their stationery ranges from customized, illustrated, and perfumed to messily penciled-in. Their handwriting is as plural as their life-stories, but their tone remains constant: confessional, colloquial, driven, an energetic blend of convention and slang.

Declarations of fan love abound. The typical "fan love confession" rehearses an Arthurian code of conduct where the deferential knight makes his devotion to an adored lady known, but decorously and from afar. For instance, a working girl from Chicago wrote to inform "Dear Miss Lawrence" that she is "only a poor worshipping girl" without means, but one who vows to be forever "lovingly yours,"[4] while from New York City, a "constant admirer" confessed to be "but a girl of seventeen who has fallen in love with sweet Flo."[5] Analyzing "the complex linguistic field of lifewriting" as it manifested in nineteenth-century correspondence and journals, Sharon Marcus discovered that it was common for educated women to call on "the tradition of amatory literature" to express unconsummated same-sex infatuations. Marcus presents a compelling case-study on the rhetoric of accumulation, intensification, and sublimation crafted by these lovestruck past women: "Like a medieval ascetic," they "eroticized their lack of sexual fulfillment, . . . [ultimately] representing their unrequited sexual desire for other women by extravagantly combining incompatible terms such as mother, lover, sister, friend, wife, and idol."[6]

Moviegoing girls drew from these established vernaculars to articulate wants, fantasies, and desires sparked by the new medium. Steeped in affect, the feminized language of sentiment is the blueprint of film fandom and the lifeblood of queer reception. Forging a common language is instrumental to the maintenance of both youth and marginal communities. Lawrence's fan mail captures a reception idiom as it was being first drafted by working- and middle-class movie-loving girls. The result is a hybridization of vernacular and literary sources, as fans mashed together elements of epistolary sentimentality and amatory poetry with film lingo and juvenile terminology. Twenty-year-old Theodora Antony, for example, used slang to convey her attachment to Lawrence: "I have a great many girl friends which often remind me of my 'crush' [for] you."[7] Another schoolyard colloquialism entering film-fan idiom in the 1910s is the superlative expression "I am crazy about," predominant in literate girls' life-writing, as previously seen in Medora Espy's diaries. In 1910, sixteen-year-old Marie Hiller from Minneapolis opened her letter to Lawrence by announcing, "I am just crazy about moving pictures and have seen your face appear so many times I thought I should like to correspond with you."[8] A year later, sixteen-year-old schoolmates Virginia Kramer and Helen Wood reinforced the widespread appropriation of neuropathological language as a stanchion of fan expression by proclaiming "We are so crazy about you and you are so pretty. . . . All the girls here are crazy about you."[9]

If the hyperbolic idioms of sentimentalism and amatory poetry elevated movie actresses to heavenly muses, colloquialisms brought them right back to earth. As twenty-two-year-old Isabel Rae (a minor film player and aspiring screenwriter) told Lawrence in 1911, "Kindly excuse the slang used in this lengthy epistle but it expresses my feelings better than anything that I can think of."[10] Speaking in their own vernacular freed girl fans, while slang humanized stars, as did pet names and fan-coined soubriquets.[11] It is not a coincidence that the film industry promoted their first female stars with sentimental monikers like "Goldilocks" and "Little Mary" (Pickford), many of which had originally been devised by fans. Seeking to replicate that instant intimacy, sixteen-year-old Jessie Wakefield signed her fan letter "Golden-Head," while Nance O'Neill asked Lawrence to call her "Nan," in return dubbing the star "Flo-Flo."[12] "You haven't said I may call you that," the Massachusetts fan quipped in 1914, "but 'Miss Lawrence' sounds, or looks, so formal."[13]

Fan neologisms stemmed from girls' slang recycling and remixing the sentimental idiom. One movie-loving correspondent promised not to behave like a "masher," while another hoped her letter did not come across too "gushy."[14] In 1916, Dorothy Swart told Lawrence, "Do you know I am a *grafter*? I am, although I am only fifteen years old." The New Yorker followed up with an explanation of the fan term: "grafter," short for "autograph-collector, [means] I write to all my favorites and ask for pictures. . . . I have twenty autographed photos."[15] An assemblage of high and low threads, the language of film fandom was not engineered in a vacuum; it borrowed from literary convention, medical terminology, and the popular press. The labor of linguistic patchwork and emotional stitching that went into cobbling such a dominant fan dialect was largely produced by young female hands. By the following decade, this had become common knowledge. Around 1921, a Chicago newspaper reported difficulties in delineating where juvenile female "slanguage" ended and the movies began since girls all tended to "talk like a film."[16]

Homoerotic desire saturates those sutures. Raptured expressions of film reception reproduced the mercuriality of limerence. As the girl fans repeatedly put it, they "couldn't help" contacting, following, and adoring the Canadian-born actress. After confessing to have fallen in love with the star, Cecile Holmes pleaded with Lawrence to "forgive my madness, and receive my letters kindly, for *I just couldn't help* writing you."[17] Anna Mae Oldham similarly declared, "I am not a girl for flattering anybody, but *I can't help it* with you,"[18] while Edith Crutcher admitted, "I just *could not help* from writing you—for when I love any one, it's impossible for me to keep it from them."[19] Inked on perfumed pink stationery, Rose Sachmmellen's letter asked Lawrence for her "pardon, for I've been guilty of the same offense before, Miss Lawrence, when I was bold enough to write and tell you how glad I was that the report of your accidental death proved untrue. But *I couldn't help it* and meant every word and I'm not ashamed of having done so."[20]

Such succinct expression of powerlessness, abandonment, and rapture—"I can't help it"—articulates an unusual investment in Lawrence, so urgent and all-consuming that it took a life of its own. "I can't help it" further implies that such uncommon same-sex investment threatened a heteronormative sense of female propriety, a breach that could bring embarrassment and disrepute to the fan according to Sachmmellen's defiant "but *I couldn't help it* and meant every word and *I am not ashamed*." Hilton similarly professed, "I know you will think I am bold—very bold [for writing] but I just can't help it."[21] Though emotional exuberance between educated women was condoned at the time, the type of hagiographic intensity channeled in these fan confessions pushes them well beyond the regular affective correspondence between turn-of-the-century girls. In their apologetic phrasing, Lawrence's female correspondents seem aware of this transgression. Freighted with adolescent ardor, awkwardness, and the awareness of trespass, the language performed here is that of "so-called ecstatic friendships," bonds between school-going girls openly stigmatized in newspapers and women's publications since the late 1800s.

Ladies' Home Journal, for instance, constantly warned against the "morbid emotions" girls nurtured for one another under the cover of "boarding school friendships."[22] Comprised of "a young adorer" and her chosen muse, such "excessive friendships" created a canopy of volatile emotions liable to stifle and corrupt both participants.[23] Perversion of normative schedules, attitudes, and habits symptomized the unwellness of these rapports: "The ecstatic girl lover caught in a 'crush' will probably protest that it is a friendship . . . , but if it affects her sleep, her appetite, her work, and her temper; if she loses flesh and can think or talk of nothing but her 'friend' . . . , the 'friendship' needs looking into."[24] Collapse and heartbreak were inevitable since "anything which is so extreme cannot have much stability."[25] The press discourse castigating girls' ecstatic friendships held a clear subtext of homophobia, not unlike that found in press coverage of "lesbian love murders." Vilification increased if participants were women of color or from underprivileged milieus.[26] "Normal, wonderful friendships" were hence imagined as polar opposites of these "shameful" bastardizations of young female affection; as a columnist proclaimed, "Girls can and do go through boarding school and college without *prostituting* their senses!"[27] Such a trenchant verb choice betrays that the horror inspired by women's ecstatic friendships veiled a keen awareness that homosexual desire flourished in cloistered proximity. Similar conditions of heightened same-sex tenderness and propinquity proliferated under the cloak of film fandom.

Nonheteronormative tendencies are, in fact, explicitly indicted as the problematic nodule central to the diagnosis of "ecstatic friendships as a dangerous disease." A chief characteristic of "the girl lover" is her "invariabl[e] bitter[ness] against men. She regards [them] as her a natural enemy for, in her heart of hearts, she knows that there is a stronger sentiment than affection" linking her to the adored "chum." Desire bleeds into touch: "Once free, she greets her [friend] with a rapturous kiss and a close embrace." Such demonstrative displays of physical intimacy are immediately remonstrated as improper and transgressive: "Bad manners, my dear girls, bad manners! The strongest love expresses itself in words not caresses." Perverse is also the prospect of same-sex coupledom embodied by the girl who is "willing to pass her life with her so-called 'chum,' and that nothing stronger than friendship with a woman, or a Platonic liking for a man, is demanded of her. To my mind, *there is something wrong with such woman.*"[28]

Written tirades classifying girls' "intense friendships" as dangerous and deviant generally devolved into broader criticisms of female refusal to conform to heteronormative romance, domesticity, and parenthood. The morbid "hero-worshipper" anatomized in these prescriptive articles reiterated traditionalist portrayals of the New Woman as a man-hating, biologically defective virago. And yet, such meticulous delineation of a pathological taxonomy of passionate same-sex attachment is crucial to understanding female film fandom, because ecstatic friendships are its scaffolding. The synopsis of "half friendship, half worship . . . given often to an unknown [i.e., stranger] who has some fame or [is] an ideal of womanhood" impeccably summarizes the affective behavior performed by girls writing to Lawrence throughout the 1910s.[29] Their grandstanding language of devotion, prostration, and consuming infatuation borrows both the cognizant pageantry of ecstatic friendship and its performative self-chastisement. The question of whether these emotions are absolutely genuine or partially affected is secondary; what matters is that girl fans chose to mimic a model of female rapport widely discussed as rife with homoerotic limerence and heteronormative dissent when it came to communicating with their favorite movie actresses.

The linguistic etiology Marcus traces across women's personal papers strengthens the significance of screen-struck girls selecting this particular type of fan dialect from so many other registers available to literate audiences in the 1910s. Poring over letters and diaries from Victorian England, Marcus argues that women engaged in a sexual relationship or a close friendship may have used gushing language to express their mutual appreciation, but their writing lacked the obsessive "intensity, exclusivity, and volatility" subtending accounts of unrequited lust. The woman who desired other women *without* the possibility of actualization "modeled herself on a courtly lover, made all the more devoted by the one-sidedness of her passion." She fetishized and idealized her love object, "fixating on her presence and absence, and used superlatives to describe the feelings she inspired"; sick on yearning, she was consumed and animated by the inaccessibility of her muse.[30] Author Dorothy Strachey located such conflicting responses in adolescence, describing same-sex female desire as veined by "a curious repugnance, a terror of getting *too* near."[31] Writing about a girl's infatuation with her boarding-school headmistress in the late 1800s, Strachey encapsulates a first-person perspective on the recuperative powers and superlative pleasures of one-sided queer attraction: being "hopeless . . . [was what] gave my passion dignity," the girl narrator declares, what "made it worthy of respect. No other love, *no love of man and woman could ever be as disinterested as mine. It was I alone who loved.*"[32] This seminal tug-of-war between eroticized longing and relished distance, the wanting and the having, foregrounds both the language of turn-of-the-century sapphic crushes and early moviegoing girls' fan writing.

In private letters to Lawrence, many girls conveyed their intense fan investment through a cross between the sublimated language of courtly love and the blunt obsession of "the hero-worship crusher."[33] "I could hold my appreciation and love for you to myself no longer. . . . Flo, I dearly love you, I am sure," Wakefield blurts out on pink stationery. "[I] often think of you when I should be at something else. Is your hair blonde and your eyes hazel? . . . You [are] to me like the breeze of a summer thought."[34] The actress is simultaneously addressed as a crush, an idol, and a friend; asking about something as trivial as hair color tips fan mail into homoerotic closeness. Adoring a female star from a distance walks a tightrope, then: daydreams run alongside daily obligations, an imagined caress coexists with the force of intrusive thoughts. At sixteen, Wakefield is already well aware of the razor's edge between female esteem and "unnatural" same-sex desire, for she preemptively notes that "You will have the opinion that I am [a] silly, sentimental girl—the latter I am [but] I do not wish to seem too affected or *unnatural* in my expression of admiration for you."[35]

The blend of sentimental lyricism and confessional colloquialism attests to how successfully the star system seeded the notion of "picture personality" amongst female audiences. Promoted as both astral body and everywoman, rarefied royalty and industrial employee, picture personalities embodied the perfect hybridization of desire and self-denial, proximity and remoteness, pleasure and pain. Young female spectators responded in kind, infusing their fan writings with the sharpest amalgamation of all these contiguous emotive states: longing. Charles Baxter describes longing as "a particular kind of desire that has lost its way. . . . Longing creates search parties and then sends them out into the world without a specific thing to search for."[36] Shaped by limerence, the female longing in Lawrence's fan mail searches for an undefined form of same-sex closeness that cannot be parted from hope and hunger. The girls in these writings crave for more, for alternatives, for affinities that will crack open a world of possibilities: professional, economical, social, romantic.

Though the lovesick homoerotism pervading female fan correspondence to Lawrence derives from an established chivalric code, the urge
to actualize physical desire is not absent. Wakefield recounts an occasion when "I went with a young girl to see your film lately and . . .
she exclaimed: 'You must love her! I bet if you saw her you'd up
and kiss her.'"[37] Through indirect speech and a secondhand voice, the
high schooler acknowledges her physical attraction for the female star,
making it unmistakably legible through the act of kissing. Like Espy's
diaries indicate, girls conceived of moviegoing as an eroticized venue
predicated on female bodies—a world of girls going out with other
girls to be stimulated by performing young women. The potentiality
of homoerotic female pleasure and identification always threaded
through the practices of filmgoing and film reception. Some girls made
it flesh by creating written accounts of their embodied spectatorial
reactions.

Widespread engagement with the language of unrequited infatuation
cultivated by their nineteenth-century predecessors does not signify that
all movie-loving girls were putatively enamored with an actress. It does,
however, suggest a deliberate stylistic choice. These correspondents
wanted to be perceived by Lawrence as exceptionally ardent followers,
slavish suitors who reveled in the one-sidedness of their same-sex affec-
tions. In "The Psychogenesis of a Case of Homosexuality in a Woman,"
Freud identifies preference for being "the lover rather than beloved" as
symptomatic of female homosexuality. Conducted in the late 1910s, the
case-study focuses on "a beautiful and clever girl of eighteen, belonging
to a family of good standing" who feverishly pursued an aloof twenty-
something woman, romancing her with love letters and "gifts of flowers."[38] Though the erotic nature of this relationship is explicitly
acknowledged, Freud refers to the girl's lover as "a beloved friend," in
part because genital contact seemed to be absent. Such euphemism is
revealing of a pervasive resistance to recognize female sexual desire,
while reiterating the polysemic valences same-sex friendships afforded
early-twentieth-century girls.

The girl's age, language, and attitudes documented in Freud's case-
study mirror those of Lawrence's followers. It is possible that such rhetorical choice (to be "lover rather than beloved," self-presenting as unrequited rather than friendly) stemmed from a lack of available models to
draw from when seeking to articulate nonnormative film reception. When
many of these girls wrote to Lawrence, a vernacular linguistic apparatus
to articulate with nuance same-sex desire or fan behavior was still being

forged. In the wake of novelty, stable conventions stepped in to fill the void. Their power was one of multiplicity: "never classified as friendship or love," early written testimonies of same-sex fan attachment possess "the advantages and limits of remaining in the realm of suggestion, where they could expand infinitely without ever being realized or checked."[39] Twentieth-century scholars have associated such willful indeterminacy with queer desire.[40] The absence of a contemporaneous term to describe a historical occurrence should not elide nor minimize that occurrence. Past desire is still desire regardless of the changing labels used to classify it.

What is relevant about girl fans' homoerotic investments in film actresses, then, is not whether it corroborates presiding understandings of human behavior, but that it vibrates out of conventional categories. Such libidinal abundance produces its own affective central system, complete with ordinances, valences, and gratifications that texture identities and attachments historically ascribed to women. When they wear their fan hat, early moviegoing girls are able to shuttle back and forth between gendered and affective positions: spectatorship and participation, friendship and romance, deviance and convention. Animated by movie love, they become authors alongside industry insiders.

Affective overflow is a cornerstone of fandom, as it is of feminized "morbidness and sentimentalism."[41] These three instances—spectatorial pleasure, deviance, and emotional surplus—subtended most discussions of young women's homoerotic attachments throughout the early twentieth century, whether voiced by medical professionals, reformers, legislators, educators, journalists, or film columnists. Though assorted in expertise, all agreed that an excess of feeling defined nonnormative girlhood: mad girls, movie-struck girls, ecstatic girlfriends, they all felt *too much*. The externalization of excessive emotion is what distinguishes bosom friends from lovers, casual moviegoers from fervent fans, consumers from criminals. De Lauretis argues that excess— "sufficiently outrageous, passionate, verbally violent and formally complex"—holds the key "to destroy the male[-dominated] discourse on love and . . . undomesticate the female body."[42] Perhaps utopian, this feminist embrace of female-authored excess energizes girls' writings to movie actresses. Passion is loudly felt and performed, and so is pleasure. In the sphere of fan-star correspondence, girls allow themselves free rein to explore behaviors and emotional states frowned upon by society, where restraint and decorum dictated the lines separating a proper lady from the deviant underclass.

In the early twentieth century, excess also scaffolded dominant ideas on female psychology, namely Jean-Martin Charcot's and Freud's seminal theories linking neurophysiological disorders like hysteria to the fairer sex.[43] By the 1910s, the belief that pathological lability resided in women's subjectivity had become so culturally naturalized that many girls internalized it. An inculcated mentality of female shame and self-policing may explain the apologies, tentativeness, and self-deprecation permeating girls' fan letters to Lawrence. In 1916, twenty-year-old Marie Benson begs Lawrence, "Please don't think this is plain flattery, because it isn't! I wanted to write you a long time ago [since 1908, the girl implies], but I was afraid you wouldn't like it. Please find a little time [for] . . . a true admirer, wont [sic] you?"[44] That same year, a high-schooler from Massachusetts complains that, "I've looked and looked for a line from you for about a month now; but without any avail. . . . I'm inclined to think you are cross with me for something I suppose I have said or done something stupid and that you won't forgive me until I apologise [sic], or say I'm sorry. Well then, Flo,—I am very very sorry—whatever it is. There—do I get forgiven?"[45]

Polite deference or coquette demureness may account for the subservient tone. In asking for the star's forgiveness, fans may have wished to attain her good graces by coming across as well-mannered, respectful, and deserving correspondents. However, it is also likely that, by the mid-1910s, educated girl fans had grown aware of scientific discourses surveying female sexuality and, increasingly, alerting popular consciousness that romantic friendships among women could metastasize into abnormal infatuations.[46] Between 1892 and 1919, US newspapers brimmed with reports on girls who "showed unnatural affection for specifically named members of [their] own sex," most of them dead by their own hand or their lover's.[47] Those who survived found their preferences publicly broadcast as "mental perversion," and the stigma of being "unnatural" or "mad" never washed off their names.[48] Therefore, girls writing to movie actresses may have peppered a certain obsequiousness in their letters as a way to reassure the star that their same-sex investment was intense but innocuous.

Still, lest we forget, obsequiousness also entices closeness. Having the addressee enter the writer's intimacy and in return be welcomed into the addressee's bosom is the ultimate goal of all sentimental correspondence, of which fan mail is an offshoot. In her survey of Clara Bow's fan mail, Marsha Orgeron remarks that film magazines trained silent movie followers (particularly women) to "proactively attempt to control interactions with the star by scripting [their] response[s]." In reaching out to actresses through private correspondence, female fans "continu[ed] the intimacy-building project of fan magazines. Asking for favors, sharing ideas, and offering advice were all iterations of the discourse established and enabled by the movie magazine."[49] To perform coy subordination in their epistolary self-presentation thus caught two birds with one stone: it lubricated propinquity between star and fan while also casting the latter in a flattering, *knowing* light.

A TOKEN OF YOUR AFFECTION: MATERIAL
KEEPSAKES AND THE BIRTH OF A COMMERCIAL
FILM-FAN CULTURE

Notwithstanding their humility, girls frequently banded around their attachment to Lawrence as all-consuming, capable of oversetting their better judgement and disrupting their daily lives—trademarks of ecstatic friendships. Thirteen-year-old Anna Ford from Hanover, Pennsylvania, admitted in 1912 that it might seem "foolish," but "I am thinking of you every minute."[50] Three years later, Edith Crutcher from Dallas, Texas, attributed her unhappiness to constantly yearning for Lawrence and having limited resources to satisfy her heart's desire: "When I was in the convent, I was so very miserable for I never could get out . . .— when I would go just as quick as I could to town to find you. I no longer go to the convent and [now] I see you *every day*."[51] Vernacular movie love encroached in the fan's religious setting until it replaced vocation altogether: as the girl grew up, the convent gave way to the movie theater. The correlation between worship and film fandom is implicitly drawn here, further deifying the figure of the female star and spiritualizing the fan's homoerotic devotion.

More explicitly likening their fan investment to romantic obsession, some girls shared that once severed, the spectatorial tie gave way to a sensation of hopelessness and hankering similar to lovesickness. When in 1914 Lawrence absented herself from the screen, Dorothy Swart exclaimed, "When you disappeared entirely, *I didn't know what to do*."[52] In 1916, Miss Myrtle Bradshaw from Somerville, Massachusetts, likewise found herself plunging in hyperbolic helplessness: "Two or three years ago I saw you a great deal. . . . Suddenly you disappeared and I didn't see you any more and my heart sank down down; I didn't find your name in the magazines and *I didn't know what to do*."[53] This urgency for an increasingly scarce proximity with stars reveals the fast pace with which picture personalities rose and fell in early cinema. A major player since 1907, by 1914 Lawrence's film celebrity was on the wane. As a sixteen-year-old fan observes, a few months away from the screen meant a lifetime in early Hollywood: "In your absence so many other stars loomed up in popularity [but] I never forgot little you."[54] Sensing a closing window of opportunity to access Lawrence emboldened girls to ask the star for a personalized token of affection. On Valentine's Day 1916, Miss Edna Hall from Bath, Maine, implored rather forcefully: "Won't you *please, please* send me your autographed picture? Also *please* write me a letter and tell me about yourself? . . . *Please answer soon.*"[55]

A commentary on the ephemerality of early film fandom, the request for material emblems of star presence and connection signals an essential fan need to preserve consumer attachments through a tactile, presumably lasting good: a personalized note, photograph, or autograph. The desire for direct correspondence reveals a longing for mutual intimacy, as well as a bid for retarding modern temporality.[56] In the contained universe of the mailed letter and autographed photograph, the ruthless linear vector of industrial time (always forward and ongoing) slows down, the past reaching the recipient on a delay and yet remaining current by virtue of being seized in affective writing and mechanical imaging. It is no accident that physical mail would be dubbed "snail mail": letters and photographs are fixed objects, snapshots of "the then," proffering respite to the neck-breaking impermanence of "the now." A product of US capitalism, the early star system exemplified its accelerated temporality, where time is money and people assets, so their value, like their utility, is bound to be fleeting—Lawrence's own stardom began free-falling six years into its making. In pleading for pictures and missives from a declining star, movie-loving girls held back the impending death of Lawrence's career, while simultaneously seeking to conserve their youth by collecting memorabilia of an actress whose celebrity brought to mind their own coming of age.

Fans' insistent requests for film ephemera also seem to confirm the conspicuous consumption characteristic of screen-struck adoration— that is, girls' reputed mindless prizing of quantity over quality. However, a rhetoric of excess and accumulation is as essential to the ethos of film fandom as it was to early twentieth-century female relationality. As Marcus uncovers through her analysis of nineteenth-century diaries and letters, educated women cultivated a habit of "accumulating analogies" to convey the contradictory pangs and delights kindled by same-sex unrequited passion.[57] Extravagant hyperboles, run-on metaphors, and countless epithets were carefully deployed to show off the exceptionality of attributes of the muse and, more importantly, the exceptionality of feeling of the fan. Excess and accumulation, of goods as of figures of speech, hence played a cardinal part in bolstering the emotional capital and affective power of a film follower who saw herself as participating in an erotic asymmetry.

Additionally, the keepsake carried "thematic and emotional complexity" in turn-of-the-century US culture, Joanne Dobson remarks: more than "a self-indulgent token or a silly relic, . . . the sentimental keepsake constituted a vivid symbolic embodiment of the primacy of human connection and the inevitability of human loss."[58] By the late 1910s, the influenza pandemic and World War I had brought ephemerality and grief to the forefront of national imagination, as to the fray of everyday life. Death and loss became pressing concerns and mundane realities. To carry a piece of a beloved, even if one as removed as a movie star, held abundant meaning, functioning as a tangible reminder that emotional ties lasted even when people or relationships did not.

Long treated as a sentimental relic, the photographic portrait centered fans' presentation of self. Girls often mailed professional headshots with their letters, personalizing and eroticizing their correspondence with the stars. They had a face now, a body, their words fleshed out with the avoirdupois of their features. Circa 1919, Theodora Anthony sent Lawrence a sepia headshot sporting a chic bob and a Peter Pan–collared uniform. An aspiring movie player, the Rhode Island schoolgirl used her image to showcase her photogenic attributes and entice the star's proximity. Hand-trimmed, the photograph resembles a valentine's die-cut, the fan's bobbed hair announcing the arrival of the flapper, a youthful figuration of female freedom and fun. Anthony, however, distances herself from the vapid archetype by acknowledging the social prejudices attached to female performers and the tenacity required to succeed in early filmmaking. "I had always cherished hopes of being an actress but my people won't consider it for a moment. *I know* it is work and [that] many *do not succeed*," the girl states sensibly, "but *I am determined* I shall, because I am not afraid to try."[59] Modern, intrepid, and hardworking, the movie lover sells herself as an ideal correspondent and professional-to-be.

In 1911, Rose Horte from Baltimore mailed Lawrence a classic studio portrait, her Gibson-Girl hairdo and white frilly dress telegraphing the girl's conservative personality, while drawing attention to her resemblance to the "ingénue," a sentimental stock type celebrated on US screens throughout the decade. Like Anthony, Horte aimed to become a film actress. She contacted Lawrence to politely inquire about "the salary a beginner gets and how to find a position of the [acting] kind."[60] As pay for services rendered, the fan left the IMP star with a professional headshot. In both cases, the fan photograph appears equal parts calling card and sentimental keepsake, rendering the unknown correspondent legible to the star.

Sometimes girl fans brazenly reversed the courtship act of picture-swapping. Self-portraits were ransomed in an attempt to retrieve messages from the movie actress. In 1916, eighteen-year-old Laura Baillargeon from New Bedford, Massachusetts, bantered: "I expect a long letter & a little picture of yourself Florence. I will send you mine soon. . . . I will write a long letter as soon as you write."[61] Other times, unprompted photos transmitted clues about fans' economic standing. In 1911, eighteen-year-old Jean Wilson Martin from Oberlin, Ohio, told Lawrence, "I am very much interested in picture posing and would like to take up the work, so am taking the liberty of writing to you for advice. . . . Do companies sometimes take a performer who is inexperienced and let them work up?"[62] While Anthony's and Horte's studio portraits projected well-to-do aspirants, Martin's grainy and unevenly hand-cropped snapshot suggests that the girl may not have possessed the means to get headshots professionally taken. Her blurry image records a dark-haired girl in an ill-fitting dress, her young features obscured by the photo's poor quality.[63] Still, in sharing "a small Kodak picture of me," Martin feels entitled to a formal evaluation: "If you think there is no hope dont [sic] be backward about telling me," she directs, while requesting that Lawrence "kindly keep this secret from any other members of the co." (figure 4).

Responding to film magazines' growing solicitation of interaction between moviegoers and stars, some girl fans began deploying epistolary communication as a means to approximate anonymous devotees to their newly available screen heroines. As Orgeron notices in her analysis of personal star mail, "to revise the anonymity of the fan-star relationship, [female correspondents] reversed the direction of the conventional star-fan photographic exchange" by demanding reciprocity. While "not inventing the nature of this exchange, [fans] chang[ed] the rules of how the game was played to suit [their] own conceptualization of the star-fan relationship" and to steer it to their benefit.[64]

FIGURE 4. An improvised introduction of self: Jean Wilson
Martin's Kodak, hand-cut and mailed to Florence Lawrence in
1911.

When photographs were beyond a fan's means, girls found creative
solutions to make themselves physically available to the star. In 1910,
F. C. Singleton told Lawrence:

> I see your sweet face everyday in the pictures and think of you at night. . . .
> Enclosed you will find discription [*sic*] of my-self.

> age 21
> height 5ft10
> weight 154
> I am a Brunette.
> I am Irish American born.[65]

In its specificity, the data supplied may seem uncannily similar to that currently listed in online profiles or on performers' headshots. If age and ethnicity conform to usual information required by early twentieth-century institutional forms and census surveys, physical details such as weight, height, and coloration imply a more intimate agenda. Since the twenty-one-year-old does not mention acting or modeling ambitions in her letter, one can speculate that fostering attraction and romance was not outside the realm of her intentions.

A chief fan practice to this day, collecting images of stars owes its propagation to a network of movie-loving girls. Asking Lawrence for a photo, Myrtle Bradshaw explains that it was "a girl chum" who first informed her that film fans could write to their "favorites for photographs. She said she received some. [So] I started to send to mine." In 1911, Anna Mae Oldham, a single girl employed at Boyle's Hosiery Mill in Philadelphia, reported that she only wrote to Lawrence after her friend Anna Geissler, an extra at the Lubin filmmaking company, "told me to write you and ask you for a picture. I told her I did not have the nerve [and] she said that's alright just mention my name [and] I am sure Florence will answer you."[66] According to Denise McKenna, in the early 1910s the role of film extra had a reputation of being fun, well-paid, and possibly life-changing work, providing respite from the menial humdrum of industry and service jobs.[67] In drawing attention to a word-of-mouth reference system, complete with calling stars by their first names, Oldham's letter confirms that young urban women perceived film acting as a viable occupation that ran on female solidarity.

By 1916, gathering and safekeeping stars' photographs were established fan practices. With pride, Bradshaw boasts to "have now fifteen [headshots]. I am just in my glory when I receive a picture. I am a typical 'Movie Fan.'"[68] Imbued with longing for same-sex closeness, and participating in the tradition of token exchange between lovers, the request for trading self-portraits also duplicates standard practices of sociability between early twentieth-century schoolgirls. Throughout the 1910s, cohorts of girls swapped amateur Kodaks as mementos of affection and schoolyard camaraderie. In one of her scribbled notes, Medora Espy asks her colleague Ruth, "How did your pictures come out?" and urges her schoolmate to "not forget me when you distribute them."[69] Seeking to personalize a bond with female stars their own age, girl fans resorted to a familiar mode of peer intimacy: they reached out and asked for a photo.

Though common, the exchange of personal headshots between girl fan and star is exceptionally charged with homoerotic tactility. The sender invariably expresses that the physical distance of a film actress can only be mitigated through possessing (and implicitly touching) her photographic likeness. As early as 1911, Miss Eileen Smith pleaded with "Miss Flo," "I would love to have your photograph . . . for if I didn't see you in moving pictures, I would have your picture, all for my self [sic], to look at."[70] In "Little History of Photography," Walter Benjamin posits that the advent of mechanical reproduction sparked in "the masses . . . a passionate inclination . . . to bring things closer." Looking at Eugène Atget's turn-of-the-century photographs of Paris, Benjamin claims that, "every day the need to possess the object in close-up in the form of a picture, or rather a copy, becomes more imperative."[71]

By the time intimacy with film stars became a "more imperative" commodity, audiences already regarded mechanical reproductions of absent loved ones as functional surrogates of emotional proximity—affective mediators accessible anywhere at any time. Aware of the slew of feelings audiences negotiated through photographs and other fungible print reproductions, the film industry began commercializing paper-based effigies of the stars. Facsimile headshots, movie stamps, playing cards, photo-postcards, and movie paper dolls were given away at special screenings, made cheaply available through mail-order catalogues, or inserted freely in fan publications. Miniaturized paper trinkets cropped up to provide the masses with a reassuring sense of physical proximity. Generally sold for a nickel or a quarter, mass-produced reproductions guaranteed instantaneous access to stars' bodies in a way that language, even in the form of fan mail, could not assuredly or immediately proffer. Touch, imagined and mediated, becomes thus an integral aspect of Hollywood's lucrative commodification of fan culture, as well as a prime conduit for homoerotic fan attachment. Already established in mid-nineteenth-century sentimental literature as a site of affective authenticity and human connection, touch enters movie promotion as "a fully loaded trope that speaks to the height of feeling and the insufficiency of language."[72]

By the late 1910s, one-on-one domestic intimacy with movie stars began being sold as a multisensory experience. Combining an "unbreakable phonograph record with a photo of your favorite star; an autograph; and an intimate chat with a star," the "Talk-o-Photo" mobilized movie lovers "not to worship from afar" but, for thirty cents apiece, welcome shadow players "in *your own home*" to have "a little chat." *Photoplay* ads promised fans that their "favorite stars . . . will talk to you on your own phonograph [and] answer to your wishes."[73] Together with two-dimensional paper paraphernalia, these novelty items exhorted spectators to "take the star home" and, through ancillary technology, enact fantasies of propinquity and interactivity denied by the very incorporeal one-directionality of film projection.

Movie-loving girls routinely incorporated images of stars in their domestic space, utilizing their readymade likenesses to nurture fan-star attachment. "Dear Flo will you please send me one of your pictures," Miss Elsie Shallaby begged in 1915. "I have a small picture of you in a frame on my writing desk but it is not very good."[74] Unsatisfied with keeping the star away in a frame, some girls placed star photographs in their bedrooms, so players watched over them as they slept, dreamt, and undressed. The act of pinning a star's reproduction to one's bedroom wall is intensely intimate. Fans often phrased it as an open invitation: "Mother did my room over as a Xmas present," sixteen-year-old Mathilda Thompson tells Lawrence in 1915. "I left a place on the wall for your photo so please don't forget to send one."[75] The empty spot in a girl's bedroom wall conjures an invitation to take up space, a door left unlatched waiting for the star to push it ajar. The void in an otherwise fully redecorated private space also holds a symbolic charge: apparitional, it acts both as a reminder of Lawrence's physical absence and as testimony of her emotional presence in the fan's inner sanctum. Constance Topping, a moviegoer growing up in the San Francisco Bay area during the Great War, confirmed the affective weight of keeping someone's photo in one's bedroom. The twenty-year-old tells her diary that it felt "too intimate" to have a crush's likeness "stuck in my mirror [as] it seemed to give him too much claim on me to have his picture in my room." Ultimately she had to take the keepsake down, hoping the gesture pushed the infatuation away.[76] It stands to reason that the inverse action (to bring a reproduction nearer) would symbolize a desire to be intimate with the person on the picture.

In fact, film magazines and young actresses promoted the notion that decorating private spaces with star pictures was a welcome demonstration of film devotion. In 1915 *Photoplay* published a photograph of Vivian Martin's "dressing room at the Fort Lee Studio of World Film Corporation," its walls papered over with headshots of other movie players. A three-dimensional scrapbook, the actress's private working space proffers insight into the bedroom decor girls describe in their letters to Lawrence.[77] Predominant reproductions of Anita Stewart and Marguerite Clark gesture to a culture of mutual admiration where commercial film ephemera functioned as a main conduit for female closeness, even for an insider like Martin, daily immersed in the physical presence of stars (figure 5).

FIGURE 5. Wallpapered in stars: actress Vivian Martin's dressing room, 1915.

Industry power brokers were very aware that "film fans longed to have intimate peeps at stars," going as far as marketing productions featuring actresses' private properties as "a wished-for opportunity" for moviegoers to indirectly visit "stars in their own homes."[78] The goal of expanding cinema's economical reach beyond the picture-house spawned an ever-growing number of film-themed consumables directed at middle-class patrons, especially those in their teens. In 1916, a student publication drolly heeded that "the movies prove valuable in stimulating certain industries which before have been in economical language limping or protected. . . . That the false mustache industry has been benefited goes without saying. Other commodities which have had a great sale due to the flickers [include] boarding house table clothes and dishes, flower-pots, . . . etc., etc., ad infin."[79]

Simulating intimacy with actors via commercialization of their material effigies thus worked as another way in which the film industry sold itself as a medium of vicarious consumption—democratic and endlessly rewarding. The disembodied nonpresence of picture players rendered them ubiquitous and always available. They could be brought home by every patron and by no patron at all; they could be enjoyed to grapple with homosocial, homoerotic, homosexual, heteronormative responses. In this context, no fan should possess a superior stake in a star's emotional real-estate: their reproductions held as much or as little value as the fan-consumer decided to attribute to them.

By the mid-1910s, as interactive opinion columns boomed in film-fan magazines, authenticity began to rely on the channel of delivery, and by extension, on manual labor. To receive handwritten letters and autographed photos directly from the star instead of through mass outlets, to be able to trace over where a star's fingers or mouth may have brushed (stamps and envelop flaps must be licked, after all) generated a hierarchy of touch, while reaffirming it as a keystone of fan-star intimacy. For instance, in 1916 Malina Wanamaker from Salt Lake City insisted that Lawrence "look around a 'wee' bit and see if you can't find a little picture of you [because though] I have some print pictures of you, you know they are not like the 'real ones.'"[80] Implicit is the assumption that chemically developed photos received straight from a star accrued an authenticity that magazines' printed halftones lacked. Provenance, presumably sanctified by the celebrity's physical touch, thus instantiated value distinctions in a marketplace dominated by mechanical massification.

Portable, tactile, and interactive, stars' images may have provoked an audience's playful touch, but they also enforced traditional gender scripts. Movie paper dolls—ephemera aimed specifically at female consumers—illustrate how deliberately the film industry sought to capitalize on fans' desire to touch a star, while censoring the shape female spectatorial fantasies should take. Distributed in women's magazines, fan publications, and dailies throughout the late 1910s and early 1920s, movie players' dolls usually anthropomorphized the two-dimensional keepsake and domesticated the interplay between female fan and paper alter. "Mary Pickford is coming to your house . . . all dressed up," a Boston newspaper announced in 1921. "So are Charlie Chaplin, Douglas Fairbanks, and Anita Stewart. . . . They'll stay just as long as you wish and they won't be a bit of bother."[81] Ads such as this presumed that the audience engaging with the colorful memorabilia would be female and adolescent: young enough to remember the pleasures of their "doll-cutting Sundays," but old enough to "say you are over your days of cutting out paper dolls," which likely meant girls in their teens.[82] That many paper dolls promoted popular girl stars (namely Pickford, Mary Miles Minter, Lila Lee, May Allison, and Norma Talmadge) and introduced their accompanying wardrobes as a selling point further attests that movie paper dolls targeted female consumers (figure 6).

FIGURE 6. Another form of playing with star bodies: colorful paper "Movy-Dols," complete with screen wardrobe.

At the same time they labored to endear girl audiences, commercial film ephemera worked to de-eroticize fans' longing for the stars. Promotional copy couched the dressing and undressing of the female doll in fans' yearning to experience filmdom vis-a-vis playing dress-up: "You can dress them up to suit yourself and have a wonderful time," ads promised.[83] In early and classical Hollywood, fashion consumption functioned as a discursive channel between female stars and fans, stimulating cinematic storytelling and audience immersion. By imitating actresses' featured looks and purchasing star-sponsored goods, female audiences were encouraged to forge an intimate rapport with movie idols in their daily routine.[84] This industry-sanctioned closeness generally sidestepped homoerotic desire, reinforcing the transactionality of female fan attachment by reducing it to material consumption, cosmetic identification, and sartorial vanity.

Conservative and disciplinary, movie paper dolls also incited girl audiences to parlay their love for female stars into honing their domestic skills. Stepping into the roles of agreeable hostess and resourceful homemaker, female fans were instructed to "have Mary Pickford for tea" and use those daydreamed moments to think of the home as a manipulable arena, ready to accommodate "any movie you choose to stage."[85] Rather than inspiring girls to enact romantic scenarios, movie paper dolls prompted them to harness fandom as a didactic trial-run that would help them fulfill the expected parts of lady of the manor and curator of the home. Reminiscent of nineteenth-century advice manuals, movie paper dolls aimed to pull literate white girls away from voluptuous desire, professional ambition, and participation in public life by redirecting them into domestic caretaking.[86]

In such a context, the materiality of fan mail swells in significance, as do the techniques moviegoing girls employed to subvert prescriptive scripts embedded in mass-produced stationery and sentimental keepsakes. In addition to including their headshots and drawing romantic iconography, girl fans eroticized their correspondence with Lawrence by perfuming their letters and selecting suggestive writing paper. For instance, Clara Moore, a daughter of Lawrence's New York City acquaintances, wrote twice in 1914. Both epistles feature a peculiar choice of letterhead: colorful live-action reproductions of two Japanese geishas, a figure historically coded with young female sexuality (figure 7). The reproduction in the second letter is particularly redolent with homoerotic undertones: the pair holds hands and stands at a threshold, the girl up-ahead leading her companion into a secluded garden. While cracking the wooden gate open, she takes her partner's hand, staring at the second girl with a sideways glance and subtly parted lips. The face of the female follower is unseen, completely absorbed in that intimate silent exchange which remains as secret and suggestive as the undepicted garden.[87] The inclusion of a visual representation so laden with exotic female sensuality cues the writer's alignment with eroticized otherness.

Girl fans reached out to film actresses for a multitude of reasons, ambition, infatuation, and identification being the most prevalent. All of these, however, stemmed from fans perceiving Lawrence as the personification of successful girlhood. Known for her stunt-ridden and well-paid performances in short comedies, dramas, and westerns, the dimpled leading lady embodied a life of prosperity, self-reliance, and public respect seldom allowed to working and middle-class girls but often desired by them. As Shelley Stamp observes, in US cinema from the 1910s, female leads like Lawrence "manifest[ed] athletic talents and a taste for adventure that belied outmoded notions of demure 'ladylike' behavior and stay-at-home femininity" still enforced in everyday life.[88]

FIGURE 7. Hand in hand: Clara Moore chose to frame her letter to Florence Lawrence with this homoerotic stationery of two doll-like geishas, ca. 1914.

"ALL THE FUN YOU EVER DREAMED OF:" QUEER INTENSITIES IN FEMALE EPISTOLARY VERNACULAR

For many girl fans, attraction toward Lawrence originated from a recognition and appreciation for the star's projected difference: the actress appeared strong, confident, and independent, characteristics society found unbecoming in average young women, but that the actress portrayed as empowering on- and off-screen. As a result, some fan correspondents explicitly filtered their gender nonconformity through identification with Lawrence's picture personality. In a letter dated from 1911, Lucile Pervas from Portland, Oregon, explains that she is at odds with her well-off aunts, who did not look kindly on the eighteen-year-old's rough-and-tumble pastimes (which included farming, fishing, and "shooting and the like") and expressed urgent concern over the motherless girl's "very unlady-like" behavior.[89] The older women interpreted their niece's favoring of masculine occupations as "full of mischief," and worried it might symptomize a constitutional inability to conform to "sensible" (read: heteronormative) womanhood. Such concerns were not without reason. Since the late nineteenth century sexologists had alerted that the female "invert" showed her abnormality by favoring from an early age "the play-ground of boys. . . . She will have nothing to do with dolls; her passion is for playing horse, soldier, and robber, . . . [and she will be] very wild and unrestrained."[90] Seeking to counteract this undesired outcome, Pervas's aunts took drastic measures: "Honey, would you believe it," the high-schooler complained, "they have actually persuaded daddy to send me abroad to a French school [of manners] *for two solid years.*" In a heartbeat, the fan asserted, "As hard as auntie is going to try she will never make a quite sedate young lady out of me."[91]

Pervas's confessional letter to Lawrence reveals a coming-of-age in conflict: on one hand, the fan admits that her "very unlady-like" behavior indicates a threatening, even unacceptable female identity; on the other, she brandishes an unwillingness (an inability) to change. Torn, the adolescent fan transfers this anxiety to her object of desire, asking the young actress to validate such untraditional way of being by sharing it with her. Calling Lawrence "my little girl friend" and "my girl hero," the moviegoer confesses to only reaching out to the star after having "read in the last issue of the [*Motion Picture Story*] magazine that you enjoy out-of-doors sports," data that intimated that fan and star were "kindred spirits."[92] In one fell swoop, Lawrence is cast as confidante, soulmate, and mentor, a queering amalgamation of affective roles. Self-improvement, however, propels such strong spectatorial reaction: if coupled with Lawrence, the troubled fan believes that she too could become a fulfilled nonconventional adult.

Perhaps the most conspicuous sign of homoerotic courtship is Pervas's attempt to seduce Lawrence with a profuse fantasy of dyadic intimacy. Confessing "to have just learnt to love you," the tomboy invites Flo to visit her Portland country house and share what resembles a romantic idyll, complete with town-and-gown options and lady-in-waiting services. "Any time we wish to go to town the auto can take us there in forty-five minutes," the girl jauntily declares, "and I will try my best to keep you from getting lonesome." Subtle but assertive, the indication of Lawrence's potential "lonesomeness" persuades that Pervas conceived of the vacation as a summer of pleasure made for two. Playfully vague, the promises to "keep Lawrence from feeling lonesome" and to avail her of "all the fun you ever dreamed of" leaves to the imagination a cornucopia of activities two young women could engage in together to keep solitude at bay.

Through manipulation of the sentimental idiom, girls layered connotation into their fan writings. Like sedimentary rock, each stratum of meaning adds to the libidinal texture. As a result, *identification with a star* could rapidly bleed into *desire for the star*. Pervas repeatedly blurs distinctions between the two spectatorial responses. Throughout her three-page letter, the girl constantly calls attention to her youthful inexperience as if this—in spite of all her wealth and education—could somehow limit her ability to satisfy the movie actress. Preemptively, the fan discloses: "I had better tell you just how old I am so you won't plan on any-thing and then be disappointed. I am just eighteen. . . . I'm just out of 'hogh' school, and not very polished yet." What could a twenty-four-year-old celebrity "plan" that would require her summer companion to be over eighteen and more "polished" than a well-read, well-off adolescent is left ambiguous, if highly suggestive of occupations requiring worldly experience.

Pervas's letter performs the kind of connotative sleight of hand feminist scholars have long attributed to the sentimental genre: on the surface, most narratives revolved around coming-of-age into heterosexual marriage, while in actuality this story line operated as "the coverplot," a literary veneer that "masked subversive elements that reside underneath and were meant to be decoded by the female reader."[93] Here the film star plays the addressee summoned to read between the lines; a confession of gender nonconformity and generational strife functions as a gateway to signal homoerotic desire and propose a sensual escapade.

It is important to recall that, in early-twentieth-century United States, self-identified "inverts" reported feeling deeply isolated; according to medical literature, "many felt no possibility of finding like-minded individuals." Pervas's epistolary intensity may thus have been motivated by the euphoria of self-recognition, the promise of elusive succor. To historian Bert Hansen, most homosexual patients recorded in turn-of-the-century clinical studies seemed to be "seeking not only social and sexual relations, but also a confirmation of their odd feelings, for numerous cases refer to persistent efforts toward self-understanding."[94]

Letters like Pervas's demonstrate that, a century after its halcyon days, the sentimental idiom continued to be employed by female writers to articulate self-understandings of difference and longing for freedom of choice. In the 1910s, girls turned to Hollywood cinema for inspiration. Echoing sentimental correspondence from the mid-1800s, their fan mail shows "the reader and author [establishing] an intimacy made possible through the exchange of the written word and negotiated around the personality constructed in the [star] text."[95] In the newfangled picture personalities, girl audiences found interlocutors through which they could negotiate an adolescent craving for dissident models of womanhood. Fans also latched onto certain narrative hooks in female star texts, manipulating them to fit their own needs. Homoerotic desire, gender nonconformity, and an appetite for plurality crisscrossed the fabric of fan production from the very beginnings of the star system.

Nance O'Neill is another screen-struck girl who used epistolary sentimentality to bring Lawrence into her struggles with nontraditional identity and impending adulthood. Like Pervas, O'Neill believed she defied paradigms of middle-class feminine propriety: she self-characterized as "a holy terror . . .—sliding and running instead of being ladylike—like other girls."[96] She also preferred horses and her dog (suitably named Lady Raffles after a serial heroine) to male company, enjoyed going "about mostly in overalls [because] you can navigate better in overalls than skirts," and openly admitted that "keeping house and I are not congenial."[97] O'Neill's case is peculiar because she wrote multiple times to Lawrence between 1914 and 1917, while Pervas and other correspondents seem to have written only once. Also, if we are to believe O'Neill's letters, she came to befriend the star and spent private time with "Flo-Flo" in her New Jersey homestead during the Summer of 1915.

Again, O'Neill's correspondence documents the recurrent queer phenomenon where a female fan's identification with an actress seamlessly overlaps with her desire for the star.[98] Desexualizing herself by self-identifying as "a kid," the eighteen-year-old observes that her "unfeminine" proclivities are deemed eccentric by those surrounding her; only with Lawrence could the movie fan shed the "nice and conventional" pretenses and be her true unconventional self.[99] The performance of authentic female personhood nonetheless comes enveloped in sensuous desire, communicated through very specific rhetorical choices.

In one of her first letters, O'Neill muses:

> Just now I feel as though you were sitting opposite me and smiling your inscrutable smile, because perhaps, you know just what I'm going to write. . . . Somehow you are smiling at me from that deep chair across the room—you are all wrapped in rose-clear light from the lamp on the table. . . .

If I dare to go near you, I know you'll vanish, like smoke from a witches'
pot! Because although it's pleasant to have you there, smiling *queerly* and
knowing all about this letter, I'm not so stupid as not to know that you are
really in New Jersey, among your flowers and trees and bulldogs. . . . [But]
do smile as wickedly, as aggravatingly as you please, petite. I can stand it—I
rather like it! Did you ever feel very, very near to someone you love? I feel so
now . . . Now, isn't that *queer?*"[100]

Familiarity and domesticity act as backdrops for romantic seduction.
As Marcus notes, it was part of the vernacular of one-sided female infatuations to "create an atmosphere of pent-up longing" and paint "an
erotic aura around [one's muse] through the very act of writing about
her, through liberal use of adverbs and adjectives, and by infusing her
most ordinary actions with dramatic implications."[101] The "rose-clear
light," a "deep chair," the gesture of "smiling queerly and knowing," all
become props in the staging of O'Neill's (or is it Lawrence's?) bewitch-
ment. In addition to sentiment, the overemphasis on gesture also brings
into play melodramatic conventions popular in turn-of-century stage,
film, and literature. Peter Brooks remarks that in the modern melodramatic imagination "gestures cease to be merely tokens of social intercourse whose meaning is assigned by a social order; they become vehicles of metaphor whose tenor suggests another kind of reality," subjective
and superlative. By virtue of its own exaggerated indetermination, "gesture is read as containing such meanings because it is postulated [by the
recipient] as the metaphorical approach to what cannot be said."[102] A
smile is not only a smile then; as devised by the fan, the movement of
Lawrence's lips becomes intentional—a telegraphed clue and a veiled
come-on.

Melodramatic meaning and mood are baked into the act of fan letter-
writing, as into the practice of star-worshiping. "If I dare to go near
you," O'Neill breathlessly confesses, "I know you'll vanish, like smoke
from a witches' pot!" More than a dramatic flourish, the fan's phrasing
captures the pivotal deification of stars' immateriality, their lack of a
live presence rendering them both enthralling and foreboding to moviegoers. Cast in theatrical apparitionality, Lawrence emerges visible but
untenable: she is chum and siren, approachable and aloof, both a mystic
soulmate projected by telepathy and a faraway friend being conjured by
reminiscence. It is remarkable how volatile O'Neill's colloquial mode of
address is, conveying the type of masochistic, mercurial rapport Marcus
claims belonged not to the sphere of female friendships but to the province of uneven and unconsummated same-sex passions.

The placement of a seduction scene in two domiciliary spaces (O'Neill's Massachusetts rooms overlapping with Lawrence's New Jersey home) casts light on how the star system supplied female audiences with new backgrounds to rehearse intimate fantasies. Marcus proposes that to write about a female beloved in exalted detail was in itself an exercise in autoerotic play—what the historian calls a "self-dramatizing" in "the private theatre of [women's] journals."[103] Melodrama, Brooks argues, first offered industrial consumers "a habitat where imagination [could] play with large moral entities."[104] The practice of receding into the private theater of the mind and transposing female desire onto the written page gained supplementary dimension when cinema became the leading medium entertaining the masses. The igniting of fan ardor, until then tied to physical proximity (stage performers and friends could only be experienced in the flesh), widened with the ascendency of narrative cinema and its mediated stars. Now available daily for a dime, clipped from magazines or purchased as memorabilia for a lifetime, the image of movie stars entered both the domestic space and the psychic real estate of worshipping fans. The private theater of girls' correspondence and diaries, as well as their bedroom walls, swelled with raw material to adore. Simultaneously, girls' psychological fora dilated with possible willing participants: film stars reputedly wrote back, sending headshots and autographs along with their letters, as well as volunteering information about their private lives.

Put in another way, female intimacy remained a matter of language in the 1910s, but the star-driven film industry introduced a performative closeness to it through the commercialization of tactile star ephemera, which in turn created an additional layer of fan demands, deficits, and expectations. The need to be closer to a star grew once proximity seemed possible. In fan mail, screen-struck admiration and courtship merged together, ebbing and flowing into a palimpsest of affects. Often it is impossible to distinguish homosocial appreciation from homoerotic desire because these are not articulated as separate. "An essential pleasure for those who loved a remote figure," Vicinus notes, "was the very distance itself, which gave room, paradoxically, for an enriched consciousness of self. Without gratification, countless fantasies could be constructed, a seemingly continuous web of self-examination, self-inspection, self-fulfillment."[105]

It is that saturated hybridity, that union of self-discovery and self-denial, identification and want, diplomacy and disclosure, that renders early girl fandom constitutively queer. In their correspondence, fans coalesced autoerotic expression with demure chivalry, conjuring an idiom that privileged coded messages and gender questioning. The result is a type of sentimental life-writing where imagined touch and witnessed screen mannerisms are elevated to prime currency. Both movie fans and sentimental writers privileged descriptions of facial expression, willing it to "contract the distance between narrated events and the moment of their reading."[106] Baldassare Castiglione's influential manual on courtly love, *The Book of the Courtier* (1528), counseled that a lover should "make his eyes the faithful messengers to bear the [hidden] embassies of his heart, since they often show the passion that is within more clearly than the tongue, . . . [and] kindle love in the beloved's heart."[107]

Following in this amatory tradition, O'Neill channeled the male courtier, fixating her gaze on Lawrence's erogenous features. In all her letters, the star's mouth (goading, teasing, sly) anchors the high-schooler's attraction, concretizing an imagined intimacy between female star and fan. Later that year, Lawrence's smile becomes a bargaining chip: "Honey, I'll send my photograph if you'll send one of yours, one in which that famous, saucy dimple appears."[108] The fan's attachment to the star's facial orifice, attended by sensual terms of endearment ("honey," "petite") infuses the epistolary barter with eroticism. By recasting Lawrence's trademark dimples as a personalized gesture, O'Neill ultimately sexualizes the star's physicality, investing homoerotic desire with the power to narrow the intimacy deficit between a picture personality and her dispersed followers.

O'Neill's strategic performance of exposure and concealment further gives rise to a historiographic inquiry into the transformative usages of self-defining language, particularly terms that have come to be associated with LGBTQ+ history. In the letter quoted above, O'Neill employs "queer" twice in reference to herself. As discussed in the introduction, in early twentieth-century parlance the adjective commonly meant "strange" or "peculiar" and was liberally employed in everyday communication. Since the late 1800s, however, pejorative connotations had affixed themselves to the term, so that "queer" became a whispered noun deployed to disparage people who displayed same-sex desire or gender nonconformity. By 1914, the slur seeped out of street slang and made its way into local and national newspapers as an umbrella descriptor for nonheteronormative acts, including homosexuality, female impersonation, male transvestism, and even suffragism.[109] Gaining a second meaning in press discourse, "queer" resurfaced as code for "different from the norm," conveying an innate divergence or deliberate resistance to performing the strict binaries of gender identity and sexual attraction upheld by heterosexist society.

At the same time that this linguistic shift took place in the public domain, girls repeatedly employed the adjective form of "queer" in their personal writings to characterize intensely unsettling, unparsed, or discordant responses to people and situations. They also regularly applied it to describe themselves when wrestling with gender noncon-formity and homoerotic attraction. Taking into account O'Neill's sug-gestive tone—dotted with pet names and flirtatious references to Law-rence's body—the insistent usage of "queer" in her correspondence can be interpreted as knowingly playing upon the double meaning the word had come to harbor. Propping this theory up is the frequency with which O'Neill reminds Lawrence of her distaste for male company. "Darling Muse," the girl fan writes once she has settled in New York City, "Don't you suppose two girls can steal away for dinner by them-selves without being weighted down by a couple of males?"[110]

Performing and building a public persona is integral to the pleasures afforded by female fan writing, as manifest in girls' self-perceived iden-tity as a "proper lady," a "holy terror," or a "movie fan." Gender per-formance thus brought young female fans near to a star—literally and figuratively. If some moviegoers approached Lawrence seeking profes-sional advice on how to become a movie actress, others understood "act-ing" as a constitutive demand of their shared gender. Pervas worried that being sent to a school of manners for two years would compromise her core self, forcing her to adopt a parody of "sedate" femininity the girl decried as "an act."[111] O'Neill collapsed both instances when she admit-ted to prefer acting on the silver screen to "acting" on the confined pla-teau of middle-class domesticity. The girl demonstrates piercing insight when assessing the social expectations limiting well-to-do white women in the 1910s: if pretending to be "nice and conventional" is what should be demanded of her, then an acting career in the company of Lawrence would prove more authentic. In a letter predating her presumed stay with the star, O'Neill promises, "You can rely on my word, Flo-Flo—I'm not going to be nice and conventional when I go [to Westwood]—because I know you too well and if I dared to be—I know you'd laugh and say *I was acting* wouldn't you?"[112] For O'Neill, Lawrence embodied an empowering alternative to a lifelong impersonation of "nice and conven-tional" femininity. The star symbolized freedom to be oneself: unapolo-getically nontraditional and joyful. According to a later letter, the Mas-sachusetts fan seems to have fulfilled her adolescent dream, growing up to live an independent, eventful life as a bachelor socialite in Uptown New York.

Still, it is important to linger on girls' self-fashioning as a "star worshiper" and to map how such performance of self took shape through female fan writings, both private and published. Making a spectacle out of one's unparalleled admiration for a famed actress was not an innovative praxis in the early 1910s. Stage divas like Sarah Bernhardt, Maude Adams, and Gaby Deslys had been attracting such feverous followings for years; star-struck men of privilege, however, received most of the public spotlight.[113] Cinema democratized the opportunities to adore a female performer. With its cheap mass availability—ranging from low prices of admission to shareable promotional items like magazines and exhibitor brochures—motion pictures supplied girls from diverse backgrounds with an accessible venue to fawn over female celebrities and act as lovesick as male audiences had in the past. Further, fan love may have anteceded movie-struck girls, but the public dramatization of extreme fan attachment surged in the early twentieth century, a byproduct of what historian Warren Susman termed "the cult of personality." Defined by a "performing self" that banked on broadcasting "the quality of being Somebody, [either] . . . famous or infamous," "personality" quickly became a prerequisite for the profitable implementation of Hollywood's star system and, by extension, of a homegrown celebrity media culture.[114]

Movie fan girls' attempts to "distinguish [one]self from [the] crowd" by curating a nonpareil interiority for a target audience coheres with a cultural moment embracing narrative cinema, public performance, and psychology as vehicles to render selfhood fungible for mass consumption.[115] Probing the theater of the mind becomes the subject of hundreds of literary texts, biographies, and scientific treaties published throughout the early twentieth century, their film adaptations mushrooming in the mid- to late 1910s. Imagining oneself as a movie star's most committed acolyte functioned as a similar push toward public visibility, toward transforming the self into an accessible consumer good. Self-casting as a star's number-one fan ultimately replicates the individualistic cult of personality amplified by the early film industry, in which a chosen few rose above the anonymous masses. From this perspective, Pervas's and O'Neill's stated identification with nonnormativity may operate as a means to stand out among the imagined throngs of fans who daily accosted stars of Lawrence's import. Presenting themselves as the unpolished misfit or the amorous free-spirit introduced a measure of distinction, a strategic "expression of difference from other women" (particularly the vain, ultra-feminine "screen-struck girl" painted by the press), and a rhetorical device that authenticated the fans' "wish to leave the female world and to escape its conventions," a commonality with the exclusive picture star.[116]

We witness this intentional spectacularization of the atypical self play out across Lawrence's fan mail. Stars of their own narratives, girls employ private correspondence to shine a light on their singular personhood, vaunting tragic aspects of their lives to court a player's favor. When asking for a photo, twelve-year-old Louise Johnson from Washington, DC, leads with having just survived typhoid fever.[117] Theodora Anthony discloses that her father, "a very great physician, committed suicide three years ago [due to] loss of money" and illness (figure 8).[118] On Valentine's Day 1916, a twelve-year-old immigrant girl wrote to Lawrence from Canada. Originally from Holland, Angelina Mary Kovez professed to be "having an awful time with Dad [.] He chase [sic] us out at any time and mid night [sic] when he gets drunk." Dramatically self-effacing, the narrative of domestic violence and paternal alcoholism is positioned as a come-hither for further star contact: "I am afraid you won't like [me] because I am writing you but I thought you was [sic] the only friend I could write to as I have no body [sic] else to write." Though harrowing, the contents of this letter rehearse hallmarks of sentimental temperance fiction in which a young heroine's worth directly correlated with her suffering at the hands of an abusive father.[119] Not seeking to dilute the authenticity of Kovez's account, I am instead gesturing toward interrogating the various strategies girl fans may have deployed to establish instant intimacy with elevated movie idols. Confessions of extreme hardship and need for rescue sought to speed up affective bonding while carving a lasting place for the fan in the star's memory. Kovez herself makes these intentions clear by closing with the following statement: "Now Florence I hope you will like me after you get this letter. . . . I will look for a letter every day from now on, I will be very much disappointed. Be sure you wont [sic] forget me."[120]

Girls' bids on actresses' intimacy may seem to merely partake in a longstanding culture of female sentimentality, but the forwardness and gusto emanating from their writings are striking, especially when taking into consideration that, according to historian Francesca Cancian, early twentieth-century US culture did not consider erotic love and courtship pathways to female self-development.[121] "Good girls"—illustrations, newspaper articles, and pedagogical manuals instructed—purportedly

FIGURE 8. Theodora Anthony, whose father killed himself, sent this portrait to Florence Lawrence asking for friendship and professional advice, ca. 1919.

grew up to find fulfillment in the roles of wife and mother, not in that of pursuer. Individual pleasure and independence fell under the purview of masculinity: turn-of-the-century culture expected boys to become self-knowing social agents, while girls were to develop a nurturing selfless-ness. In other words, the concept of "love" may have become feminized in the nineteenth century, but romance and courtship did not emerge as a means to advance women's personhood and freedom until the 1920s. In the 1910s, the gender-coded construct of romantic love buttressed a heterosexist economic structure trading on women's homebound sub-servience and monogamous reproductivity.

That moviegoing girls openly employed the charged language of romance to communicate instances of self-discovery, aspiration, and fantasy thus holds a measure of queer subversion. It reveals that in the confines of epistolary fandom, girls combined the inchoate syntax of filmdom with the rhetorical conventions of heteronormative courtship to convey persuasions perceived as going against the grain of dominant cultural scripts, specifically those regulating female attachment, advancement, and well-being. Avoiding the long-term transactional goals promoted by the patriarchal society of which moviemaking partook, girls wrote love letters to film actresses mainly for their own enjoyment and enhancement: to momentarily capture a celebrity's attention; to receive a personalized response or expert advice; to be briefly seen and recognized as a distinct audience member; or to claim autoerotic gratification. Simply put, when applied to female fan-star communication, traditional sentimental conventions afforded an affirming venue for female self-exploration and self-development at a time when gender and sexual identities, like emotional states, remained socially and legally restricted to determinist binaries: male/female, active/passive, power/love, public/private, compliant/deviant.

Most of these governing oppositions, Cancian argues, sprouted in US culture during the mid-nineteenth century, fruit of novel labor and spatial divisions induced by the rise of an industrial consumer society. Women, now confined to the home and its caretaking obligations, were expected to prioritize the well-being of others over their individual potential, pleasure, and ambition. In their writings to young film actresses, movie-loving girls pioneered a paradigm of same-sex support where "self-development and love [are] mutually reinforcing."[122] In other words, a moviegoing girl loves an actress, and by making her love known in writing, she fuels the star's radiance while deriving repute or expertise by proxy. According to US historians, such a model of equitable self-development gained traction only in the 1960s, and exclusively within the traditional structure of middle-class heterosexual marriage. Lawrence's fan mail bears out that girls from both well-off and working backgrounds chased after alternatives to a heteronormative model of love and self-actualization as early as 1910, casting female stars as their muses, mentors, and peers in a pursuit of elastic and fulfilling growth.

Framed by sentimental modes of female bonding and memory keeping, such quests for acceptance and recourse must have resonated with Lawrence as well—after all, she saved over two dozen of these letters.

Taking into consideration that Lawrence's film career spanned more than a decade, the amount of fan mail received in her lifetime surely surpassed that number. Yet the actress chose these, an overwhelming majority of girl-penned letters, their envelopes pink and perfumed, their cursive words dripping with raptured admiration, audacity, and innuendo. What may have led the star to keep these and not other fan communications can only be speculated. Though possible explanations range from utility to vanity to happenstance, I suggest that it was due to a measure of self-identification, likely tinged with the kind of pride and pleasure that did not bloom under the attentions of besotted male suitors but in the company of eager, plucky, appreciative girls. A parasocial version of homophily hence approximated early star and fans. Sociologists Paul Lazarsfeld and Robert Merton first delineated the notion of homiphily as "a tendency for friendships to form between those who are alike in some designated respect." With a picture personality harmonizing feminine and masculine attributes, Lawrence functioned as a lightning rod for nonnormative audience responses as early as 1909, the date of the earliest letter found in her fan archive.[123]

Despite saving personal letters and published materials dating from 1909 to the 1930s, the bulk of Lawrence's curated collection focuses on the early-to-mid 1910s. Since her stardom rapidly declined around 1913, it is also possible that Lawrence kept girls' correspondence as a talisman against loss, a melancholic means to relive her own girlhood and fast-fading glory days. Many of the fan letters from 1914 onwards are nostalgic in tone, reminiscing about Lawrence's earlier parts, bemoaning her absence from the screen, and vowing that she "still has [a] 'big' place in my heart."[124] By the mid-1910s, industry and audiences considered fan mail a tool capable of reliably measuring a star's magnitude, so it stood to reason that if the written praise kept coming, a player's relevance ought to remain. As Florence Turner (another early picture personality with a short-lived stardom) argued in 1924, "No, I don't believe the public is fickle—I know it isn't. . . . How do I know? How does any of us know? By the fan letters, of course."[125] The impetus to save fan mail thus betrays a moving parallel between aging stars and adolescent fan writers: both sought to affirm a sense of unique selfhood through personalized ephemera exchange, to preserve a material record of individual value and importance that could stand the test of modern temporality. Off the screen, Lawrence was besieged by unhappy romances, unfortunate business decisions, and failing health from injuries sustained on-set—all of which culminated with her suicide in 1938, at age fifty-two. In an indirect way, stars' fan-mail collections spotlight this negative side of early film celebrity, palled by the ruthlessly swift demands of the medium, as by the undiscussed toll moviemaking took on pioneer actors' bodies and minds.

Exhuming the homoerotic/homophilic bonds fastening silent-era girl fans to female movie stars (and vice versa) helps destabilize the misconception that girls' engagement with popular media is predominantly centered on heteronormativity. Personal fan mail also complicates the lingering notion that female romantic friendships play a secondary role to heterosexual coupling. Neither was true in early twentieth-century film fandom. Within the protected framework of private fan correspondence, movie-loving girls engendered a language of same-sex intimacy and identification that would come to blueprint future expressions of fan adoration and star consumption. These material traces of adolescent want ultimately shed light on the emotional fabric of female relationships—on a "hunger" that, as Nell Dorr conveyed in her impassioned letter to Lillian Gish, tangled aspiration and admiration with fantasy and sensuality, while also holding space for homoerotic uneasiness and gender defiance.

CHAPTER 3

"If I Were a Man"

Gender-Bending in Girls' Published
Fan Poems

Went to the movies. Tried to be affectionate.

—Helen Pease, August 17, 1915

In a personal letter dated from 1911, twenty-one-year-old Miss Mabel Hilton expressed her feelings for Florence Lawrence through the conditional usurping of an imaginary male identity: "I love the pictures where you play opposite Arthur Johnson and I'll bet if I were a man you wouldn't be Miss Lawrence very long," the Connecticut fan cheekily declared.[1] Drawing on amatory conventions, some girls wrote poems to actresses in the voice of a male suitor. Usually published in movie magazines, these compositions evidence the diversity of identificatory mechanisms early Hollywood instantiated and how they flowered under the shelter of sentimental rhetoric.

Although tributes to male players were not unusual, fan-submitted panegyrics frequently addressed young actresses. Like other first-person statements found in film magazines (including letters to editors, talent interviews, and advice columns), fan poems tended to reinforce binary standards of gender and sexual normativity. For instance, under the guise of advice, in 1914 "Blondina" told other young film lovers that

If you've never had a sweetheart
(Boys and Girls, this is for you)
Go to a picture playhouse
There you'll find your love most true.
For the girls there is Earle Williams
Warren K. and Wallie Van

. . . .

90

For the boys there's Lillian Walker
Alice Joyce and dear Pearl White.

Reasserting a heteronormative mode of reception, the fan finishes her limerick by proclaiming:

For me I'll take Jack Standing
He's my hero, it sure seems;
Pathé claims him now for acting
But I claim him in my dreams.[2]

As is the case with letters girls sent directly to female stars, the distinction between homoerotic passion and homosocial admiration is manifest in linguistic choices. Most same-sex compositions found in the periodical press lacked any heat or innuendo. Instead, they relied on a laundry list of generic compliments and well wishes to relay fan appreciation. For example, Betty Ethridge of Fulton, New York, paid homage to Clara Kimball Young by remarking how

Of all the maids who are so sweet
Of all the maids who are so neat
There's not a single one who can beat Clara Kimball Young.[3]

In the same issue of *Motion Picture Magazine*, "Ernesta Hoawald, of Astoria [who] . . . has not been long in this country," begins by admitting that

I never saw a face and form
So fair as yours, Edith Storey—
Your artistry takes all by storm
Your acting is a glory,

only to conclude solemnly:

May your future life be all sunshine
And many hope it, too
May every joy in full be thine
I wish it thru and thru.[4]

The language of respectful admiration and polite greeting seen in published fan poems sought to set an appropriate tone for star-fan public interactions. However, in adopting a homogenous mode of proper engagement that overvalued gender and sexual binaries, movie magazines threw an incidental spotlight on any fan composition that diverged from those well-drawn lines. Male-voiced love poems penned by self-identified girl fans occupy such a space of relative subversion, both playing *with and outside* conventions set by the film press. Subject to editing, movie magazines and newspapers complicate a definitive ascertainment of fan authorship. Nevertheless, their pages brimmed with poems in which female-identified moviegoers took up a male subject-position to court screen actresses. Edited or not, by the mid-1910s gender-bending performances had become commonly associated with female film reception.

"AN ALIBI": MALE POETIC VOICE IN QUEER FEMALE RECEPTION

Evidence suggests that the practice of openly taking up a poetic voice opposed to one's assigned gender was particularly popular among female fans; if male viewers did it too, they left less visible traces than their counterparts. Some feminist scholars would argue that such behavioral disparities stem from Hollywood cinema being built around the heterosexual male gaze. Mary Ann Doane proposes that to find "a mastery over the image and the very possibility of attaching the gaze to desire," a female viewer must "pretend that she is other" through a "recuperable" gender reversal. By adopting a gender-crossed position, female audiences could temporarily reclaim a governing male gaze while simultaneously reiterating the systemic undesirability affixed to femininity by a heterosexist society. As Doane concludes, "It is understandable that women would want to be a man, for everyone wants to be elsewhere than in the feminine position."[5] In surrogating a male perspective, female moviegoers essentially reached for authorial agency and sexual autonomy whilst existing within a patriarchal power structure that often denied them both.

Straying from an overdetermination of sexual difference, I argue that the queerness of girls' male-voiced poems resides not in the reversal of gender binaries but in fans' play with erotic fluidity, which, in turn, strains biological essentialism. Twice printed in 1917, the poem "A Film Fan's Favorites" exemplifies this polymorphous mode of reception. In it, twenty-five-year-old Emma Card Stewart transforms herself into a gray-haired professional man, complete with an "office boy" named Jimmie, a "Miss La Rue the typist," and a nosy, homebound "Friend Wife." Enjoying the free, liminal hours at the end of the business day and before the return home, this imaginary male interlocutor luxuriates in his fondness for actress Lillian Gish:

In snowy ruffles, crinoline, hoop-skirt and pantalet
Miss Lillian Gish is all the rage—one great big hit, and yet
This winsome belle of 'Sixty-one,' appealing and demure
Stirs old romantic feelings that I thought were dead for sure.

Awash with sensuality, Stewart imagines herself as a married man already past his sexual prime: the dormant "romantic feelings" Gish awakes are only embers, long faded and therefore innocuous. The old male narrator confesses to being lifted from "the wear and tear, the grind of life, and [the stress of] all those unpaid bills" by the sensuous thrall Gish casts over him.[6] By taking the voice of a desexualized middle-aged man, Stewart attempts to distance herself from her own erotic investment in a female star: first by filtering her infatuation through a heterosexual male voice and second by annulling any active sexual impetus by aging the male narrator into nostalgic impotence. However, if the girl fan's subterfuge telegraphs caution and restraint in publicly confessing to same-sex stirrings, having sent this composition for publication in a leading film magazine suggests that Stewart wanted her desires to be known to a wide readership. More importantly, the decision to impersonate a male fan implies that Stewart understood, or wanted her fan investment to be understood by readers, as resembling that of a heterosexual man.

The prematurely aged, wistful male narrator is a fixture of nineteenth-century sentimental fiction, particularly that penned by men.[7] On its own, the appropriation of this stylistic device does not signify female empowerment or subversion. As Marianne Nobel remarks, by embodying a fictive male gaze, nineteenth-century female authors reasserted the sentimental genre as "a discursive agent for the proliferation of oppressive ideologies . . . [that] trained women to experience their desire vicariously through that of a man."[8] Masculinity in Anglo-American culture is aspirational, so borrowing a man's perspective to communicate the most sublime emotions only reiterates femininity as lacking finesse or range. The point is well taken, but I propose a different interpretation.

Throughout the 1910s, medical writings on female inversion burgeoned. By the time Freud published "The Psychogenesis of a Case of Female Homosexuality" in 1920, the equation of female homosexuality with the surrogation of masculine characteristics had become so well-established that the psychoanalyst mentions it only as diagnostic shorthand. In fact, his young patient's manifestations of "physical masculinity" (i.e., taking after her father, being tall and chiseled) are not what gives Freud pause; it is her lovemaking strategies. The nameless girl "had not only chosen a feminine love object but had also developed *a masculine attitude towards this object*. . . . That is to say, she manifested the humility and the tremendous over-estimation of the sexual object so characteristic of the male lover."[9] Freud further links female homosexual desire with film fandom, comparing the "enthusiastic passion" the unnamed girl dedicated to her "adored lady" with that of a "bashful youth for a celebrated actress," and commenting that such lady's "bad reputation" stemmed from her seeking "the company of a cinematograph actress at a summer resort."[10]

Male-voiced fan love poems prove that a sizeable number of movie-loving girls used the concept of gender inversion to express homoerotic responses and harness the queer potentialities of a transitional period. Stable classifications for female homosexuality and transgenderism had yet to solidify in US culture in the 1910s, but a popular perception relating lesbian desire with masculinized courtship and attire already permeated collective imagination at the time girl fans published their male-voiced poems. In fact, the practice of gender reversal to convey same-sex female attraction had become commonplace a century prior. Reminiscing about the late 1800s, author Dorothy Strachey described coping with sapphic desire by daydreaming a gender-swap of her love object: "It was a man I loved as I loved her, and then he would take me in his arms . . . and kiss me . . . I should feel his lips on my cheeks, on my eyelids, on my—No, no, no, that way lay madness."[11]

Even if in passing, turning one of two same-sex partners into the opposite sex allowed admittance into the social privileges attending heterosexual courtship. It also minimized feelings of shame, inappropriateness, or self-loathing heterosexist society cultivated in those experiencing nonnormative tendencies. Surrogating a male poetic voice to openly romance female stars thus holds elements of both transgression and traditionalism: emboldened by modern technology but articulated through sentimental convention, driven by female fantasy but cloaked under aspirational masculinity, flashing queer desire while reasserting heteronormative codes of binary gender conduct.

In this way, film fandom became a coverplot for negotiating female queer attachments—"an alibi," to use Luce Irigaray's terminology. According to Irigaray, in classical Hollywood heterosexuality (supplemented by normative womanhood) operates as a veneer, deflecting homosexual and homoerotic male bonds: "Reigning everywhere, although prohibited in practice, hom(m)osexuality is played out through the bodies of women, matter, or sign, and heterosexuality has been up to now just *an alibi* for the smooth workings of man's relations with himself."[12] Built on emotive plots and haptic feeling, US silent cinema eroticized female bodies on the screen and on the page. Some moviegoing girls responded by deploying the cover of female romantic friendship and heterosexual courtship as a subterfuge for trying out intensities deemed impermissible in everyday life. Some likely applied gender-inversion as a literary flourish, while others used it to convey felt gender complications. In either case, a clear intention to play with gender conventions underlay this subgenre of fan writing. As seen in Stewart's poem, screen femininity was often exaggerated, actresses' physical attributes and fashion choices reduced to frilliness, pinkness, and softness. By exacerbating essentialist gender binaries, fans experimented with the slippage between masculinity and femininity, ultimately rendering bare their nearly cartoonish arbitrariness and artificiality.

When discussing female fan agency, it warrants recalling that, historically, sentimental life-writing supplied girls with a repertoire of rhetorical means to communicate intense nonsexual ties between women, namely those of sisterhood and spiritual friendship. And yet many female moviegoers specifically chose to liken their response to actresses to heterosexual lovemaking, deliberately infusing their fan reception with homoeroticism. Building upon what literature scholar Lisa Spiro calls "detached intimacy," I suggest that taking up a first-person male voice afforded female filmgoers a satisfying negotiation between distance and identification, disavowal and self-awareness. Spiro coins the term when analyzing the fan letters mid-nineteenth-century US readers wrote to Donald Grant Mitchell, the author of the famous sentimental novel *Reveries of a Bachelor* (1850). According to Spiro, "detached intimacy" enabled a female consumer to "engage in a profound identification even as she remains conscious that she is actively constructing a fantasy. Detached intimacy is somewhere between narcissistic escapism and rigorous discipline: although the reader is aware of social responsibilities, she is inspired . . . to dream up different ways of fulfilling or stretching these roles."[13] In the context of girl fans' gender-bending love poems, detached intimacy underlines their appropriation of a male gaze. Protected by the alibi of compulsory heterosexuality and borrowing the sexual frankness socially granted to men, girl fans did not disconnect from their erotic desires. Instead, they placed a safe buffer around them, simultaneously revealing and concealing their attraction to young movie actresses.

Although some female fans chose the male perspective to express their investment in movie actresses, these poetic narrators are far from surrogating the asexual "female boy" Laura Horak claims male impersonation helped romanticize on the silent screen. Male-voiced fan compositions frequently dripped with limerence, the sentimental idiom applied as a thin coat covering sexual desire. Casting themselves as smitten gentlemen and forward flirts, fan writers did not use gender-crossing primarily to "produce an idealized masculinity" but to facilitate female pleasure and agency.[14] In fan panegyrics, masculinity is used less as a sentimental *idealization* and more as a sentimental *masquerade,* a covert means to queerly eroticize women without immediate reprisal, since a borrowed male gaze could pass same-sex desire as heterosexual courtship. By cosplaying a poetic male voice, in short, some female movie lovers found a safe way to publicize complicated affective responses that would have attracted criticism were they made explicit without the disavowing alibi of film fandom.

CONDITIONAL MALE IDENTITIES: FAN POEMS AND BIOGRAPHY

Consider Stewart once more, but now fleshed out by biographical data culled from public records. Born in the last decade of the nineteenth century, she frequented the University of Alabama in 1909 and had a daughter during World War I; a few years later she produced a son. No records were found of a marriage. In 1940, she is listed as the head of her Etowah, Alabama, household. A much younger male lodger had joined the premises, presumably to help Stewart make ends meet. Stewart, out of circumstance or design, grew up to lead a nontraditional life by early twentieth-century standards. On paper, her life sidestepped the heteronormative markers her poem painted in dismal colors—the passionless marriage, the childless couple, the rote job and routine only alleviated by daydreams of a young film actress. Whether happiness was achieved is not the question. The point is that the affinity for nonnormativity contouring her youthful expression of movie fandom found a match in the filmgoer's adult choices.

While Stewart deflected sexual attraction for a movie actress by aging and marrying off her male narrator, Minna Irving cast herself as a young, pining "chap" who treats the screen goddess as his steady date.

I cannot sit at eventide
Or spoon with her while softly shines

The silver moon above.
I cannot take her for a spin,
Altho I own a car,
Or out to supper, or to hear
The latest opera star.
I see her almost every night,
Yet cannot press her lips,
Or tell her that her sparkling eyes
The brightest arcs eclipse.
I cannot ask her to be mine,
For lo! the little queen
Is a celebrated heroine
Upon the movie screen.[15]

The absence of physical intimacy ("cannot press her lips" or "spoon with her") immediately sexualizes the romancing of the unnamed female star. That same erotic absence adjoins unrequited lovers to movie fans: both revere a beloved who resists being grasped. In addition to rehearsing moviegoers' rising desire to be intimate with "little movie queens"— a desire fueled by the propagation of film magazines' interactive columns, behind-the-scenes materials, and tactile ephemera—Irving performs detached intimacy by "abstract[ing] herself from the body and from concrete reality, yet remain[ing] awake and conscious" of her distinct roles as spectator, fan, imagined suitor, and lived author.

In actuality, Minna Irving was the pen name of Minnie Oddell Michiner, a published New York poet. Already in her fifties, once divorced and twice married by the time her poem made it to the pages of *Motion Picture Classic,* Irving presents a useful foil to Stewart: while the latter ages her male narrator as a means to desexualize fan attachment, Irving's rejuvenates her male poetic self to make screen-struck yearning relatable to modern audiences. Reading the poems in tandem evidences the overlaps between nineteenth-century sentimental literature and the emerging dialect of movie fandom, as well as signals a continuity between an older and younger generation of fans. It is telling that Irving, a known sentimental poet and avid theatergoer, found such resonance in the idiom of movie love that she decided to tackle it and publicly share it with other (generally much younger) fans.

Irving's is not an isolated case. The homoerotic possibilities of film fandom spoke to other mature female authors, including Florence Gertrude Ruthven, a forty-something published writer turned movie lover. Part Scottish, part New Zealander, Ruthven lived in Detroit, Michigan, when she wrote her plaudit to another unnamed "photo-queen."

Failing to gender her narrator, in 1917 Ruthven created an ambiguous confessional poem where a moviegoer's exasperation with same-sex attraction remains indistinct from frustration with early cinema's structural incorporeality, distance, and silence.

> Only a face on the screen,
> A woman's face I have seen;
> But it haunts me still,
> Against my will
> Stormy, and then serene.
> . . . .
> Lips that to me will not speak
> Oh, eyes that in vain I seek!
> . . . .
> Should we be fated to meet
> Some day, on the crowded street,
> Would they hold my gaze
> Amid the maze,
> Orbs of my photo-queen?[16]

The tension between remoteness and proximity, the fantasized and the everyday, is at the core of the fan-star dynamic; historically, that same tension animates film fandom and celebrity culture. However, characterized as "stormy and then serene," the fan's attraction to the movie actress holds an unusual volatile charge, sparked by unresolved homoerotic desire. Female fan attachment appears as a "haunting," an unpredictable and liminal influence nurtured by the star's ongoing screen appearances but acidulated by the impossibility of quotidian contact. The verb "to haunt" gestures toward lesbian spectatorial desire. In her seminal work, Terry Castle defines lesbian reception as "apparitional," hinged on "ghostly" glimpses of same-sex desire queer spectators could interpret as visual representation: a fugacious kiss between two female characters, an actress wearing menswear onscreen.[17] Unspoken, the queerness of these cinematic moments persists, legible only to audiences versed in the codes of telegraphed alterity. From this perspective, queer film reception becomes akin to a haunting: only those attuned to the invisible, the marginal, the disenfranchised can experience it. Ruthven, a first-generation immigrant, seemed to be such a medium. In fact, her concerns with early cinema's technical limitations can be read as "a coverplot." The uneasiness with "the photo queen's" physical impermanence masks a subtext of uninvited queer longing, embedded in the fan's admission that attraction to the player's body (her face, her eyes, her lips) troubles her day-to-day "against [her] will."

Publicizing same-sex crushes through conditional male identities depended on the mediation of the popular press: fans' love declarations generally debuted in newspapers' opinion columns and movie magazines' reader-submission sections. For instance, in 1914, Constance Only from Memphis, Tennessee, told the *Chicago Daily Tribune* how much she adored "the darling Mary Pickford" and how "much pleased" she would be "to see Jack W. Corrigan [*sic*] of the Feature Film company play opposite her. The two together would be divine. I simply adore them both." As a somewhat awkward afterthought, the fan adds: "*If I were a man* she would be my ideal girl, but I am a girl, so Mr. Corrigan [*sic*] is my exact ideal man."[18] The disavowal of same-sex attraction is exacted at the same time Constance recognizes the impropriety—and implicit impossibility—of said longing.

Trapped by the expectations of compulsory heterosexuality, Constance settles for idealizing a male star known for his "emotional" acting (and later queer suspicion). Only after voicing that conditional buffer ("if") does the fan confess that her natural inclination is to desire Pickford, not Kerrigan. The subtle unanswered question lingering behind this wording, as in many of other writings where girl fans take up hypothetical male identities, is appended to Constance's gender identity: did the moviegoer favor Pickford as a sign of her own identification with masculinity (i.e., a gender-nonconforming subjectivity), or did she only know how to express same-sex desire via opposite-sex models of sexual attraction (i.e., only a man could lust for a woman and vice versa)? Whatever the case, it remains clear that the appropriation of a sentimental male voice helped female fans like Only assert a measure of control over uneasy spectatorial responses, as well as evade conventional presumptions concerning film reception that dismissed female fans as uniformly fame-hungry and boy-crazy.

In this way, girl fans who took up a subjective male voice in their declarations to film actresses brought to life the sort of pleasure and recognition Susan Potter postulates lesbian audiences derived from watching Rudolph Valentino play across media platforms in the 1920s—a sense of identification contingent not on explicit screen representations of same-sex intimacy and gender-crossing but on dispersed nonnormative markers surrounding a star text that made queer female moviegoers feel interpellated.[19] In other words, a moviegoing girl's affinity with a male player could potentialize a transcending of the embodied female experience, substantiating Doane's theory that some female audiences found pleasure in being able to step away from their biological sex and socially imposed gender vis-à-vis surrogacy of a screen male perspective.

If a literary gender-swap intimates a certain subversiveness on the girls' part, most actions fans imagined conducting with their female idols still duplicated staples of heteronormative courtship: gifts of flowers, comped dates, physical caresses, and romantic proposals are bestowed on actresses by these imaginary male suitors. On one hand, such stylistic choice shows that from its early days film fandom appropriated a chivalric idiom and etiquette that not only followed somewhat universal societal conventions but was also upheld by fans and the magazines that catered to them. On the other hand, these poems attest to an internalization of dichotomies of social and sexual difference, even as the writings reveal fans' far from homogenous relationship with gender identity and erotic attraction.

Moreover, the limitations of fans' epistolary gender-swapping render visible the limitations inherent to the grammar of film stardom, where top billing, if shared, was typically reserved to those starring in the heterosexual love plot. Female moviegoers like Constance Only may have lacked the language to express a desire for sharing in Mary Pickford's screen ascendency. The promotional mechanics of the star system prevented other female-assigned diegetic roles (like those of sister or friend) from receiving the same attention as that lavished on the named female star; the only character that came close to being seen as Pickford's match was her leading man. Casting themselves as a female star's male lover thus may have been a response to girl spectators' desire to abridge power differentials between themselves and celebrities, as between men and women. Tempting as it may be to read them as exclusively empowering, such self-inserted fan scenarios also reiterated the rarifying stratification of early star culture, including its zero-sum understanding of fame and obscurity.

WRITING THEMSELVES INTO STARDOM: A FAN LANGUAGE OF QUEER AGENCY

Though not the norm, some female fan poems did vocalize homoerotic responses without the alibi of heterosexual male desire. In 1916, Mabel W. Burleson from Temple, Texas, straightforwardly informed *Motion Picture Magazine* that she fantasized locking lips with Lillian Gish:

There is an appealing young Gish
With a quirk to her mouth, and I wish
I might have the delight
Of being the knight
She kisses—it must be delish![20]

Although a gender switch is implicit (the fan casts herself as the masculine figure of the "knight"), Burleson's fantasy of being intimate with the young actress remains boldly acknowledged.

This limerick demonstrates the amalgamated nature of fan language in the early days of filmdom. A patchwork of high/low references and double entendres, Burleson's composition marries tropes of courtly love poetry (e.g., the knight figure) with contemporaneous youth slang (the abbreviation "delish" for delicious, the colloquial "smacks" for kisses). Cleverly titled "Her Smacks Are All Certified and Screened," the tongue-in-cheek poem also plays with the overlap between a fledgling film dialect and clinical jargon: the term "screened" can refer to movie technology as to medical inspection. By 1916, Temple, Texas, was a hub for American healthcare, its hospitals leading the nation in medical services. Burleson's linguistic blend may thus reflect a moviegoer's lived experience.

In fact, movie-fan poems capture a moment in US history when a younger generation wrestled to fashion their own modes of self-expression by reworking established matrices. That push-and-pull between tradition and progress underwrote girls' relationship with their own bodies, their selves, their social roles, and the world around them, swiftly undergoing cultural and technological change. This push-and-pull also directed girls' endeavors to craft a functional fan shorthand while calibrating the intense affective responses elicited by those elusive creatures, the picture personalities. In mobilizing hallmarks of heterosexual courtship to express queer ways of feeling, moviegoing girls enacted "the process of reaching for an identity through a social ritual." Patricia White speculates that "spectators with marginalized social identities" engaged with classical Hollywood through a process of identification based on self-perceived difference and interpretative code-reading.[21] Gender reversal poems prove that, not finding themselves explicitly represented onscreen, early queer moviegoers tuned into the negative space surrounding heteronormativity, seeing themselves in subtly subverted depictions of archetypal maleness: the knight speaking in girl slang, the female fan posing as charming cad or ponderous old man. Queer reactions attached themselves to these fragments, female movie fans projecting and reworking feelings of divergence and homoeroticism through habitual narrative

tropes that already trafficked in female desirability and un/availability:
the muse, the damsel, the bride.

Forged in the seesaw between yearning for belonging and recognition
of difference, the language girls engendered in their fan writings could
be cheeky and witty as well as startlingly conventional. In 1915, Dorothy M. Hills adopted Petrarch's style and borrowed Shakespeare's
phrasing to articulate her devotion to twenty-two-year-old World Film
player Gerda Holmes:

> Shall I compare her to a crimson rose
> A sweet June-rose, deep-hearted and full-blown?
> In what Olympian garden was she grown?[22]

Such quilted language—sentimental and classical, original and remas-
tered—signals the unappreciated labor of the imagination. In the 1910s,
girls created a functional fan idiom as they went along, stringing
together references, styles, and expressions that struck them as able to
convey the range and nuance of their responses to female stars. Both a
collective and an individual undertaking, this work of pastiche was not
unlike that of a movie scrapbooker scavenging for compelling fragments, arranging them into deeply subjective new creations. Repetition
or repurposing of literary clichés and hetero-romantic tropes thus
should not be interpreted as evidence of girls' lack of creativity or ingenuity, nor as testament to the compulsory normativity of their spectatorship. On the contrary, this repurposing evinces a willingness to play
with convention, to adjoin it to a novel star system. Grafting sentimentalism with new media, girl fans felt around for a vocabulary that could
aptly communicate spectatorial reactions that exceeded heteronormative binaries.

Martha Vicinus notes that, since "neither a pornographic nor a scientific vocabulary provided women with the language of love,
nineteenth-century educated women fashioned their sexual selves
through metaphor."[23] A generation later, movie-loving girls picked up
where their forerunners had left off. Like them, literate girl fans turned
to metaphor, to simile, to allusion, to hyperbole, to conditional, fictive,
and fluid figures of speech that allowed them to try out identities that
were not available around them—whether in US popular culture, scientific discourse, or everyday life, where the pressures to marry, secure
economic stability, and bear children loomed over most girls coming
out of their teens. The favoring of figurative language also implies secretiveness. Vicinus reads nineteenth-century usage of "metaphor and allu-

sion" as a preventive measure, indicative of women's awareness of how precarious and surveilled their existences were. To transmit preferences that broke away from the expected patterns of female sociability and desire, early twentieth-century movie girls concocted a code, a cover-plot, in which the sentimental abundance of figurative speech abetted the affective performativity of fan love. Old conventions joined cutting-edge media technologies to secure a dialect and a venue where gender-queer proclivities and same-sex fantasies could be safely explored.

In this way, female fans accomplished another creative feat: they wielded the prompts imparted by actresses' star texts as a springboard for building their own narratives. Most picture personalities may have promoted scripts of proper heterosexual femininity, but in their self-crafted poems, girl fans widened the breadth of possible identities, cross-gendering as brazen dates, modern knights, and wistful inamoratos. In their poems, fans' interiority, not the actresses', commands the spotlight. Stars are reduced to templates whereupon audience members project their rich emotional lives.

Besides providing a stimulating canvas, star-driven narrative cinema triggered spectatorial self-insertion and creative storytelling. In her 1919 autobiography, serial queen Pearl White posited that "one good reason why the moving pictures have become so popular is because each one of us like to create. . . . In the picture theatre we sit silently, watch the actors perform on the screen and imagine what most of their conversation might be. Thus do we supply our own dialogue, and when we come out of the theatre we have accomplished something for we have employed our minds and the picture play has become part of our own creation."[24] As the actress acknowledges, successful silent productions invited moviegoers to slot themselves in the film diegesis and let their imagination take off, "mentally supplying fitting conversation or even read between the lines [to make their] own story."[25]

In the 1910s, US moviemaking resulted from the collaboration of industry workers and fan consumers, a creative process that could not be dissociated from the prevalence of female labor: both on the screen and in the audience.[26] Female imagination and fabulation translated into handsome rewards in early Hollywood. The press advertised film journalism and scenario-writing as women's work.[27] Young female columnists and screenwriters graced the printed page with their rags-to-riches biographies, often educating other unmarried movie fans on how to turn their fantasy scenarios into a paid writing career. Some girl fans thus felt compelled to do more than reading *between* the scripted lines:

they wrote themselves *into* star narratives, arrogating authorial power by playing the leading man in a queer fictional courtship.

In reworking the sentimental idiom in this way, girls' male-voiced declarations render visible what Patricia White dubs "the same-sex star crush narrative," an undercurrent of homoerotic desire and queer identification subtending Hollywood cinema and activating lesbian responses to female stars.[28] For that reason, girls' male-voiced love poems complicate reception theories positioning compulsory heterosexuality as the default of female spectatorship. In her analysis of Valentino's followers, Miriam Hansen famously grounded female spectatorial pleasure in the actor's "sadistic" screen persona.[29] Though Hansen recognized Valentino's androgynous star text, she still credited his success with female audiences on the actor's embodiment of violent virility, hence reiterating a normative erotic dichotomy where female viewers assumed the "feminine" passive position against Valentino's masculine dominance. Such a fan-star dynamic relied not only on the presumption of compulsory heterosexuality and internalized gender binarism, but also on female fans' sublimated masochism, which supposedly blossomed through the mediated "prospect of being humiliated" by Valentino's "barbarian" protagonists.[30]

Connecting female spectatorial pleasure with heterosexual fantasies of eroticized male dominance pervades feminist reception studies from the 1980s and 1990s. In her groundbreaking ethnographical work *Reading the Romance,* Janice Radway argues that suburban communities of self-described straight white female readers derived most gratification in being exposed to eroticized representations of male brutality toward female characters.[31] Unevenness in physical size and strength threw into stark relief gendered power imbalances women felt in everyday life. This endeared middle-class consumers who wanted their media of choice (romance novels) to smooth out the lived struggles with "missionary sexuality," a dominant mode of social control theorist Marilyn Frye sees as "organized around male-dominant, female-subordinate genital intercourse."[32]

The limitations of this type of audience scholarship rest as much on gender essentialism as on implicit homogenization: invariably, the female audience is conceived as a white educated monolith, its desires distinct from those of its male equivalent but bracketed by universal heterosexuality or marginal homosexuality. When individual moviegoing girls loved and desired female stars in the 1910s, binary thinking did not disappear, but at times it morphed into something else. Casting themselves as pining male suitors replicated traditionalist models of heterosexual courtship, as did the use of amatory language, a formula steeped in eroticized power differentials. But the gaps produced here— of gender as of station—are consciously manufactured and intentionally performed.

At the heart of female fan-star homoerotic interplay thus rests a perceived sameness, not difference. Girls wrote to Florence Lawrence seeking advice, approval, and complicity because they saw themselves in the star. In fact, the term "kindred spirit" features repeatedly in their fan letters, revealing that girls considered themselves Lawrence's equals in spite of professional and economic disparities. The perception of a women-only support network propelled girls' identification with and desire for self-made young actresses like Lawrence, Gish, Pickford, or White. As an acting aspirant confessed to the first in 1911, "I thought it would be better to write to you than the management as a girl is generally willing to help a girl [out]."[33] It is important to stress that such perceived sameness went beyond a shared age, skill, or pastime. Again and again, girls accredited their kinship with Lawrence to the awareness that growing up female in the 1910s was in itself a type of performance, socially imposed and strictly determined by heterosexist expectations and demands. Women were all performers on the stage of life; Lawrence was simply getting a more rewarding return. So, it stood to reason that adolescent girls would reach out and ask the star "to throw in any advice," whether on how to turn performative talents into a lucrative career or simply on "how [to] have the happiest life."[34]

Therefore, even when girls embodied a male persona to romance film actresses, their gender masquerade did not follow what other studies of heterosexual reception identify as the principal modes of female spectatorial pleasure and consumer engagement. Queer girls did not perform their attraction to actresses through traditional role-play based on male-coded dominance and female humiliation—their vocabulary never embraced the brashness attributed to the virile screen hero or the rakish cross-dresser featured in newspapers and medical journals. The gender-crossed courtship of a female star did not depend on subjugation or violence; power was not licensed through force but through praise, seduction instantiated by shared wit and experience, not crushing conquest.

In sum, the idiom of fans' lovestruck male voices retained that of sentimental femininity. An understanding ear, an identarian affinity, is what endears many girl fans to girl stars, coupled with the promise of compassion, cooperation, and validation. Actual reciprocation was not a complete impossibility either, if we are to believe Lawrence's private correspondence. Letters from at least two of her followers (Nance O'Neill and Clara Moore) indicate that the Canadian actress responded to their requests and even met with them, O'Neill's letters detailing an ongoing friendship, complete with late-night dinners and joint vacations. The love poems fans published in the film press also did not go unnoticed by the stars. Lawrence kept clippings of a couple, and there is evidence that she wrote some of her own. Unlike heteronormative courtship, centered on sexual difference and friction, female fan-star intimacy thrived in consonance.

Last, the ways girls employed the lyrical gender reversal to achieve intimacy with movie actresses contradicts pioneer feminist theories proposing that female audiences universally "assume the male point of view" when watching Hollywood cinema.[35] Chris Straayer alerts that this persistent "misaligning" of women-identified viewers with a heteronormative male perspective not only undermines the autonomy and plurality of queer spectators but also becomes particularly damaging when discussing lesbian (and, I would add, transgender) audiences.[36] Theories based on binary spectatorship perpetuate a determinist split in which, by virtue of their love object, woman-loving audiences are forced into a false equation with male viewers, their identifications forcefully masculinized and thus foreclosing gender and erotic variance.

Instead of uncritically assuming a compulsory male gaze, girls' male-voiced impersonations corroborate a spectatorial desire for polymorphous closeness with women that chafes against fixed categories. Borrowing the role of an actress's male suitor granted nonnormative fans admission into a women-only world of performance and pleasure from a different perspective. Through male masquerade, moviegoing girls could fiddle with gender and sexual differences from the safety of film stardom. Atypical lifestyles defined US filmdom and the women who emplaced it, fantasy, uniqueness, and self-reinvention being publicly lauded as early Hollywood's lifeblood. Queer fans may have felt that in such a motley milieu, to be "different from the norm" would be welcomed, their gender and emotional fluidity regarded as a strength, not a flaw.

For these fan poets, closeness with movie actresses thus derived energy from a shared interest in gender polysemy: it is no accident that most stars addressed were businesswomen praised for their versatility, successfully masquerading as dewy heroines onscreen while prospering in a male-presided industry. It is telling, too, that when occupying a poetic male voice, many female fans never attempted to disguise their feminine birth names: they did not resort to masculine pseudonyms or neutral initials, modes of covert disidentification popular at the time. By openly juxtaposing a male poetic perspective with a lived female identity, girl fans called attention to the artificiality, and hence intrinsic performativity, of sexual and gendered differences, while enjoying the potentialities released by toying with that awareness.

In the end, the concurrent feminization of early film-fan culture and the star system precipitated an affect-driven, female-centered youth subculture that provided its members with a multiplicity of avenues for same-sex identification, communion, complaint, and desire. Some of those avenues challenged what would later be theorized as Hollywood's dominant male gaze.[37] The most recurrent responses recorded by individual girl fans—the desire to *be like* the female star/to *be with* the female star—purposefully blended the traditional and the progressive, the personal and the professional, the homoerotic and the homosocial. For a number of female moviegoers, the appeal of movie fandom rested on its plasticity, its many transformative outfits. Like the burgeoning industry they adored, these fans privileged novelty, entertainment, and experimentation, with all the impermanence and permutation inherent to these.

Fans' first-person writings, in sum, expose the nuanced spectrum of affective investments populating female film reception during the 1910s. In private and published documents, we find traces of dissent and discontent with the conventional social roles attributed to white women and girls. A desire for escaping the bounds of heterosexism, domesticity, and conservative femininity are communicated in unpublished epistles to Lawrence, where girls vie for an opportunity to partake in the actress's prosperous and atypical lifestyle. In poems featured in the periodical press, girl fans took up a masculine subjectivity to perform social inadequacy, same-sex attraction, superlative feeling, and gender nonconformity, while older female fans culled from their long-lived knowledge of sentimental literature to both participate in an emergent media fandom and experience the freedoms and pleasures it availed a younger generation.

CHAPTER 4

Girls, Pick Up Your Scissors

The Queer Makings of the "Movie Scrap Book" Fad

Your obsessions lead to your vocabulary.

—Richard Hugo

Movie-fan scrapbooks and their kissing cousin, movie-illustrated diaries, operate as concurrent archives of ephemerality and queerness.[1] Structurally, the scrapbook lends itself to staging the heated, fitful, and shapeshifting nature of adolescent desires. A multimedia artifact defined by its personal affective voltage and shrouded in idiosyncrasy, the scrapbook has been imagined as having an elemental affinity with queer identity. José Esteban Muñoz speaks of queerness and its grassroots archives as scrapbook-like, "makeshift and randomly organized, due to the restrains historically shackled upon minoritarian cultural workers."[2] Gay novelist Neil Bartlett draws a direct line between queer history and the scrapbook, asserting that "the scrapbook is the true form of our history, since it records what we remember, and embodies in its omissions both how we remember and how we forget our lives. We are always held between ignorance and exposure."[3] For Bartlett, the scrapbook's opacity and fragmentation mirrors the historical experience of queer people: a continuum of elision and marginalization, intermittent exposure and persecution, and a constant struggle to leave meaningful dents, empowering signposts, personal breadcrumbs, in a punishingly heteronormative official record that continuously renders LGBTQ+ people either pathologically visible or constitutionally insignificant, easily forgettable or memorably cautionary (AIDS victims, queer criminals, suicides, fallen stars, etc.).

Personal scrapbooks and queer identity can also be regarded as epistemologically kindred: both centered in introspection, intimacy, and autobiographical disclosure, both understood as requiring a distinct cipher to be made readable to a mass audience, their message calibrated to knowing sets of eyes (whether those of the scrapbook-maker, a close friend, a star, another fan, or another queer subject). Historian Barbara Benedict describes "the cipher" as sharing an affinity with sexuality. Designated by "doubleness," it works "as both evidence to the eye yet concealed from the mind;" "like sexuality," the cipher can be "simultaneously seen and unseen" at will.[4] Suppressed by an oppressive heterosexist patriarchy, queer identities, Muñoz claims, have historically "existed as innuendo, fleeting moments, and performances that are meant to be interacted with by those within its epistemological sphere—while evaporating at the touch of those who would eliminate queer visibility."[5] The dual motion of making itself momentarily legible while remaining cloaked under plausible deniability brings sentimental writing near to queerness, and queerness near to ephemera, all sharing an openness to possibility, interpretation, and impermanence.

Due to their structural dependence on curiosity, personalization, and overlay, scrapbooks can further be seen as serving the interests of early Hollywood. As a commercial apparatus, the early star system relied on the promotion of identificatory data, secrets, and exposures. As Richard deCordova relays, throughout the 1910s, "all discourse about those who appeared in the films emerged in a secretive context. . . . The fascination over the players' identities was a fascination with *a concealed truth, one that resided behind or beyond the surface of the film. . . .* A set of secrets was introduced beneath a set of secrets, *en abyme,* [where] the private finally emerged as the ultimate and most ulterior truth."[6] In the pursuit of stars' most "authentic self," film fans were tasked with becoming amateur detectives and archivists. Their documenting of stars' screen credits, print interviews, and promotional pictures achieved physical shape in the accumulative movie scrapbook, which functioned as a tactile rendition of the many facets of a loved shadow player. In this way, personal movie scrapbooks preserve a material record of the industry-driven process of humanizing film stars through fan labor.

An idiosyncratic form of data storage, scrapbooks further refuse linear temporality; pinning down the timeline of their assemblage, for instance, can be challenging. In excavating the affective traces individual girl fans etched in their ephemera collections, this chapter sets to narrativize a film cache that is queer by virtue of its homoerotic affect and gender fluidity, but also by virtue of its constitutional resistance to being readily classifiable or rendered transparent. Both objects and compilers analyzed here embrace a straining of fixed dualisms regulating heteronormative time, female development, identity, and desire.

FOR GIRLS ONLY: REIMAGINING MOVIE SCRAPBOOKING IN THE AGE OF PAPER CONSERVATION

Though the practice of scrapbooking long traverses class, race, age, and gender, sociological studies conducted in US schools in 1907 claimed that "cases of girls collecting were much more numerous than those of boys."[7] By the following decade, the practice of scrapbook-making had become linked with young femininity, more specifically school-going girls in their teens and early twenties. In their studies of early twentieth-century memory albums and yearbooks, historians Kelly Schrum, Jane Greer, and Leslie Midkiff DeBauche argue that girls took up scrapbooking because it allowed them to form same-sex peer networks and express conflicted attitudes toward heterosexual romance, matrimony, motherhood, beauty, and other socially constructed requirements associated with becoming a woman.[8] Economically affordable and widely accessible, motion pictures and film-fan magazines provided a cheap, communal, and stimulating pastime to many girls growing up in both rural and urban regions of the United States. The marriage of community, affordability, and affective reception birthed the movie-themed scrapbook, an artifact commonly sourced, created, and circulated within a close-knit group of adolescent fans, many of them girls.

Movie scrapbooking became the province of girlhood for myriad reasons. In the early twentieth century, the leisure activities recommended to school-age girls clustered around reading, handcrafts, and life-writing (i.e., correspondence and journaling).[9] Original movie fan practices followed in this tradition, taking two principal forms: scrapbooking and letter-writing, followed closely by illustrated journaling. Not unusually, the first two appeared intertwined: movie-loving girls frequently proved their devotion to the medium by writing to favorite stars and asking for personalized ephemera that would later be preserved in their "movy albums."[10] Fan letters and scrapbooks crafted during the 1910s demonstrate that, in collaboration with newspapers, fan magazines, exhibitors, and studios, North American adolescent girls helped delineate what would become cornerstone praxes of media fandom. Actualized in communal acts and everyday performances of the self, such praxes combined pastimes and skills culturally tied to femininity with the film industry's increasing valorization of female labor, patronage, and affect.

Despite aggregating an assortment of mixed-media sources (e.g., newspaper clippings, ticket stubs, exhibitors' bulletins, autographed headshots, personalized fan mail), movie albums focus on safekeeping film-related ephemera. The first generation of moviegoing girls readily adopted scrapbooks as a self-expressive platform, a trusted place where tastes, aspirations, and desires could be simultaneously made pictorial and oblique. Researching movie scrapbooks produced by Deanna Durbin's followers, Georganne Scheiner claims that ephemera collages dedicated to the teenaged film star allowed girls growing up after World War II to make meaning (and sense) of their coming-of-age process in a supportive same-sex community. "The pleasure, histories, and personal memories associated with scrapbooks are a tangible artifact of identity formation," Scheiner claims, "and the pride of creating a collection was an alternative arena of achievement. Instead of concentration on their man-pleasing and -catching skills, girls could take pride not only in their unique creative endeavors but in displaying their expertise."[11] Working- and middle-class girls in their teens assembled 80 percent of the signed scrapbooks I was able to locate in online auctions and research facilities. Most of the remaining albums produced during the 1910s are either unsigned or have been compiled by older women.[12]

The press played a pivotal role in the gendering of movie scrapbooking as a young female occupation. In the mid-1910s, film-fan magazines, alongside local and regional newspapers, began marketing scrapbooking as an efficient method of converting idle female fandom into useful hand- iwork. As early as 1914, dailies promoted scrapbooking as a "brand new fad in movie land" aimed specifically at its female patrons.[13] Published under the heading "Special Features of Interest to Women Readers" and authored by a beauty columnist, the "My Movie Scrap Book" ad appeared in various papers across the country, including Pennsylvania's *Wilkes- Barre Times Leader,* Chicago's *Day Book,* Kansas's *Wichita Beacon,* Mis- sissippi's *Vicksburg Evening Post,* Texas's *Courier-Gazette,* and Washing- ton's *Tacoma Times* (figure 9).[14]

On the printed page, scrapbooking rapidly became a shorthand for young ladies' civic dedication to wartime patriotism. In 1918, a Texas paper commended "a bevy of attractive young girls" for assembling "scrap books which are to be sent to the convalescent soldiers in France."[15] The *New York Sun* reported on a "Scrap Book Ball" being thrown by "Brooklyn's fashionable set. . . . Each girl will bring a scrapbook made

FIGURE 9. Found in multiple newspapers, the "My Movie Scrap Book" ad targeted female moviegoers with exclusive advertisements and content.

by herself for a wounded soldier and a prize will be awarded for the best one."[16] The next year, "scrapbooks had proved [such a] popular diversion in hospitals" that a Scrapbook Department of the War Camp Community Service was created. An unmarried young woman, Miss Ruth Campbell, presided over the operation and exhorted other girls to help in the relief effort by compiling all-paper scrapbooks for wounded soldiers. The most suitable materials for "grown men," Campbell instructed, were "pictures of actresses."[17]

Already relying on "pictures of actresses," scrapbooking became part of the press discourse humanizing female film stars. In May 1918, a year after the United States had entered the European conflict, the *Washington Herald* reported that "having knitted all the available yarn into sweaters for the boys in France, *the feminine portion of the film colony* is now busily engaged on a new enterprise. The morning greeting on the studio lot is: 'Have you a little scrap book in your dressing room?'" According to a Hollywood correspondent, the news that "convalescent soldiers [needed] something that they could look at or read for amusement [had] spread around at various studios and now everyone, *including stars and extra girls,* were [sic] compiling a 'Nonsense Scrap Book' to be sent over to the hospitals. These scrapbooks contain[ed] snap shots, still pictures of productions and comic cartoons many of them made by the stars."[18]

Not only did movie actresses donate their images and time to the war effort, but they reportedly also kept scrapbooks of their own, which provided moral edification and cultivated emotional depth. A correspondent of Florence Lawrence "enclosed a snap[shot] for [her] scrap book" in one personal letter, quipping that "it won't add much to your book, because I'm not in the least bit pretty [but] I can send you my very best wishes along with it which may improve it a little."[19] At the same time, a couple of New York City newspapers mentioned that "Mary Pickford is strong on human nature [because] she has a scrap-book full of incidents and finds them useful as suggestions."[20]

A unifying call to duty and a mindful manual reappropriation of mass-produced paper resources continued to frame the practice of movie scrapbooking in the late 1910s. Movie love did too; only now, performed by film stars as well as fans, it appeared rosied by self-interest. In publicizing film actresses as patriotic scrapbook-makers, newspapers not only gilded the public persona of female stars but also promoted the act of scrapbooking as a noble and charitable occupation, a utilitarian outlet for girl fans' all-consuming movie devotion. In addition to legitimizing film fandom and female acting, these features further endeavored to endear actresses to their fans by suggesting that, in their domestic pastimes as in their daily concerns, they were just like the regular folk who followed them in the pictures.

Newspapers encouraging domestic scrapbooking harked back to public debates on the conservation of national resources, debates Theodore Roosevelt's presidency (1901–9) and a plethora of preservation acts had recently brought to the fore.[21] However, the outbreak of World War I in July 1914 changed the prescriptive narrative attached to scrapbook-making, exacerbating both the emphasis on domestic conservation and the direct interpellation of young female consumers. By 1916, while Europe lay devastated by conflict, the US began reimagining itself as a two-faced Janus: on the one hand, "the barn of the world," an oasis of resources ready to rescue the war-riddled Old World, and on the other, a war-bound country whose natural plenty ran the risk of running dry if not duly protected.[22] Recycling paper goods within the home was a relief activity that required no special skill and was thus accessible to girls from all backgrounds. Other relief efforts targeting adolescent girls included knitting for Allied orphans, organizing charity bazaars, and joining the Red Cross.[23]

Newspapers were not alone in attempting to standardize female film reception through the manual manipulation of movie ephemera. In

1916, *Motion Picture Magazine* and its sister publication *Motion Picture Classic* began advertising film-themed handcrafts as an excellent method to redirect female readers' passive movie consumption into useful home-making. One feature was dedicated to a female fan letter from Sayles-ville, Rhode Island, that taught readers how to weave a "bead portiere from *Motion Picture Magazine* covers. . . . The unusual quality of the vellum parchment used for the covers of *Motion Picture Magazine* make it, Nina Kilgore found, the only practical material from which these link-beads can be successfully made."[24] Another column had Rose Tapley, the publication's Answer Lady, instructing female fans to follow her exam-ple and, after exhausting *Picture*'s and *Classic*'s "reading matter . . . , cut off the cover of a couple of them and have them framed. . . . I have them in my den because of their beauty," Tapley concluded in a "big-sister-like" tone aimed to elicit camaraderie from her female readers.[25] Once again, the magazine championed the repurposing of its outdated content into household decor, hailing film-based "handicrafts" as "the very latest fad" about to revolutionize female fans' "idle hours" and dethrone "knitting and crocheting and embroidery" as their favorite pastimes.[26]

Explicitly directed at female patrons, the language used to promote movie scrapbooking coupled ludic consumerism with a homemaker's frugality and industriousness. That union was not coincidental. Scrap-books became popular at a time when film promotion and exhibition began relying heavily on printed ephemera. Colorful window cards, lobby displays, and illustrated programs proliferated in movie theaters across the country; yet the fast-paced production of new film releases rendered these promotional artifacts obsolete almost overnight. In a war-stricken period, concerns with resource conservation seemed inimical to the paper-based lavishness practiced by the emergent film industry.

Furthermore, paper—historically a cheap and accessible material in US industry—saw a dramatic price hike during WWI, its scarcity crest-ing in 1916. Writing that year, historian Lyman Weeks reported a wide-spread panic when the sudden "demand for paper, especially printing, increased, and, although mills were running at top-notch, the market could not be fully supplied. . . . The public was exhorted to help by sav-ing old paper. The United States secretary of the interior and the United States chamber of commerce sent out notices . . . and newspapers car-ried advertisements urging the saving of waste paper."[27] Film-fan publi-cations soon began echoing this national concern: twice in December 1916, *Motion Picture Magazine* remonstrated female readers for "want[ing] the [Picture] Gallery doubled. Alas! It costs too much money—paper is so high!"[28] It is within the context of a conflict between paper scarcity and overproduction of film ephemera that female audiences came to be recruited to rehabilitate movie ephemera from decorative waste into household essentials.

Newspapers and magazines also advocated that, more than eye-catching visual content, "a valuable movie scrapbook should include" significant informational content such as "press stories of your favorite stars and names of plays in which you have seen them."[29] "Movie fans who keep scrapbooks of their film favorites" were urged "to do well and clip" Theda Bara's series of syndicated articles on the struggles of female stardom.[30] Emerging amid global conflict and an economy of thrift, the definition of fan value had to shift away from leisure and toward the functional agglomeration of usable knowledge—not just the facts, sources, and lessons physically preserved in the movie scrapbook but also those experientially gathered by the moviegoer. Through its declarative emphasis on amassing hard data, the movie scrapbook ultimately sought to upgrade the emotional movie fan into the discerning movie collector, and the valuable collector into the useful connoisseur.

In their urgency to encourage fans to become diligent record keepers, the press articulated another anxiety related to the swift turnaround of early film manufacturing. According to film distributer Harry R. Raver, in 1916 the US movie industry produced players and pictures with such neck-breaking speed and volume that "it [was] hardly possible for the most enthusiastic fan to keep up with the pace."[31] The practice of scrapbooking trained fans to memorize the names of stars and productions during a period when weekly movie releases ran in the dozens.

Scrapbook-making also sought to counteract the intrinsic ephemerality of filmgoing. As one journalist pointed out, the only feature distinguishing films from magazines in the 1910s was that "last week's film does not go into the waste basket as does last week's magazine. . . . [Instead,] the film fan takes home and cherishes . . . the image—the mental image of the picture."[32] In directing fans to gather, paste, and annotate film ephemera of treasured icons and screenings, the movie industry attempted to secure the profitable permanence of that transient "mental image of the picture." Women, long appointed as familial memory keepers and newly minted as the most invested movie consumers, were entrusted with the task. Repackaging the consumption of film ephemera as a recycling-oriented endeavor, nonetheless, did not aim to diminish female fans' material purchases but to reframe them as patriotic, useful, and multivalent, instead of self-indulgent, wasteful, and disposable.

Determined to incentivize fan scrapbooking, *Motion Picture Magazine* implemented a series of telling alterations to its popular image-only section, "Art Gallery of Popular Players." The feature first appeared in the magazine's second number, issued in March 1911. Then called "Personalities of the Picture Players," it generally resembled a collection of annotated *cartes de visite*: one star's studio portrait per page, occasionally captioned by a biographical note. The gradual shift to an image-heavy feature encouraging curation and safekeeping—signified by the inclusion of "Art Gallery" in its title—culminated in June 1917. Gone were staged headshots floating in a sepia void or adorned with filigree frames. Various kinetic stills of picture personalities appeared in elaborate photomontages that mimicked scrapbook collages. These alterations expressly targeted female moviegoers, since theirs were the voices most often quoted in the magazine's Answer Department commenting on the gallery.

By January 1916, *Photoplay* explicitly connected scrapbook-making, female film stardom, and girl fandom. To illustrate the breadth of contestants entering the girls-only star-searching pageant "Beauty and Brains," *Photoplay* issued two collages: one with the decoupaged headshots of participants pasted on a line map of North America and another where, haphazardly overlaid, the girls' headshots created a textured visual tapestry of female movie love and aspiration. Blatantly drawing on handcraft aesthetics, the two-page photomontages resemble a personal movie scrapbook, the hopefuls' headshots occupying the same central placement a star's cutout would were it a collage handmade by fans (figure 10).[33]

Newspapers and fan magazines may have hawked movie scrapbooking as a fashionable female occupation, but they certainly did not invent it. Scrapbook-making spanned centuries; historians trace its protean lineage back to Renaissance commonplace books and Victorian keepsake albums.[34] Since the early 1800s, admen and manufacturers on both sides of the Atlantic distributed appealing paper scraps as low-cost publicity. A few years later, newspapers began urging their readers to recycle old printed scraps in the interest of self-enrichment and home savings. What Hollywood introduced, then, was not the practice of scrapbooking but the humanized figure of the star, ultimately imbuing representational ephemera with affective capital. Collecting the image of a darling film celebrity flexed a fan muscle; it carried emotional value. It also carried individual expression: that of the star, and vis-à-vis, that of the fan. Because scrapbooking was advertised as an activity for movie-loving girls at the same time that the star system depended on a

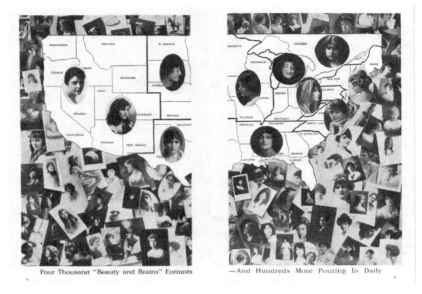

Four Thousand "Beauty and Brains" Entrants   —And Hundreds More Pouring In Daily

FIGURE 10. A tapestry of female fan want: *Photoplay*'s collage of "Beauty and Brains" pageant entrants mirroring the aesthetics found in girls' personal movie scrapbooks.

majority of female picture personalities to draw revenue, exploring the ways diverse girl fans engaged with film ephemera affords new insights into the gendered scripts subtending a nascent star system, illuminating not just how these were accepted by a key audience but also how they were tweaked, ignored, or subverted.

Many feminist film historians acknowledge that fandom has always been an inherently erotic activity, yet they fail to excavate *how* exactly that manifested. Fandom is predominantly a thing you do with your hands, an attachment you perform with your body, so to examine how girls creatively and materially expressed it is central to feminist film historiography. DeBauche's research on memory books assembled post-WWI is one of the few examples addressing the embodied erotics in early girl film fandom.[35] DeBauche finds pictures of Theda Bara pasted next to snapshots of schoolgirls imitating the Jewish star's vampish style. These fan collages reveal that middle-class girls not only adopted a provocatively exoticized picture personality as a model of womanhood but also deployed their dressed-up bodies to test the boundaries of socially acceptable performances of white womanhood. As Richard Abel indicates, "Theda Bara always attracted large audiences" throughout the 1910s.[36] However, she appealed to many female moviegoers less due to her acting and more due to "her beautiful face and body, which," a woman reviewer observed in 1915, "she can twist and contort into the most fiendish of postures."[37] In other words, Bara's film figure—sensual, skimpily clad, mercurial—ignited haptic spectatorship, inviting female fans to connect with their own bodies through three-dimensional mimicry, pantomime, and autoeroticism. Marilyn Frye links queer subjects with this heightened awareness of embodied desire and difference: "Since our marginality has so centrally to do with our bodies and our bodies' nonconformance with the bodily and behavioral categories of the dominant cultures, we have access to knowledge of bodies which is lost and/or hidden in the dominant cultures."[38]

Early cinema thrived on these tensions between the sensed and the seen, the projected kinetic bodies of stars and their physical absence from the audience. To bridge such asynchronous incorporeality, exhibitors and admen disseminated highly tactile and durable giveaways (i.e., actors' headshots, brass spoons, textile banners), while film magazines banked on colorful covers and detachable star pictures to lure consumers. Though the lux tactility of early film promotion primarily attempted to compensate for the perceived lack of stars' physical presence, it incidentally enabled an erotic engagement with silent players that easily careened into queer reception. Because the star system depended considerably on a female working force, and female moviegoers constituted more than half of all patrons, cinema became a privileged medium for exploring same-sex attachments, of a kind that persist today in online fan cultures.

Shaped by experiential desire, the transformative abilities inherent to fan handcrafts are activated by sensory stimulation, particularly touch and sight. "Tactility, achieved through the inclusion of sensuous textures and interactive features, such as flaps that lift to reveal hidden messages, are vital components of the nineteenth-century valentine," art historian Christina Michelon notes. "By having to hold, touch, and interact with the valentine, recipients were made to *feel materials in order to feel sentiment.*" Indeed, through scavenging, leafing, cutting, pasting, coloring, and writing, manual labor turned into an extension of affective spectatorial attachment, a prime stage for a haptic fan cathexis. Fan scrapbooks can thus be read as media reception made flesh, if flesh is paper and glue and ink, lovingly assembled by hand. They also inherit the touch-prone three-dimensionality of nineteenth-century valentines. Like "sentimental or 'fancy' valentines," early film scrapbooks grew "more ornate with every added layer of material," striving to communicate via paper abundance fans' "hope, fondness, and desire" for incorporeal shadow players, as for the identities and lifestyles they embodied.[39]

TOUCHING A STAR WITH PAPER: EMBODIED EROTICS IN PERSONAL FAN ARCHIVES

One of the ways girl fans achieved intimacy with movie players was by manipulating their paper likenesses in tandem with their own bodies. At fifteen, Edna G. Vercoe, from Highland Park, Illinois, took great pains in cutting and pasting published data on players' love lives. Many of these informational clippings are magazine replies to letters by fans such as herself, eager to humanize the stars, to discover what lurked behind the picture veil. Unsatisfied with print sources alone, Vercoe also transcribed players' press interviews by hand, repeatedly underscoring personal details. Such a labor of love suggests that the movie-loving girl wished to somehow surmount the ineluctable distance separating fan from star by using her body (her hand, her calligraphy) to become a Hollywood insider, the actors' all-knowing Boswell. The process of transcribing first-person star accounts is also not unlike that of secretarial stenography or letter dictation, entry-level work typically done by young women who wished to go up the Hollywood ladder. In short, in the context of Vercoe's movie scrapbook, data accumulation produced spectatorial intimacy when filtered through female manual labor.

This accretion of investigative knowledge cannot be separated from sexuality, both the fan's and the star's. According to deCordova, the star system was built around secrecy and disclosure, actors' private lives mainlining the curiosity and attachment of fans. At turns veiled and flaunted, stars' biographical information clustered around queries of intimate nature. Incessantly moviegoers asked: Who were players married to? Who had been their sweethearts? What was the nature of their relationship with costars? Did they have a type? Could they spare a private token of affection—a lock of hair or a handkerchief to be remembered by? Magazines obliged, often framing the divulgence of stars' personal particulars as bartered confessions available only to loyal patrons whose "intense and insistent involvement [could result] in discovering the truth of the star's identity."

Integral to its promotional mechanics, deCordova claims, was how "the star system . . . accorded [to] the sexual the status of the most private, and thus the most truthful, locus of identity."[40] Avid for accessing celebrities' "true sel[ves]," Vercoe and many other movie-loving girls gathered print sources unveiling stars' romantic histories and marital statuses, distributing them throughout their movie scrapbooks. In this way, fan behavior corroborates deCordova's postulation: audiences understood that the ultimate "truth" stars withheld from their followers "was, at its limit, the truth of sexuality." Disclosure of sexual desire went both ways though: when Vercoe exposed Crane Wilbur through a chronicling of his personal life, she concurrently exposed her own erotic investment in his picture personality. In other words, to self-define and behave as "screen-struck" presupposed a response to celebrity cognizant that "the very modes of knowing the star, of investigating the truth of his or her identity, were linked to a broader strategy of deploying sexuality in modern times."[41] This means that, through their private fandom practices, silent-film girl fans like Vercoe already centered the discursive nomination of sexual desire not only on a social decoding practice and public performance but also on an experiential self-avowal.

Vercoe's hand returns as an eroticized site of embodied fandom when one of her classmates, Florence Schreiber, teases her for hammering a "thumb just because you were trying to find a place of honor for [Wilbur's photo] in your bedroom." Schreiber urges Vercoe to "please write & tell him about your pounding finger. If you don't, I will."[42] The surprising informality of this threat indicates an imagined familiarity with the movie star, potentialized through the handling of his paper image. Such desired closeness holds an erotic charge, grounded in the "pounding" body. As discussed in chapter 2, the act of placing a reproduction of an adored player in a girl's bedroom spoke of a yearning for physical proximity, one that could straddle cinema's notorious ethereality and in/corporeal distance. Vercoe's thumb pays the price for the girl's fan ardor. The fan body wants and the fan body labors and the fan body suffers the aborted stabs at intimacy with a star.

The practice of decoupaging and hand-coloring commercial headshots exposes yet another layer of embodied fan erotics. As Susan Tucker, Katherine Ott, and Patricia Buckler reflect, "The experience of reading a scrapbook is intensely physical and sensual. The pages must be touched to be turned, and the turning creates movement between objects and amasses visual stimulation."[43] Assembling a movie scrapbook—particularly when manually modifying stars' paper images—taps into a similar sensuous pleasure that supplies the compiler with added transformative agency, while rendering visible erotic investments.

For Betty Ross, a Catholic movie lover born in 1903 to cotton-mill workers in Milltown, New Brunswick, Canada, a desire for proximity with female stars shaped her scrapbook arrangements and reception language. Likely crafted between the late 1910s and the 1920s, many of Ross's collages are of young actresses showing off their trim figures and glamorous wardrobes in full-body shots. Scantily clad and caressing their own bodies, the vamps Theda Bara, Alla Nazimova, Betty Blythe, and Pola Negri evince the fan's longing to contemplate the skin of exoticized screen actresses, their paper reproductions simulating a voyeuristic feeling of intimacy (figure 11).[44] Other collages depict ingenues lounging in their homes while accomplishing mundane tasks, including Betty Compson playing violin by a hearth, Alice Brady in bed with her dog, and Juanita Hansen answering letters at her desk. Handwritten captions describe these collages as "With the 'Gishes'" or "With the 'Talmadges.'" Such familiar language implies that clipping and pasting images of movie actresses' domestic spaces allowed a working-class fan to vicariously enter stars' private lives, while simultaneously introducing them into her own. Voyeurism infuses both types of scrapbooked collages, homoeroticism underpinning the fan desire to gaze at a female star's body at its most eroticized (the foreign vamp), as at its most prim and proper (the white lady of the manor).

Between 1915 and 1916, fourteen-year-old Margaret Harroun from Saint Joseph, Missouri, the third of five siblings, also pasted manually modified images of young female stars onto her self-titled "Picture Book."[45] Clipped from *Motion Picture Magazine*, Beverly Bayne's parted lips are bloodied with red ink, her face dabbled with pinkish crayon, her eyelids glistening with a faded green layer. Using household supplies, Harroun's transformation of the nineteen-year-old actress from one-toned ingenue into multichromatic vamp calls to mind late nineteenth-century descriptions of "the painted woman," a soubriquet attached to stage actresses whose profession required constant appliance of rouge and lipstick. The derogatory term linked female performers with exhibitionism and sexual promiscuity.[46] In this case, however, the hand-coloring practice seems to convey the scrapbooker's longing for animating her idol, to inject some life and warmth into the only effigy fans possessed of elusive movie stars: their two-dimensional paper surrogates.

Tinting of star headshots may also evidence fans' swelling interest in the mechanics of filmmaking and the behind-the-scenes routines of picture actors. Throughout the 1910s, audience members wrote to movie magazines inquiring about stars' attire, hair styles, and makeup. In the

FIGURE 11. Embodied collage of female skin: ephemera collected by Betty Ross, ca. 1919.

age of blue-sensitive film stock, "rouged cheeks were taboo since they made people look alarmingly gaunt onscreen. Men usually left lips bare, but women applied a bit of red—or brown—lipstick."[47] If an actress was "a dark-haired person with eyes of deeper blue or green or hazel" like Bayne, experts advised "green color" to be applied in "the space between the eyelid and the eyebrow, the object being to bring out the white of the eye and make the latter more brilliant."[48] Hence, a star's crayoned lips and cheeks may be a testament of fans commuting their acquired knowledge of screen makeup to their private consumption of movie celebrities. It may, however, also disclose a girl's desire to be closer to a film actress, the painting of her paper duplicate a makeup mockup from a lady-in-waiting in-training, an excuse to caress a simulacrum of Bayne's untouchable face.

Further proof that girl fans conversed with the film industry via their coloring of star reproductions is found in the three scrapbooks Thelma Laird Lauer Majors (b. 1902) dedicated to Lillian and Dorothy Gish.[49] While growing up in Seattle, Washington, Majors replicated artisanal coloring aesthetics found in film magazines and official promotional materials. A fan of the Gish sisters, Majors used wax crayons to color production stills from D. W. Griffith's *Orphans of the Storm* (1921), starring both actresses. The adolescent fan attributes icy blue to Lillian's costume and warm pink to Dorothy's, a color palette that not only echoes each sister's star text—Lillian the reserved tragedienne, Dorothy the vivacious comedienne—but also duplicates the color scheme employed in the motion picture and its promotional ephemera. Lobby cards and an exhibitor's booklet sold when the film first premiered in December 1921 present Lillian in blue and Dorothy in pink costume. Color was likewise significant for the film itself with Griffith using tinted filters on several action scenes to magnify emotional impact. It is thus possible that the fan's coloring choices reflect the recollection of her own viewing experience.

While duplicating official color schemes, Majors nonetheless found a way to insert her own creative subjectivity into the manufactured images. She took pains in delineating details in both dresses, so that Lillian exhibits rather thick black stripes on her skirt and bonnet, while Dorothy's bust is adorned with a fiery magenta rose. Both sisters' fallen curls have been filled in with yellow ink, Dorothy's lips tinted red and Lillian's barely touched. This disparity in manual coloring may once again convey girl fans' understanding of appropriate screen makeup and its implicit associations between an actress's darker lips and flirtier picture personality.

Fans' hand-coloring of star ephemera also reveals early film manufacturing's uncredited reliance on women's manual and creative labor—in the home, but also in the studio, specifically when it came to film editing, individual frame coloring, and color tinting. The aesthetics of handmade coloring that girl fans embraced in their movie scrapbooks harken back to die-cut advertisements and mass-produced postcards which, in the second half of the nineteenth century, popularized the unfinished hand-painted look. Since the inception of moving pictures, producers had used similar coloring techniques for prints. The most predominant were individual frame coloring (applying multiple colors within each film image) and color tinting (applying a single-color wash to an entire film sequence), tasks performed almost exclusively by dexterous young women.[50] By 1913, these coloring techniques appeared in lobby cards and coming attraction slides. Aiming to entice audiences, both artifacts emphasized actresses' red mouths, colored hair, and rouged cheeks. Their imperfect look may have laid bare the inchoateness of color reproduction technology, but it also likely captivated female audiences, many of them amateur decorators and lifelong handcrafters.

The artisanal nature of scrapbook labor thus lays bare an inherent tension between duplication and creativity, manual and machine labor. In another collage, the Seattle moviegoer carefully decoupaged around Lillian's face, treating the headshot borders as a "cut here" suggestion. Placed in the center of a black cardboard page, the oval headshot resembles a paper cameo or a photographic keepsake, one of the candids girls used to snap, swap, and paste on their journals. If that retreatment implies intimacy—the fan's craft labor approximating the star to a friend—it does not preclude a desire to emulate the "professional" visual aesthetics found in leading publications, namely in *Motion Picture Magazine*'s "Gallery of Photoplayers." Excising an ornate trim from an unknown image, Majors overlays it around Gish's headshot, making the composite seem mechanically produced. In fact, the two-tone differences between the star's sepia face and the grey wreath surrounding it are the only seam giving away the fan's almost seamless handiwork. Betraying her attachment to mechanical reproduction, Majors's circular composition further brings to mind the view from a camera keyhole, the enlarged face of the star resembling a movie closeup.

Preoccupations with rendering labor invisible informed the production of early picture personalities, deCordova and Danae Clark remark.[51] In stimulating fans' fetishistic consumption of star images, the film industry tried to sublimate the work of performing celebrity, obscuring all the injuries, struggles, abuses, silences, and injustices that undergirded the behind-the-scenes of US moviemaking. The elision of fracture lines and messy scaffolding promoted by Hollywood's star system extended to the sanitization of players' public images, including their bodies and troubled biographies. In Majors's collages of the Gish sisters we find a similar manufactured smoothness, where, under the cover of accomplishment, personal physical labor is effaced to the point of near invisibility.

QUEER SUBTEXTS: MALE HOMOEROTICISM IN GIRLS' FAN COLLAGES

If Majors's collages played within industry-sanctioned conventions, Alice Shefler's challenged them.[52] Born Alice Edith Shefler on August 2, 1899, the youngest of seven siblings moved around between Illinois, South Dakota, and Iowa until her parents finally settled in Portland, Oregon, when she was ten. A month after her twentieth birthday, Shefler would marry a Canadian resident and relocate to Southern California, where she would live until her death in 1979. In the years prior to her shotgun wedding at the Peace Crossing in Canada, the adolescent girl voraciously stored away film ephemera in an enormous scrapbook, its materials dating largely from 1915 to 1917. Built at the threshold between teenage leisure and marriage, Shefler's star collages exemplify how fan scrapbook labor could stretch open gender and erotic scripts launched by a developing movie industry.

At a first glance, Shefler's collages seem to follow press dictates: they are typically themed around individual stars, a labeled cornucopia of pictorial, print, and handwritten information glutting the page. I claim that such material excess enables queer spectatorship. For example, in a collage dedicated to actress Edna Mayo, Shefler gathers four clipped pictures: two duplicates of the same studio shot and two stills from Mayo's popular 1916 serial *The Strange Case of Mary Page*. Overlaid, these two promotional images focus on the young star's body: the oval cutout depicts a disembodied hand prowling over Mayo's naked back, while the rectangular one shows a maid helping the heroine with her evening gown. The two women stand close together, their mobile bodies seemingly caught in an act of domestic intimacy. Neither of them face the camera; the maid is entranced by her lady's movements, and Mayo is distracted by an offscreen presence. The image, as Shefler preserved it, simmers with homoerotic innuendo: two young women huddle in a boudoir and evade the camera's voyeuristic gaze, while one of them partakes in either dressing or undressing the other—the direction of the act is left unclear. Through overlaying, the seventeen-year-old fan also created a visual continuity that exceedingly eroticizes Mayo's two-dimensional body and magnifies its tactility: in the bottom clipping the creeping male hand makes a grab for the star's exposed back, while on the top one the maid's hands tend to it. In emphasizing its bareness and vulnerability, Mayo's skin comes alive in the fan collage as a touchable and desired surface, simultaneously an eroticized site of male violence and of female care (figure 12).

A few pages later, it is revealed the extent to which Shefler's manipulation of this image played up homoerotic potentialities latent in the original. In a collage honoring Mayo's *Mary Page* costar, Henry B. Walthall, Shefler includes the original version of the still showing Mary with her maid. In the complete image, a smartly dressed Walthall stands on the right, addressing the heroine. Walthall's inclusion not only diffuses the homoerotic charge between lady and maid but also definitively pins their actions as those of helping the former get ready for an outing with a gentleman caller. Mayo's diegetic gaze also moves from uninterested in the camera to focused on a man, thus rendering the maid extraneous, a third wheel lurking behind the elegantly dressed and centrally placed heterosexual couple.

That Shefler decided to literally and figuratively cut Walthall from the picture when including it in Mayo's shrine speaks of a fan's desire to both retain and enhance the fraught closeness between two female characters. Walthall's exclusion evidences an intentional skirting of the inevitable heterosexual voltage a male presence brought to serials—a film genre known for its reliance on female physicality, ingenuity, and independence but one that regularly concluded with returning its heroines to home and husband. By excerpting Walthall from Mayo's *Mary Page* collage, the moviegoing girl did not just amplify a serial heroine's queer potential but moreover reiterated her position as diegetic protagonist. In recontextualizing the movie still via handcraft, Shefler rewrote corporate messaging. She cast female independence and same-sex intimacy as pivotal to her fan purchase in an episodic film narrative instead of accepting serials' depiction of both as disposable.

Like Ross's, Shefler's movie scrapbook exposes an interest in young actresses centered on the kinetic eroticism of their exposed bodies. In one of many images occupying a full page, Mary MacLaren swirls in a gauzy dress, her bare legs and splayed arms caught in exuberant motion; Mae Murray, Theda Bara, and Molly King are all clipped in similar positions and revealing attire. In another *Mary Page* still, Mayo swoons on the floor, head thrown back, eyes closed and arms limp, her bare décolletage at the mercy of Walthall's crouched figure. Rapture and vulnerability coalesce in the images of film actresses Shefler chose to keep. In the pictures as in the press, female bodies were generally set up as objects to be looked at with curiosity and desire. In the fan-made scrapbook, the adolescent girl not only becomes the bearer of the look; she is also the curator of the performers on display, fiddling with their figures and star texts at will (figure 13).

The very tactility of the paper cutouts Shefler compiled—essentially poseable body simulacra—reiterates that cinema functioned in the 1910s as a unique catalyst for erotic spectatorial investments, ephemera being handled by industry and fans alike as proxies for resolving the in absentia ardor players triggered in certain moviegoers. It is no coincidence that Shefler's scrapbook includes memorabilia distributed at actors' live appearances, such as a pocket-size autographed photograph of William Farnum and exhibitor cards announcing giveaways of "photos of favorite stars" at Portland's newly refurbished T. & D. Theatre, or that the young movie lover adorned her photomontages with printed eyewitness statements disclosing that a veteran player like Earle Williams "is much better looking off stage than he is in pictures and has a very pleasing voice. . . . He pronounces the 'I' long as in 'high.' "[53]

Fans' paper collages, in sum, act as extensions of commercial advertisements dispensed by film impresarios and newspapermen intent on retaining moviegoers by supplying them with a surrogate proximity to stars. However, by rearranging film ephemera to suit their pleasure, girl scrapbookers teased out a queer redolence otherwise unregistered in official star promotion. Such fan-found intensities seem to respond to what Roland Barthes termed "the punctum of a photograph . . . : that accident which pricks me (but also bruises me, is poignant to me)."[54] Discussing affective media, Jennifer Bean adds to Barthes's definition, describing the punctum as "nothing the photograph *strives* to convey" but that still manages to arrest the beholder's eye, triggering an impactful contingent response.[55] Early queer reception likewise does not depend on explicit content to come into being: it burgeons as response to a perceived electric current, an instinctive reaction instantiated by the queer punctum of certain film images and stars.

If her scrapbooking labor transmits a homoerotic investment in young actresses, Shefler's attraction to atypical masculinity exemplifies the sundry queer ways of looking that silent moviegoing girls generated through paper play. In over two hundred pages, Shefler convenes shots of leading men deviating from their virile star texts. George Walsh and Harold Lockwood, for instance, garnished praise in action genres, including westerns, crime thrillers, and military dramas. Lockwood, credited as one of the first movie heartthrobs, reached stardom in the

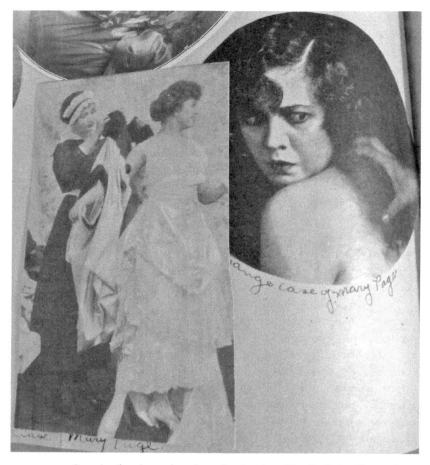

FIGURE 12. Queering female stardom through scissoring: Alice Shefler's collages of Edna Mayo with lady-in-waiting . . .

mid-1910s, playing patriotic heroes against ringleted May Allison. Walsh, a former athlete, received praise for performing his own stunts, becoming a rival to swashbuckling Douglas Fairbanks in the late 1910s.

Though Walsh's celebrity, like Lockwood's, hinged on physical prowess and gallant heterosexuality, Shefler favored promotional images in which both actors appeared against type. In a still from *The Island of Desire* (1917), Walsh is seen stranded on a beach. Bowing defensively, he stands with long matted hair, shirt open and askew, a gun in his

FIGURE 13. . . . and with male beau.

uncertain hands. Unusually vulnerable, Walsh's face is caught between alarm and confusion while a dog and a girl (Margaret Gibson) sit by his side on the sand, dirty and despondent. That the heroine regards the dog with dismay instead of looking up at Walsh with hope and awe undermines the typical castaway narrative, in which the male lead wins

a maiden's heart by conquering natural disaster with resilience and athleticism. Whereas the film narrative likely progressed in that manner,
the instant Shefler decided to preserve is one of male fragility and female
disinterest, thus circumventing the inevitability of heterosexual romance.

A similar queering occurs in the elaborate collage Shefler devoted to
Lockwood. Great emphasis is given to his performance in *The Buzzard's
Shadow* (1915), a WWI drama. Despite Lockwood playing a dashing
all-American sergeant alongside May Allison, his onscreen sweetheart,
Shefler chose to highlight stills in which the actor engages other men. In
one cutout, Lockwood holds intense eye-contact with a young officer,
the man's hand covering Lockwood's in a tight grip. The moment teems
with such tension that, excerpted from context, their exchange can be
read as homoerotic or homosocial, threatening or sensual. In another
film still, Lockwood appears among working men who cheer as he is
patted on the shoulder by an older officer on horseback, a female child
secured between his legs. The image celebrates rugged masculinity, while
presenting a picture of male bonding centered in an alternative familial
formation. Again, without contextualization, this fragmented scene
shows a community of men physically reassuring each other and nurturing a child without any adult female presence to signal heterosexual
romance or reproduction. Though two additional clippings depict Lockwood with Allison, those do not exude the same charge as the images of
Lockwood with men—in part because photographs of the opposite-sex
duo so saturated their shared stardom that the studied pervasiveness of
their in-text romance dulled any erotic tension.

That Shefler bestowed as much attention on Lockwood's closeness
with men as she did on his closeness with his leading lady implies an
affective equivalence in the scrapbooker's eyes. It also points to early
stagings of female fans gravitating toward screen representations of
male-male intimacy and finding them in screen glances and touches. This
reading is strengthened by many other film stills Shefler selected, all
depicting "pretty boy leads" being physically intimate with men, including Jack W. Kerrigan having his hand kissed in *A Son of the Immortals*
(1916); Lou Tellegen caressing Tom Forman's shoulder and holding his
gaze in the *Explorer* (1915); and Owen Moore, in a small still from *Betty
of Greystone* (1916), entangled with another man on a carpeted floor,
their limbs so closely intertwined one cannot tell the two bodies apart
(figure 14).[56] Blurring wrestling and lovemaking, the latter is an unusual
still to highlight from a dramatic five-reeler starring Dorothy Gish,
more so because both men's faces are obscured, precluding star identifi-

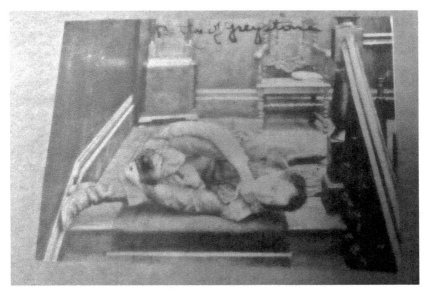

FIGURE 14. The entangled bodies of men: a film still from *Betty of Greystone* (1916) collected in Alice Shefler's scrapbook.

cation or optimal handsomeness. The emphasis on homoerotic male intimacy—on strapping masculinity turned brutishly on itself—likely drives the inclusion of this grainy film still, a thematic thread amplified by adjacent clippings showing Moore exchanging heated glares with an unidentified male player or sitting in a studio portrait adoringly gazing at director D. W. Griffith while screenwriter Dell Henderson "hang[s] on his chair."[57]

Queerness attracts queerness. Seeing two men being intimate may have appealed to female spectators who identified as divergent because such depictions gave visibility to their own misalignment with heteronormativity. As furtive or comedic as these moments of male homoeroticism may have been intended, they proffered a glimpse of titillating actualization, a possibility of queer feeling at a time when same-sex attraction did not find much positive representation in popular culture. Laura Horak theorizes that in the 1910s, the "range romance" film subgenre deliberately elicited queer readings by "linger[ing] on images of two apparent men flirting, falling and love, and embracing." Though one of the men turned out to be a "disguised girl boy," her temporary gender masquerade "allow[ed] cinema to visualize same-sex attraction" without committing to authenticating its existence.[58] Movie-loving girls, therefore, would have been familiar with male homoeroticism as a common component in narratives that troubled, however fleetingly, traditional gender and sexual binaries.

In short, representations of male-male affection, violence, and rough-housing may have operated as proxy for a young moviegoer, allowing her to probe nonnormative attachments from a safe remove. Susan Potter connects such spectatorial displacement with the "lesbian fantas-matic," a mode of early queer reception where a male star provided female audiences with "access to an alternative discursive space for the recognition and expression of women's same-sex desires . . . : not only as a figure with whom spectators might identify—or who enables a homoerotic spectatorship in relation to the female figures he is associated with—but also as a particularly generative node in a cinematic discursive field, enabling the production and experience of shared ideas or emotions . . . less amenable to explicit representation in dominant culture."[59]

Potter's theory that androgynous male stars could instantiate queer reception in early female audiences takes fuller form in Eleanor G. Fulton's movie scrapbook. Entirely devoted to silent screen heartthrob Jack Warren Kerrigan, it amasses ephemera mainly distributed between 1913 and 1915, including giveaway headshots from movie magazines, clippings from daily newspapers and trade publications, penciled lists of Kerrigan productions seen (sixty-four total), and personalized memorabilia the girl fan retrieved directly from the star. A well-connected Los Angeles resident, Fulton was the only child of John Addison Fulton, a civil engineer and the construction superintendent for the first Los Angeles aqueduct, which broke ground in October 1908 and continued until November 1913.[60] Born in the late 1890s, Fulton was an avid filmgoer who, in her youth, had unprecedented access to studio lots. As a result, her ephemera collection provides rare insight on fan scrapbooks functioning as a complex material go-between, preserving transient spectatorial experiences as well as seizing queer star (sub)texts.

If at first glance Fulton's neat chronological collages may resemble a visual resumé of Kerrigan's film career, it quickly becomes apparent that the girl fan privileges newspaper articles foregrounding Kerrigan's non-traditional masculinity. Numerous clippings comment on his unusual "beauty," remarking that even "directors agree with matinee girls on this. He is one of the men who can command several hundred dollars a week for his looks alone." Seemingly flattering, this line of discourse carried underhanded criticism, the specter of effeminacy, prostitution, and homosexuality haunting the association of physical beauty with venal transaction. In fact, papers often undercut Kerrigan's good looks and professional success, describing the actor with terms applied to female stars. A clipping from 1915 has the *Los Angeles Herald* cooing, "Oh Jack/your features so fine/your kissable lips and your soft, wavy hair," while painting Kerrigan's fans as an army of sentimental kooks: over-coddling mothers who "urge him not to smoke cigarettes in pictures, and not to drink," "their sons, who copy everything he does," and "the love-sick lassies . . . who write on pink perfumed paper from their boarding school" mooning over Kerrigan's hair color. Two of Kerrigan's most salient nonnormative characteristics—a consuming love for his mother and a distaste for female company—are also highlighted in Fulton's scrapbook. The fan gathered and underlined interviews where the actor stated that "my only interest besides my work is my mother" and where the press warned that "in spite of his good looks, Warren Kerrigan does not care for girls. He is seldom seen with women; he says he loves the ladies devotedly—and then adds 'when they leave me alone.'"[61]

Queer rumors attached themselves to Kerrigan before 1914, when seventeen-year-old James Carroll Vincent moved in with the star and his mother at their Hollywood Hills estate.[62] Often photographed in debonair poses, Kerrigan did not hide his penchant for finery, including fashion, flowers, and high art. Kerrigan's celebrity would only tarnish three years later, when allowances for his androgynous masculinity finally expired as the actor spoke against serving in WWI. However, Fulton's scrapbook creates a roadmap to the writing on the wall: early queer whispers, slivers of newspaper pulp quipping that "Jack Kerrigan's favorite flower is the pansy," calling him "a great big baby doll," and announcing that the star was to write a syndicated column "to teach men dress properly," since he reported having "boys actually mob me to get my handkerchief away for a souvenir." A precursor of Valentino by nearly a decade, Kerrigan would undergo the trials of challenging dominant notions of red-blooded American masculinity while being heralded "the ideal of the feminine heart." His sartorial panache, "emotional" acting, fervent female following, and apparent asexuality made for an impossible double standard: to be "as much of a man's man as he is fitted to qualify as a woman's man." Fulton's collages energetically track Kerrigan's ambiguous star text, juxtaposing photos of his delicate features and "soulful" acting with press items boasting that "big-limbed, big-bodied, square-jawed, . . . [Kerrigan] is virilely [*sic*] and vigorously Man." Extending the gender binary to affective film reception, Fulton pasted "maudlin 'mash' letters" by girl "Kerriganites," next to tributes by male fans, like Edward A. Liftka's "I'll Think of You," a poem *Motion Picture Magazine* commended for singing "a man's praise of man [with] no lurking sentimentality in it."[63]

This managerial enforcement of essentialist gender performances spoke of broader anxieties questioning the extent of the influence movie stars held over impressionable fans. It is meaningful, then, that Fulton, a self-confessed "screen-struck girl" and "Kerriganite," seemed to have found the queer idiosyncrasies mining Kerrigan's star text not a deterrent but a driving force of her fan attachment. Her collages constantly emphasize the emotionality of Kerrigan's acting and the feminized vulnerability of his body, selecting stills of him lying in bed, lounging in silk pajamas, disrobed, brooding, cowering, touching other men, or long-haired and skirted as Samson in the 1914 biblical short. More telling, Fulton clipped verses penned by male-named fans that gush with homoeroticism. In 1916, William De Ryee, from Santa Cruz, California, crowned Kerrigan "the player of my heart." He proceeded to assess the leading man's physical attributes with whistling appraisal: "And talk of being handsome— he's living Belvedere! / With dreamy eyes, whose wistfulness had made him e'en more dear." The poem concludes with possibly one of the first instances in filmdom of a deflecting "no homo": De Ryee hurriedly asserts, "Of course, 'I love the ladies,' but commend I must this man; / This peerless Sovereign of the Screen—J. Warren Kerrigan." The scare quotes around the fan's disclaimer of manly heterosexuality is perhaps as damning as his swooning over Kerrigan's "dreamy eyes."[64]

Kerrigan's divergence from the conventional he-man stereotype clearly charmed the Los Angeles moviegoer, stimulating her desire to follow, document, and meet the movie star. Fulton's scrapbook holds photographic evidence of two such encounters, one on November 28, 1913, and another on October 12, 1915. The first is a personalized commercial headshot, the black ink reading "Truly Yours, Jack Kerrigan." The star's handwriting dialogues with the fan's, Fulton having underlined the memento with a penciled caption: "(he gave me this picture after autographing it. Nov.28–17, E.G.F.)." The second image is a full-body photograph of Kerrigan standing against a sun-bleached trailer, awkwardly holding his bag after a long day's work. "Warren Kerrigan posed for this picture at Universal City, October 12–1915. I took it with my Kodak," Fulton scribbles, proudly signing off, "E.G.F." The fan's shadow can be seen projected against the actor's feet, her flowery hat a ghostly intrusion and a reminder of the power differential undergirding star-fan relations, even when they met in the flesh (figure 15).

FIGURE 15. Snapped: Eleanor Fulton's scrapbooked collage and self-produced Kodak of Jack W. Kerrigan, October 12, 1915.

Both reproductions are remarkable, not only for their singularity but also as poignant testaments to the lengths a well-off movie lover would go to alleviate the anxiety of loss conjured by both the moviegoing experience and film fandom. Surrounded by mass-produced facsimiles, the amateur Kodak condenses the overlapping longings to be serially intimate with a star and to safekeep one-of-a-kind live encounters with him, to stretch temporality beyond a face-to-face instant, and to guarantee an embodied afterlife that moviegoing actively precluded. As Christian Metz observes, unlike cinema, "the photographic *lexis* [i.e., the socialized unit of reading, of reception] has no fixed duration (= temporal size): it depends, rather, on the spectator, who is the master of the look."[65] In its visual fixity and libidinal fluidity, Kerrigan's snapshot invested Fulton with rare mastery over a star's body. Twice arrested by the girl fan's hand (the mechanical click and the manual pasting), the male player goes from a larger-than-life projection on the big screen to a butterfly pinned down with loving care in the fan's private scrapbook. Reduced to pocket-size, the personalized star photograph becomes a simulacrum of intimacy *and* a measure of control, affording an unknown admirer the sensation of collaborative authorship when rewriting their—star, fan, cinema—intersecting life-narratives.

The material tactility of printed paper, being an amateur snapshot or an autographed mass reproduction, galvanizes spectatorial cathexis, the portable representation of film stars nearing and endearing female fans who favored alternatives to normative gender performances. The possibility of alienation and otherness threads through nonetheless, for the act of photographing a star, like that of clipping and gluing their commercial likeness, is imbued with the watermark of loss. "An instantaneous abduction," photography constantly reminds subject and creator of the relentless march of time.[66] Film ephemera, as a result, affords intimacy by foregrounding distance, and remembrance by evincing transience, possibly throwing an ardent fan into a queer loop of yearning, where temporality refuses to follow teleological linearity but instead keeps snaking back to a fixed attachment.

It is relevant then, that the only other Kodak included in this scrapbook is half-ripped from the page; all that survives is a residual streetview and a small disembodied head, presumably Fulton's, if the stylish headgear and California landscape is anything to go by.[67] Read as companions, this photograph and the one Fulton took of Kerrigan comment upon the power asymmetries sustaining film fandom. The violence exacted against her self-portrait, its near obliteration, contrasts deeply

Where is Warren Kerrigan's "lion strength" in "Scooped by Cupid"? Oh well, a star reporter cannot show much strength when scooped by a pretty girl.

FIGURE 16. Scratched off: Eleanor Fulton's own photograph, a ghost on the page.

with the care deployed in every clipped ephemera dedicated to the actor. The white scars on photographic paper where the surface image was scraped off, as the negative space delineated by glue remnants, tell a story of fan self-erasure both parallel and essential to the enshrinement of movie celebrity (figure 16).

While the act of taking a snapshot of a movie star may seem apothe-otic, Fulton kept adding unique Kerrigan ephemera to her scrapbook, including a strip of nitrate film containing sixteen frames of an actor (presumably the man himself) on horseback. In this one piece of memo-rabilia, the photographic image coalesces with the filmic print and the picture personality, denoting the fan's urgency to own physical indexes of Kerrigan's presence.[68] Fulton also gathered a stamp-size cutout from the Victor short *The Man Who Lied* (1914), depicting Kerrigan in a policeman costume. Underneath, the fan inscribed in grey pencil: "Was in this uniform when he gave me his picture." Eagerness for bodily contact and serial closeness with a star subtends this cumulative archiving of written and visual sources. Such eagerness extends, as well, to Fulton's repeated screenings of Kerrigan's picture work: handwritten notations indicate that the Los Angelina often saw the same production two or three times, likely in an effort to integrate the actor's spectral projection in her daily life.

The plural materiality of the movie scrapbook and the diligent manual labor of piecing it together thus produce a polyvalent site of interactivity, imagination, and intimacy where early queer discourses crisscrossed, star images and their promotional texts shellacking the dispersed constellation of possible queer readings retrieved by fans. In mixing commercial and personal sources, mechanical reproduction and handcraft, the fan-made movie scrapbook refused to relay one single message; instead, its "general signaling of 'sentiment' or 'feeling' opened a space for [the maker and the beholder] to elaborate specific personal meanings [of] her own."[69]

LAYER UPON LAYER: EXCESS, JUXTAPOSITIONS, AND THE QUEERING OF FEMALE STARS

In a similar vein, Shefler's collages of individual actresses and romantic screen duos illustrate the sprawling queer potentialities of scrapbooked film reception. For instance, in a multipage shrine to Blanche Sweet, the Portland fan aggregates a panoply of magazine interviews, studio portraits, decoupaged headshots, and production stills inked with movie titles. The material excess and touchable texturing are rife with eroticism. Each page is stuffed with black-and-white renditions of Sweet's face, the gauziness of her hair and dress echoing the leafy layers of paper captions and banners, the folds of magazine pages tucked in the scrapbook spine beckoning to be fingered open. Posing in menswear or evening gowns, the actress's gaze never meets the eye of the camera, the beholder, the scrapbooker; yet the repetitive surplus of her print likeness forces a sense of physical presence that suggests that collecting an abundance of film ephemera might succeed in conjuring an approximal corporality between female fan and star. In its customized peekaboo overlay, as in its attempts to render affection tangible through commercial paper, the fan scrapbook once again resembles the sentimental valentine card: an image-forward object crafted "not merely to be looked at, but rather to be touched and sensually experienced."[70]

The three-dimensionality of scrapbooks facilitated a recuperation of cinema's immaterial flatness through multisensory indulgence. Scrapbooks' material tactility magnified the intimacy of witnessing Sweet at home with her dog or working behind the camera with Marie Doro. These backstage stills are pasted next to Shefler's handwritten list of watched movies starring Sweet. There are eleven titles in total, all released between 1915 and 1917, listed in chronological order and including the names of Sweet's romantic leads. It is revealing, though, that no pictures of her leading men are inserted in the actress's shrine. The inscription of their names in the fan's moviegoing ledger enables only a spectral presence without granting their male bodies any space. As a queer fan technique, it evokes an apparitional sort of heterosexuality, accessible only through a prior knowledge that the names tallied next to Sweet's filmography are those of her male costars. This type of indexical obscurity subsumes diegetic heterosexuality to a moviegoing girl's stake in Sweet's image, thus preserving a microcosmos of same-sex investment.

If print excess underpins early fandom, it did not do so apart from industry dictates. Not only did newspapermen and exhibitors continually solicit moviegoers to amass star ephemera but, as mentioned above, film magazines played with scrapbook conventions (including artisanal-looking collages) in the visual presentation of their content. Such dynamic traffic of influence comes alive in girls' movie scrapbooks. In one collage, Shefler included a photomontage of Sweet holding a miniature version of herself, manufactured by *The Motion Picture Magazine* in 1917. Some pages later, it is Lillian Gish who smirks impishly at her own poised self, a fan-made composite that flirts with notions of mass duplication, narcissism, and same-sex interest, trademarks of early female stardom and reception.

Such mirroring extended to moviegoing girls aligning their personal Kodaks with that of stars, engendering intimacy through visual homology. Circa 1916, Kitty Baker, a teenage moviegoer from Norfolk, Virginia, pasted a sepia snapshot of a female friend with a male date next to a colorized lithography of Irene and Vernon Castle fox-trotting. On another occasion, Baker juxtaposed a family picture of a young girl in a kimono with a promotional still from *The Secret Sin* (1915), a multireel drama warning against the dangers of Chinese opium dens. In the still, Blanche Sweet and Japanese actor Sessue Hayakawa appear in oriental garb, their distinct attire creating an aesthetic parallel with the photo of Baker's friend. This visual twinning suggests movie-loving scrapbookers used photography (commercial and vernacular) to blur the lines between real and reel life via an engineered narrative of symmetry and similarity.

The potentialities of queer female reception, in short, dialogued with the film industry, homoerotic reception playing *with, within,* and *against* official heteronormative scripts. We find this most explicitly in Shefler's collages of Anita Stewart. An adolescent in the mid-1910s, Stewart skyrocketed to fame as "the sweet symbol of alluring maidenhood" and screen partner of much older Earle Williams, a stout stage actor turned movie star.[71] Stuffed with bare necklines, bedroom eyes, and coquettish smiles, Shefler's shrines to Stewart exude corporeal eroticism. Yet the homoerotic charge simmering under a profusion of female limbs, ruffles, and curls peaks in promotional stills Stewart shared with Williams. In these images, Stewart is palpably sexualized, passion dripping from Williams's embraces, touches, and stares. By including a few "couple stills" in an otherwise Stewart-centric montage, the girl fan both acknowledges and deflects the actress's sexual appeal: it is Williams, not Shefler, who regards Stewart with heat. However, by displaying desire on a manipulable surface (screen, paper), the actor afforded the moviegoing girl a conduit to vicariously lust after a young actress. To enjoy watching a male-female duo make love onscreen may not automatically signify heteronormative reception, then; it may instead have provided some female fans with means for queering engagement with star texts. By strategically placing heterosexual "courtship" shots within a paper tapestry soused with female eroticism, Shefler crafted an interactive queer aperture that may have allowed her to slip into the male role and woo a lovely actress; to identify with the romantic heroine and become the center of sensual attention; or to imagine herself the lover of both players in a gleeful triangulation of desire (figure 17).

The spectatorial impetus to touch an actress's skin via ephemera manipulation and male gaze mediation manifests more explicitly in a scissored film still of Pauline Frederick. Bare back turned against the camera, the star sits naked on a bed while a fully clothed man appraises her. On the creamy white skin, Shefler has inked "Sold." The insert likely refers to the title of a 1915 Famous Players–Lasky five-reeler where Frederick played a coerced artist's model. However, the manual caption ("Sold") doubly conveys the vulnerable positioning of Frederick's screen body (naked and on display as if on auction) and the fan's definitive appreciation for the actress's figure (she is "sold" on Frederick).

In deploying scrapbook labor as a pathway for queer fantasy, girl fans executed the type of genderbending reception Potter conjectures Valentino elicited from early female audiences. In theorizing avenues

FIGURE 17. Textured desire: Alice Shefler's collage of Anita
Stewart, in which ruffles, paper excess, and heterosexual passion
elicit an erotic fan gaze.

for tracing lesbian reception in the silent era, Potter proposes that "Valentino's stardom generated a specific queer appeal for his female audiences, one that permitted the recognition not only of desire between
women but also of an interest in same-sex eroticism that could be shared
by both women and men." Scrapbook collages created by screen-struck
girls during the 1910s enjoin concrete evidence of such a queer mode of
looking, one capable of evading "the totalizing and heteronormative

accounts of identification, sexual desire, and subject formation" promoted by early Hollywood.[72] While Potter claims that Valentino's spectatorial lesbian appeal resulted from a scandalous private life and sexually ambiguous screen persona, movie scrapbooks assembled a decade prior confirm that young female moviegoers derived queer affinities from a broader spectrum of sources, including promotional stills depicting same-sex intimacy, vulnerable masculinity, and lovemaking between opposite-sex couples. Not contingent on one specific set of conditions or characteristics, the possibilities for early queer reception did not depend on an eccentric star text as Hansen, Potter, and others have posited, but on a female spectator's eye: she determined the homoerotic charge punching out of an actress's gesture or the queer subtext in two actors' entangled bodies, and she gave it visual shape through fan craft labor.[73] The variations on how and why certain pictures and players spoke to silent film female audiences multiplies then, open-ended and playful according to each individual's queer funny bone.

Centering the historiography of queer reception around personal fan materials rather than star texts ultimately shifts the agency for producing queer readings away from industrial intent and onto spectatorial perception. It also shines a light on female fans' long subtended tendency to privilege maleness and masculinity as a lens for exploring queer recognition and identification. Consequently, girl fans' attraction to male emotionality and/or female masculinity complicates what Jackie Stacey characterized as the many "forms of intimacy between femininities" structuring the "spectator/star relationship."[74] According to Horak, Stacey sees cinema as able to eventually "contain the 'homoerotic' response it evoked [in female audiences] by channeling it into heterosexual constructions of femininity."[75] Instead of being absorbed into heteronormativity, I argue that early female fandom fed off homoeroticism (male and female), using it to explore frissons of nonconformity not unlike those historians attribute to lesbian moviegoers during the classical period. Building upon theorist Biddy Martin, White speculates that lesbian spectatorship of the 1930s and 1940s primarily manifested through closer affinity with boyish rebels and dandyish women than with the catalogue of conforming wives and sweethearts Hollywood cinema foisted on female audiences. "Lesbian autobiographical narratives," Martin claims, "are about remembering differently, outside the contours and narrative constraints of conventional models. ... Whether their emphasis is on a tomboyish past, on childhood friendships, or on crushes on girl friends . . . , these narratives point to unsanctioned discontinuities between biological sex, gender identity, and sexuality."[76] Queer female spectatorship of the silent era makes itself discernible by similar deviation from heteronormative norms—whether through a refashioning of gendered star texts or a favoring of the electrically divergent, conveyed through an innuendo, a mannerism, or an outfit. Such standing apart is self-appointed and self-expressed in fan-made scrapbooking, correspondence, journaling, and dress-up, practices where gender and sexuality are portrayed as discontinuous, affective, performative.

The collages, snapshots, and mixed-media diaries early movie-loving girls created also corroborate digital scholar Alexis Lothian's claim that "creative fan culture makes ephemera endure" by rendering durable, not only disposable paraphernalia, minor stars, and forgotten productions, but also transitory spectatorial reactions and unmarked minority identifications that engage ethnicity, immigration status, sexuality, mental health, and creed.[77] As a result, paper-based fan repositories bring into sharp relief the transformative labor performed by female audiences across history. In the creative hands of early moviegoing girls, teleological paper scraps and heteronormative narratives reemerge as refractive artifacts, cropped and decontextualized, turned polysemic with lust, willfulness, curiosity, possibility, and self-affirming verve, characteristics Sara Ahmed identifies as symptomatic of queerness's "stubborn attachment to an unassimilable difference."[78] Such transformative labor practices are commonplace in feminist analyses of twenty-first-century fan communities, but their history reaches all the way back to the birth of Hollywood's star system.

To historicize the presence of female desire in early film reception also helps normalize women's erotic engagement with mass media. Female participation in gaming and online fan communities continues to be reduced to an essentialization of their sexual/romantic responses, which in turn are derided as irrational, self-indulgent, and puerile. What scrapbooks put together by movie-loving girls in the 1910s testify is that eroticized spectatorship did not preclude critical engagement with a star system. Desire and discernment, fantasy and self-discovery coexisted, as they do in current female-dominated fandoms. Platforms of fan performance may have changed in over a century, yet scrapbooking remains a staple of fan reception and belonging. In paper or digital iterations, scrapbooks are a visual distillation of the complex ways individuals process information and stimuli at one point in time. Those assembled by the first generation of screen-struck girls are no exception, seizing variegated modes of adolescent spectatorship that contradict the perdurable homogenization of female viewer engagement as irrational or solipsistic. While libidinal energy does thread through these media artifacts, it takes many eclectic shapes.

It is important to recognize the embodied erotics and transformative labor underscoring female consumers so long gone that we may feel tempted to erase their physicality. It is important to recall that these original moviegoing girls labored with their hands and loved the pictures with their whole body while in the throes of adolescence. The personal archives film historians encounter today are the spoils of these fans' exploits—they are a concrete collection of life fragments, of fleeting attractions, not unlike the film ephemera that form them. Scrapbooks are what survived after the body did not. But fan artifacts are not separate from the body, nor were they when first created over a century ago.

Queer ways of looking and feeling, in the end, originated with each and every early movie-loving girl who materialized their affective cathecting through transformative paper play, formulating praxes of female media engagement and identification active to this day. Such praxes persist in the fan fiction, virtual journaling, digital scrapbooks, and fan art circulated in online communities, with female fans excerpting licensed images from mainstream media and repurposing them as loci of same-sex desire, gender nonconformity, and divergent fantasy in self-authored reception materials. Scrapbook pages and star pictures may have shifted from paper to pixels in the last one hundred years, but the modes of making queer female reception legible to self and others have not strayed far from their early film beginnings.

CHAPTER 5

Different from Others

Movie-Illustrated Diaries, Cross-Dressing, and Circulated Discourses on Female Deviance

Even the sun-clouds this morning cannot manage such skirts
Nor the woman in the ambulance
Whose red heart blooms through her coat so astoundingly.

—Sylvia Plath

No two fan-made "movy albums" look the same. Some are entirely comprised of clipped pictures, no marginalia included. Others incorporate a mix of images and written content, the former outweighing the latter. A third type privileges handwritten film impressions, lists of movies watched, and commentaries on social outings, friendships, and daily happenings, occasionally festooning these with screen ephemera. I call these artifacts "movie-illustrated diaries," the sororal twin of the image-dominated movie scrapbook.

In her movie-illustrated diary, Helen Edna Davis—a first-generation immigrant, born affluent in Johannesburg, South Africa, on July 4, 1898—repeatedly turned to moviegoing to tackle complicated feelings of psychological divergence, social inadequacy, and gender nonconformity.[1] While attending Smith College from 1915 to 1919, the white girl crafted mixed-media diaries where she engages in epistolary soliloquies with an imaginary male interlocutor named "Jonathan." Like Davis, Jonathan is a US-based adolescent who grew up in Berlin and witnessed the outbreak of World War I with conflicted allegiances.[2] In the diary, Jonathan operates as a projected male ideal, an understanding ear to whom Davis could safely self-describe as "a queer guy" and

146 | Chapter 5

a "conceited jackass," masculine identities Davis seems to deem damning if ever spoken out loud. Unresolved gender nonconformity thus stirs an inner strife between secrecy and disclosure that congeals around oblique venting: "I wouldn't let Cora or Beth know it for the world. But there are times!"[3]

Davis's epistolary diaries echo the fan letters where girls confessed to a movie actress their discomfort with traditional femininity, often by identifying with a male subject and casting the star as an eroticized muse. "Queer," in its subtextual equation with nonnormativity, is once again employed by a moviegoer who struggles "to make [themselves] out."[4] A fear of morbidity pervades Davis's letters to Jonathan, their self-accusatory tone as constant and troubling as that threading through Medora Espy's contemporaneous diaries. Drawing on clinical terminology, Davis characterizes her "moods and strange feelings" as symptoms of being "supersensitive or extremely sentimental." "Queer isn't it?" the nineteen-year-old muses, rhetorically conflating multiple vectors of divergence under perceived pathology.[5] Davis goes on to describe herself as "supersensitive—or else crazy!," a "sentimental nut," "a huge joke," and "plain nuts." Self-diagnosed abnormal psychology is regarded as innate ("some people are just born nuts, Jonathan!") and originating from identarian indeterminacy ("I really was beginning to think I knew myself, Jonathan but I'm terribly at sea now!").[6] Being "queer" in this inceptive moment of linguistic self-articulation is seen as a state of being different, conflicted, unfixed and desirous, streaming out of orthodox categories.

Early vocalizations of teen angst, Davis's confessional writings always circle back to the perception that her emotional life is disruptive because it diverges too markedly from normative parameters. Much like Espy, discussed in chapter 1, Davis fleshes out this self-diagnosed deviance through film consumption. Her college diaries are dotted with drawings, newspaper clippings, stage programs, and amateur Kodaks, but only one image of a celebrity: Lillian Gish. A pocket-sized headshot, the sepia ephemera is collaged next to an entry where the moviegoer shares her secret "queer" yearning: "I wish I were a man." Davis continues in a pressed speech, "I wouldn't let Cora and Beth know it for the world. But there are times!—. . . I wonder, sometimes, that they don't suspect. I hunger for it so, & they never understand!" "Isn't Lillian Gish appropriate up there?" the girl blurts out at the end of her admission.[7]

The ties between female fan, queerness, and movie actress are strengthened when the diarist discloses that Gish's headshot was bestowed by another girl. Nothing more is added regarding the gift

giver, but Davis implies the exchange was fraught with forbidding inti-
mations: "Perhaps she's alright, though might mislead people as to what
it's really about!" Implicit is the idea that receiving a picture of Gish
from this anonymous girl may give onlookers the wrong impression: if
about what may be passing between the two girls, or what Davis may
feel for the star, is left ambiguous. What is plainly suggested, however,
is that the act of swapping the photographic reproduction of a movie
actress could be read as a trespass. Homoeroticism is activated by the
triangulation of female affect (from the nameless girl via Gish to Davis)
and channeled by the hands trading, handling, and safe-keeping that
image of the young screen beauty.

Annotated records of movie attendance similarly reveal that same-sex
desire found articulation through the ongoing consumption and admiration of female film bodies. In addition to Gish's reproduction—a heavy-
lidded, gauzy headshot—Davis only found worthy of note fantastic productions starring Marguerite Clark (e.g., *Snow White* in 1916, *The
Seven Swans* in 1917) and Australian-born Annette Kellerman, a white
immigrant like the South African fan herself.[8] Focusing on female physicality, Davis praises Clark for being a doll-like "darling" and Kellerman for her "amphibian" prowess in underwater scenes. Multireelers *A
Daughter of Gods* (1916) and *Queen of the Sea* (1918) stimulated
the adolescent moviegoer to ink a rendition of the star in her mermaid
role. In both feature films, Kellerman appeared nude and on display in
natural settings, a star trademark heavily promoted by fan and trade
publications. Besides saving exhibitors' programs for these productions,
Davis inked a sinuous line drawing highlighting the eroticism of Kellerman's long, lean body. The star is seen hiding naked behind a rock,
smirking and flaunting her flowing hair at a confused mountain goat
(figure 18).[9]

In the context of first-person fan archives, paper images of film
actresses—whether mass-produced or handmade—accrue affective
value beyond that of facilitating proximity between moviegoer and star.
Passed between girl fans, star likenesses become symbolic tokens of
queer feeling and belonging. Whereas in star-fan correspondence the
exchanging of headshots induced female closeness within an asymmet-
ric framework, between queer girl fans, gifted film ephemera becomes a
tie that binds horizontally, a visual cypher that communicates identarian kinship. Historian Julie Inness argues that "the act of sharing information with another is intimate when that being shared is a scarce,
restricted commodity."[10] Disclosure of same-sex attraction or gender

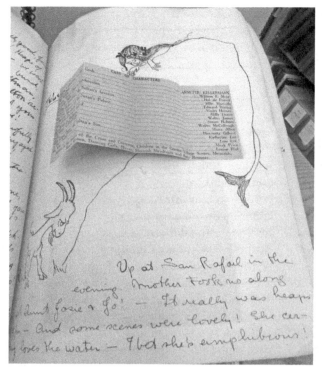

FIGURE 18. Helen Davis's journaled film review and sinuous line
drawing of Annette Kellerman in *A Daughter of the Gods*, 1916.

nonconformity can be read as "a restricted commodity," and in Davis's
case, a protected secret only whispered in a journal entry centered
around Gish's image.

Beyond showing moviegoing girls harnessing star ephemera to articulate queer feelings, Davis's diaries provide evidence that educated girls
growing up in the 1910s were well aware of psychoanalytical debates on
female interiority. In 1917, Davis mentions that she attends "confessional talks" (or "confidentials") with a specialist, her code for therapy.
Sardonically, she calls the field by name ("poor old Psychology!") and
likens psychoanalysis to bloodletting ("It's good to get the poison out of
one's system at whatever cost"), a longstanding medical procedure used
in the treatment of mood disorders.[11] The need for such "bitter medicine"
arose after the girl had a breakdown at Smith the previous year.[12] Circumstances are kept deliberately vague, but Davis implies that a relationship with another schoolgirl triggered the disruptive emotional episode.

Davis's commonplace knowledge and integrated engagement with psychoanalysis confirm that, by the mid-1910s, clinical discourses on sexuality and mental illness had already escaped the walled garden of medical journals and were actively influencing how educated individuals conceived of their divergent identities. These journal entries also undermine general claims that film audiences watching actresses in male drag during the Great War would not be able to link cross-dressing with female inversion because clinical discourses on sexual deviance developed apart from popular consciousness. The traffic of influence between US cinema and psychology was much more porous where college-going audiences were concerned. Psychology experts like Victor O. Freeburg, a professor at Columbia University, wrote extensively about film for trade and fan magazines. Moviegoing schoolgirls had regular access to courses on psychology, philosophy, and literature, disciplines where discussions on gender, aberrance, and desire took center-stage.

In fact, psychology became a mainstay in US women's colleges during the 1910s. A report issued by the president of Vassar College in 1912 affirms that "psychology continues to be one of the most popular electives,"[13] while one of the most quoted catch-phrases among the class of 1914 was "psychologically speaking," popularized by a Vassar senior named Harriet Plimpton.[14] Extant examinations from the 1910s also prove that top-tier women's colleges Vassar, Smith, and Radcliffe tested students in "abnormal psychology," prompting them to "outline a discussion of psychotherapy" and "identify a case of hysteria."[15] By 1919, "psychology" had become such a crowded elective at prestigious public schools like the University of California, Berkeley, that female students dubbed the class "mob psychology," a pun suggesting familiarity with Gustave Le Bon's popular sociological study *The Crowd: A Study of the Popular Mind* (1895).[16] Reproductions of movie actresses enshrined in personal fan archives like Davis's thus indicate that female stars' bodies, their styling, and their performed emotions could hold indexical valences that helped girl fans work through self-perceptions of abnormality and difference, and supplemented the clinical knowledge provided by their formal educations.

Davis's movie-illustrated diaries, in short, prove the existence of early movie-loving girls who were familiar with clinical debates on female psychology and pathology while being groomed, by virtue of their social gender, to speak in code. This is a relevant combination because it evinces the existence of pockets of female filmgoers who possessed the necessary tools to regard female cross-dressing in a light alternative to that proposed by Laura Horak and widely accepted by other silent film historians.[17] To these audience members, homoerotic identification, same-sex desire, and gender nonconformity would have been immediately available as spectatorial readings. It bears noting that Davis's adult life followed the nonconventional path seeded in her movie-loving adolescence. After graduating from Smith, she completed doctoral work at Columbia University and the Union Theological Seminary, publishing her dissertation on ethics and literature in 1929. Never marrying or mothering children, she would spend her days between Buffalo and New York City, involved in various social causes and penning pedagogical treatises on women's rights.

SEXOLOGISTS AND PRESSMEN UNITE: CROSS-DRESSING AS SYMPTOM OF FEMALE DEVIANCE

Helen Davis, a white, well-off immigrant secluded in a women's college in New England, may seem an outlier among the heterogenous audiences attending motion pictures across the United States in the late 1910s. Her status as a cultured and cosmopolitan young lady may encourage a presupposition that she had unusual insight into medical jargon classifying sexual and gender categories. That is not the case. Since the mid-1900s the link between cross-dressing and female deviance had percolated in the cultural ether, making appearances in local legislation, newspapers, and, eventually, movie actresses' star texts. With so many diverse outlets cautioning audiences against the marriage of female deviance and cross-dressing, it is unlikely a majority of filmgoers remained unaware of perverse interpretations, at least not to the degree Horak proposes. According to Horak, female cross-dressing carried virtuous associations throughout the WWI years, because scientific debates yoking male drag to female inversion did not reach most US audiences. Such spectatorial "blindness," Horak argues, persisted until 1927, when a nationwide scandal surrounding the lesbian-themed play *The Captive* (1926) catapulted medical codifications of female homosexuality into popular awareness.

The clinical association of female cross-dressing with same-sex attraction has roots in the last quarter of the nineteenth century, when renowned European sexologists Richard Krafft-Ebbing, George Beard, Auguste Forel, and Havelock Ellis began positing that homosexual desire resulted from a literal biological inversion of gendered characteristics and societal roles, which led to sexual inclinations incongruent with one's anatomy. In Beard's words, inverted "men became women and women men in their tastes, conduct, character, feeling and behaviour."[18] In his pioneering work *Psychopathia Sexualis* (1886), Krafft-Ebing explained that the female "homosexual loves to wear her hair short and have her clothing in the fashion of men," as a way to "manifest the masculine soul" inhabiting her "female bosom."[19] Two decades later, Forel would further conflate sexual inversion with cross-dressing: "The pure female invert feels like a man. The idea of coitus with men is repugnant to her. She apes the habits, manners, and vestments of men. Female inverts have been known to wear men's uniforms and perform military service for years."[20]

Sex specialists interpreted the act of donning clothes culturally attributed to the opposite sex as one of the chief behaviors externalizing female deviance—from suffragettes to demimondes and inverts. Other telltale symptoms included an "incapacity for needlework," "a toleration for cigarettes," and an overly athletic nature or assertive disposition.[21] Nurture and nature worked hand in hand to produce inverts, so adolescence played a key role in early detection and curtailment. Eugenicist physician Arabella Kenealy alerted parents that "young girls," like moldable pieces of clay, had to be shepherded out of their "tomboy" stage, otherwise they would be "forcibly shaped to masculine modes, become more or less irretrievably male of trait and bent, losing all power to recover the womanly normal."[22]

Women's fashion became contested territory as this strict binary model of gender, sex, sexuality, and well-being took root in US culture.[23] Medical debate treating cross-dressing as an externalized symptom of female inversion quickly trickled into everyday life, initially clustering around girls-only institutions. A supposition that cross-dressing in girlhood foretold a "mannish" queer woman drove many of the early writings on female development to share in Kenealy's alarm. By 1905, however, the moral concern that juvenile cross-dressing forewarned sexual inversion infiltrated localized legislation. That year, the prestigious women-only Radcliffe College issued "an edict that . . . any student who clothes herself in masculine attire . . . will at once report to the dean. When [a stage] part calls for mannish attire, bloomers, short skirts, and any other feminine article of apparel may be substituted."[24] A slew of newspaper articles followed, drumming up that "Radcliffe girls can no longer wear pants."[25]

This single prohibition signposts a broader cultural sea change. Cross-dressing was an esteemed tradition in the performing arts, a revival of female impersonators had swept the US stage at the turn of the twentieth century. Etiquette manuals from the antebellum period saw girls wearing "masculine habiliments" as a "harmless fancy," a matter of playful aesthetics divorced from "any moral or proper legal question."[26] Historian Peter Boag presents compelling evidence that cross-dressing was a normalized practice in the United States before mid-1905. Drawing from diverse print sources, he argues that in the nineteenth century, cross-dressing was taken up by male and female Western settlers as a means to publicly redraft their social identities. In the Old West, cross-dressing became an expression of the hardworking, hard-earned, and transformative expansion of the US southwestern border. For women, wearing men's garments conveyed equality and opportunity at a time when both were dispensed scarcely. Boag notes that by the early 1900s, well-to-do ladies commonly dressed in male garb to gain temporary public agency as tourists, hobbyists, and travelers. Ubiquitous at the turn of the century, nonconforming gender performance through attire also paved the rise of a model of femininity defined by self-reliance, practicality, and athleticism. Such a model, colloquially referred to as the "New Woman," would come to be vilified by sexologists as "viragints, a term used specifically to equate feminism with female-to-male sexual inversion as a means to undermine the former."[27]

The vernacular discourse on cross-dressing and permissible female agency shifts around 1905. It is no accident that the swelling visibility of the women's movement (Martha Vicinus estimates its heyday between 1903 and 1913) parallels the implementation of an essentialist binary system opposing male to female identity and abnormal homosexuality to natural heterosexuality.[28] Determined by biology, gender/sex/sexuality/wellness dichotomies were rendered socially visible through everyday performances of self that relied heavily on dress code. Suffragists, many of whom Radcliffe housed, could be recognized by their unfeminine appearance, since "womanly women" presumably "take no interest in the cause."[29] Journalists claimed edicts such as Radcliffe's ban on cross-dressing essential because they "finally drew some crucial lines. . . . It has come to be such a common thing for women to usurp man's place . . . in every walk of life, that it is high time steps were taken to show woman her place. Intoxicated by triumphs in her competition with man, she is progressing at too swift a pace and is forgetting her sphere. . . . If she learns to wear trousers in school . . . she will be wanting to wear them after she is married."[30] The "lovely students" reportedly responded to the sanction with "downcast faces," "gloom," and "indignation." A

Radcliffe senior proposed to "get even" by punishing stage audiences with a stale performance of femininity: "We'll quit giving the plays and serve pink teas in their stead." That return to an antiquated representation of ultrafeminine girlhood, the student predicted, would solve the ban by "making the college unpopular, as it ought to be."[31]

By 1914, the denigration of cross-dressing had taken root in the slang used in women's colleges, with juniors at Vassar recording in their official memorabilia handbook that "life jests of girls in trousers and men in lacey frills."[32] Three years later, when Congress passed the 1917 Immigration Act, the list of undesirable aliens included "persons of constitutional psychopathic inferiority, persons guilty of moral turpitude, persons with a history of insanity, and persons deemed likely to become a public charge," which historian Clare Sears insightfully observes came to target "people engaging in cross-dressing practices" in their day-to-day.[33]

In short, early twentieth-century debates on public displays of cross-dressed women became a lightning rod for tackling anxieties regarding an increased fluidity of sexual and gender roles, as well as a paradoxical avatar for female possibility and perversion, outspokenness and marginality. Fear of a spike in women's public autonomy fueled the widespread embrace of essentialist polarizations, which in its turn birthed the institutional policing of both female attire and same-sex attachments. Romantic love between women had been a staple of nineteenth-century genteel culture in great part because its supposed domestic, self-contained, and asexual tenor did not threaten established gendered hierarchies of space, place, and power, divisions that had long enabled a heterosexist patriarchy to thrive. For young women to openly favor men's clothes at a time when suffragists made bids for women's civil rights destabilized those lines, as much as did women expressing sexual desire, refusing matrimony and childbearing, campaigning for reproductive rights, deploring feminine fashion and demureness, taking up historically male jobs, or manifesting their attraction to other women in public venues.

Turn-of-the-century developments in sexology and psychiatry therefore brought an end to "the age of innocence" defined by "the denial of female sexuality."[34] Noting this shift in popular awareness is cardinal to debunking the myth that, until the late 1920s, most US film audiences remained clueless of associations between cross-dressing and female queerness because these circulated only within a gated scientific community. Legislation and newspapers brought more general attention to cross-dressing as a transgressive practice with homoerotic/homosexual connotations, and they did it almost three decades earlier than pinpointed by Horak.

This is a significant historiographical reframing, because it changes our contextual understanding of early female film audiences. By 1915, female deviance, gender-crossing, and criminality had become enmeshed in US popular imagination due to local- and regional-distribution dailies. Retellings of women passing as men had been making headlines since the mid-nineteenth century, coinciding with the issuing of dozens of municipal ordinances criminalizing cross-dressing as a misdemeanor, often filed under public indecency and obscenity charges.[35] Discussions on cross-dressing intersecting with felony crime and mental illness, however, only received mass attention at the turn of the twentieth century. Lisa Duggan's study of the press coverage surrounding the 1892 murder of seventeen-year-old Freda Ward by her estranged lover, nineteen-year-old Alice Mitchell, mounts a convincing case for situating the years between the early 1890s and the late 1900s as a moment of radical transition in US culture.[36] The two decades not only laid the groundwork for the women's rights movement, but also saw the nascent field of sexology begin to marginalize women who challenged the heteronormative (i.e., heterosexual, male-breadwinning) household by presenting them as dangerous, unnatural, and unbalanced. Such alteration in the cultural narrative of gender-defiant womanhood immediately affected how the popular press reported on male-clad women.

While most mid-nineteenth-century papers framed stories of working women who cross-dressed in terms of their trying to get ahead in a man's world or playing at fancy dressing, by the early twentieth century the emphasis had shifted to sexual perversion and delinquency. In 1907, a Minnesota paper pondered the "curious mania . . . that impels women to masquerade as men [by] dress[ing] in men's clothing." The news piece pathologized female gender-crossing through the use of clinical language ("widespread epidemic") and links to criminal activity—it usually fell to police to uncloak these women's deception after apprehending them for public intoxication, gambling, loitering, and stealing. Increasingly, seduction of hapless girls also became part of the charges brought against cross-dressed women.[37] For instance, in 1910, the *Evening Statesman* published the syndicated tale of nineteen-year-old Marian Hamilton Gray, who was arrested while walking around New York City's streets "wearing a frock suit of good materials, a man's gray felt hat, glasses, spats, and a man's street gloves." The article goes on to explain that Gray's unusual attire attracted "a wealthy woman of

Newark Valley, New York, who had wanted to marry" the adolescent male impersonator. Once the woman discovered Gray's "ruse," the girl was thrown in jail.[38] This goes to show that the criminalization of female cross-dressing rapidly became coupled with the trespass of homosexuality.

In another sign of changing times, a good number of girls involved in cross-dressed scandals (both as victims and perpetrators) began to be presented as white, low- to middle-class, in their teens and early twenties. The insistent focus on their station and youth gestures to a novel understanding of female development that rekindled anxieties regarding the monitoring of reproductive womanhood. One of the most publicized cases of unlawful male impersonation was that of Nell Pickerell, "a husky woman ... dressing always in men's clothes," who went by the name Harry Allen. According to the papers, Allen wreaked havoc across the country, seducing a slew of presumably unknowing young ladies. Allen's same-sex affairs, misdemeanors, and gender-crossing adorned newspapers from 1900 to 1922, the time of their death. By mid-decade, however, the press began framing Allen's eventful life story as the proverbial cautionary tale against gender-nonconforming women. Timing suggests that an uptick in social anxieties surrounding female deviance warranted Allen suddenly becoming the face of a nationwide moral panic.

Clarions of moral outrage, newspapers leveraged Allen's colorful life story and criminal record to paint cross-dressing women as pernicious predators, luring naïve girls to addiction, debauchery, and even death.[39] The toxicity emanating from these passing men was best illustrated by the body count left in Allen's wake. By 1912, headlines reported, "three girls had killed themselves for love of [Allen]." The latest victim of their duplicitous charms was "a young girl of Seattle, who fell in love with the Amazon and, when it discovered that Harry Allen was none other than the notorious Nell Pickerell, committed suicide. Two others are said to have followed in her footsteps," choosing suicide over the dishonor of having been unwittingly courted by a "strange man woman" (figure 19).[40]

Though likely edited, quotations from suicide letters lent legitimacy to the implied ties between female cross-dressing, deviance, and disgrace. Upon discovering Allen's biological identity, waitress Dolly Quappe presumably wrote, "I love you, Harry, even though you have been to me a living lie," thereupon promptly "shooting herself to death;" Hazel Waters, having "felt the lure of the girl's false personality, in her delirium of madness drank a liquid that ended forever the disappointment that

Fighter, Bootlegger and "Bad Man" is Miss Pickrell For Love of Whom Three Women Have Killed Themselves

She Wears Men's Clothing and Is Equally at Home in a Saloon Brawl or Fist Fight— She Has Never Failed to Hold Her Own With the Toughest Men in Pacific Northwest.

SPOKANE, April 6.—A strange woman is Nell Pickrell. For love of her three girls have killed themselves. She has lived the life of a "bad man," dressing always in men's clothes, holding up her end with the toughest, whether it was in a barroom or a fist fight behind a dance hall. She has occupied a cell in most of the jails in the Pacific Northwest and seems to enjoy the reputation of being "a bad man."

Nell is a husky woman. On several occasions "Harry Allen," the name under which she has been known the greater part of the time, has exhibited a decidedly pugilistic nature. Fisticuffs is hardly the term to describe the straight arm jabs and waterfront swings the versatile Miss Pickrell cuts loose when aroused.

NELL PICKRELL IN COWBOY OUTFIT, WHICH SHE WEARS A GREAT DEAL.

Two other girls are said to have followed in her footsteps.

FIGURE 19. The gender deviant: Harry Allen/Nell Pickrell breaking hearts and breaking laws.

filled her life." In spite of Allen's repeated brushes with the law, news coverage emphasized that the male impersonator's most injurious, unnatural trait was his "clever [ability] in the art of love making" to "womanly women," which consequently doomed them to tragedy. Though Allen eventually faced charges of fraud, public fighting, and vagrancy, the corruption of seemingly heteronormative maidens became the "she man's" main crime in the court of public opinion.[41]

By conflating the male impersonator, the criminal, and the female invert in one recognizable figure of inherent perversion—her intimacy so poisonous to proper young ladies it could only be reversed by suicide— early twentieth-century newspapers and municipal ordinances stigmatized female cross-dressing and desire between women in one fell swoop. The marriage of legal and press discourse was so powerful because it "did not simply *police* normative gender by enforcing preexisting standards and beliefs, but actively *produced* them by creating new definitions of normality and abnormality and new restrictions on participations in public life."[42] In other words, newspapers made accessible to a large lay audience jargon-laden theories of binary gender and sexual identification, resultantly enabling the mass naturalization of essentialist preconceptions on normalcy and aberration. Journalists, legislators, and conservative reformers all aimed to undermine female agency by presenting female nonnormativity as inseparable from pain and impossibility. Regulatory at heart, sensational press accounts assigned death, derangement, imprisonment, and ostracization to most girls who dared to breach heteronormative models, by passing as a man, lusting after other women, or both.

In that disciplinary endeavor, tabloids were not alone. Though some sexologists did not regard cross-dressing as intrinsically destructive—it was a symptom, not a cause, of a larger dysfunction—associations with criminality did not take long to pervade the field. By 1897, Havelock Ellis alerted that, in addition to signaling homosexuality, the compulsion to cross-dress abetted dangerous tendencies in women: "A remarkably large proportion of the cases in which homosexuality has led to crimes of violence . . . has been among women." According to Ellis, because "inverted women retain their feminine emotionality combined with some degree of infantile impulsiveness and masculine energy, they present a favorable soil for the seeds of passional crime."[43] Murder-suicide incidents purportedly soared in female "intimate friendships" where one of the young women showed signs of inversion by dressing in men's clothes. Duggan's research on late nineteenth-century "lesbian love murders" attests that US papers prospered on the dissemination of grossly sensationalized reports of female intimate relationships becoming hotbeds for crime and sexual morbidity, much of their language culled from sexology studies.

Accounting for the emphasis newspapers placed on female cross-dressing is paramount to an adequate historicization of early female film reception for two reasons: First, such an accounting substantiates George Chauncey's postulation that "the medical discourse did not 'invent' the homosexual, . . . [but rather] doctors reproduced the categories and prejudices of their cultures," which gestures to a much more fluid flow of influence between popular and medical culture than often credited by silent film historians.[44] Second, though turn-of-the-century clinical debate and subsequent scholarship on early queer history tends to focus on gay male subcultures, reading newspaper coverage of female cross-dressing alongside girl fans' collages of actresses in drag evinces the emergence of a queer female sensibility pervading both published celebrity discourse and personal fan reception.

Put simply, the work of turn-of-the-century sex specialists "produced a recognizable image of the 'female sexual invert' that could be used by the legal profession as well as the police": be they college administrators at Radcliffe or law enforcement in major US cities.[45] Dailies distributed such pathologized images far and wide, familiarizing their readers with the nefarious stereotype of the cross-dressing, woman-loving, lawbreaking "Amazon."

As painted by tabloids and sexologists, the female invert made herself known through a warped adoption of male-coded conduct, apparel, and appetites. Those same visual clues commuted to moving pictures starring tomboys and heroines in menswear, though same-sex desire was either pushed to a narrative subtext or thoroughly erased. Comedy and ephemerality further dehumanized the practice, rendering cross-dressing a temporary ruse or hetero-romantic high-jinx, not a meaningful identarian expression. The felicitous rags-to-riches metamorphosis common in sentimental literature also replaced crime reports' gloomy endings: on the screen, girls in boys' clothes reconciled their biological sex with social gender via heterosexual monogamy, a passage made visible through her shedding of masculine/androgynous garb for traditional feminine dress and behavior.

CROSS-DRESSING GOES TO HOLLYWOOD:
SCREEN ACTRESSES IN MENSWEAR

Stars' clothing held a vital storytelling function during the 1910s; as Jane Gaines remarks, costume design always participated in Hollywood's "telling" of women's narratives. "Fitted to characters as a second skin," screen fashion primarily worked "by relaying information to the viewer about" a character's "personality," that is, a singular medley of interiority and social standing.[46] Silent cinema, in particular, cultivated "a tendency toward metaphorical literalization of costume design," where to play a part meant to dress like the part.[47] As a result, apparel donned by stars in any public setting could never be rid of meaning. The very mechanism that produced picture personalities demanded their meaning to be constantly actualized across multiple commercial platforms: from the silver screen to lobby displays, press interviews, promotional ephemera, sponsored goods, and public appearances.

A female star wearing men's raiment onscreen or in a backstage shot thus could not exist without "telling a story." Though responses to such sartorial prompt could be diverse—and some film reviewers interpreted convincingly playing male parts as vouching for an actress's versatility—girl stars in drag were not univocally seen as neutered. In fact, a sizable portion of press coverage discussing movie actresses in "mannish" suits or "boyish riding-togs" emanated an ongoing, barely concealed discomfort.[48]

Again and again, trade and fan publications undercut the homoerotic and masculine appeal of a young actress costumed in man's clothes. For instance, a girl star like Ann Murdock may have appeared "adorably" in a "ultra-mannish hat of silk beaver, masculine plaited-bosom shirt, and black silk tie," but she remained "the most adorably helpless-looking bit of femininity you could find."[49] The same rhetoric pervades a piece praising famous male impersonator Kathleen Clifford's "boyishly slim figure in the dark, well-tailored habit with the checked cap and boots." Despite conceding that Clifford passed for a "handsome, boyish . . . son of the nobility," the journalist quickly asserted that "as a girl she's a heart-smasher!"—hence implying that a female-born performer's sexual allure was contingent on gender conformity.[50] Onscreen, most female experimentations with cross-dressing and gender-bending were reversible, so no permanent punishment was enforced: no death, no institutionalization, required.

Narrative cinema may have sanitized the newspaper image of the fiendish "she-man," but cross-dressing remained a loaded practice in popular imagination, a legible index of female homosexuality and criminality if left open-ended. Proof of this anxiety can be found in the strenuous efforts press agents and film journalists put into reassuring spectators that actresses who played androgynous/male protagonists onscreen were nothing but "utterly feminine" in their day-to-day. Columnists often commended cross-dressed actresses' short hair and dapper figure, while immediately disallowing any possibility that they might find rewarding self-expression in masculine fashion. First-person quotes supported this press discourse. In 1918, actress Seena Owen assured audiences that, in spite of her "stunning outfit"—a tuxedo made of "French gray broadcloth, with collar, cuffs, belt and straps of black patent leather"—in the end she "didn't like this half so much as the habit [she] wore in *Madam Bo-Peep*." "I am particularly fond of the sort of clothes I wore in that photoplay," Owens confessed.[51] The "sort of clothes" the twenty-three-year old referred to were the simple prairie dresses—feminine in cut and matched by long fallen hair—that had garnered Mary Pickford the title of "America's Sweetheart." The phenomenon of female players voicing their dislike of acting in male clothing is particularly relevant if we keep in mind that, by the mid-1910s, audiences knew that "moving picture actresses [were] obliged to supply their own clothes, except for costume plays, in which the company supplied costumes."[52] In other words, if not publicly disavowed as professional obligation, fans could easily assume the male wardrobe actresses wore onscreen was their own.

Movie magazines' dogged distancing of actresses in drag from any "mannish" interests is a telling sign that, by the mid-1910s, cross-dressing could be easily interpreted as code for gender/sexual deviancy if left unexplained. The risk of associating men's fashion with latent lesbianism further undermined the possibility of bespoke riding-habits and suits truly satisfying the actresses who wore them. By the early twentieth century, Lillian Faderman notes, "Lesbianism and masculinity became so closely tied in [US] public imagination that it was believed that only a masculine woman could be the genuine article."[53] That the film press found it necessary to aggressively assert the offscreen heteronormativity of cross-dressed actresses implies a tacit recognition that women in menswear could be too readily read as something else, something untoward and unbecoming. The urgency with which both journalists and players stressed distinctions between an actress's gender-nonconforming film characterization and her everyday feminine self is searing testimony to the cultural discomfort with female masculinity and cross-dressing, fictitious or otherwise. Such glaring division between "real" and "reel" life is especially revealing at a time when the star system labored to elide gaps between a player's on-camera persona and their off-screen identity.[54]

Scholars like Horak contend that the theater—where cross-dressing and gender-swapping were long-revered traditions—taught early film audiences to regard female cross-dressing as an unthreatening practice. Actually, fear that women in drag unmoored a monolithic view of heteronormativity ran so deep in the 1910s that an actress in men's clothes caused a ripple of concern even when taking place on the legitimate stage. Such discomfort shone through the amount of press dedicated to legitimizing the inclusion of male cross-dressing in plays led by famed young actresses. When Arturo Pinero's *The Amazons,* an 1893 play about three girls raised as boys, got a Broadway revival in 1913, much of the periodical coverage dwelled on how the young star, Billie Burke, would negotiate "her first appearance on any stage in boy's clothes."[55] The act is repeatedly acknowledged as distasteful and difficult, a challenge to the star's "natural" femininity. When the *San Francisco Dramatic Review* inquired "how she liked to wear—well, 'those things,'" Burke confessed to feeling "quite distressed" at first, discreetly confirming her dislike of male drag. The twenty-something-year-old ends up having "lots of fun" on stage, but she reiterates that such outcome was "more because the play is so cute [that] . . . wearing knickers makes no particular difference."[56] The play succeeds, then, because the "cute" wholesomeness of its script and leading lady offset the potential tawdriness of male drag. This hypervigilance surrounding women wearing menswear in the public sphere—being that on the stage, the screen, or the streets—exposes a cultural unease with gender-nonconforming femininity and confirms its salient sensitivity in collective imagination.

In her study of queer prohibitions in turn-of-the-century San Francisco, Sears discovers that, paradoxically, an upsurge in municipal criminalization of public cross-dressing coincided with a swell in cultural appreciation for vaudevillian gender inversion: while female and male impersonators rose to stardom, ordinary gender-crossing people descended into the gallows. Behind such double standard lay the idea that, under the footlights, "gender crossings [were] magical illusions" performed by skilled prestidigitators. However, "for the frame of illusion to hold, female and male impersonators had to emphasize their gender normativity and sexual probity off-stage, or else their on-stage transformation would conjure up a different set of associations—not an awe-inspiring act of magic but the grotesque display of the freakish self." This judicious separation of scripted behaviors mirrors what movie actresses displayed in press interviews and public appearances throughout the 1910s. By selling male impersonation as a feat of cinematic legerdemain, female stars distanced themselves from the act in a manner that "ultimately confirmed rather than threatened the ostensibly natural and immutable gender divide."[57]

Horak theorizes that increasing social discomfort with the New Woman figure (in its many boundary-pushing iterations) spurred the film industry's managerial efforts to uncouple "mannish" performative attire from nonnormative lived identities. Though it may have been a consideration, the relentless public relations campaigns seeking to assure audiences that cross-dressing onscreen did not translate into an actress's offscreen gender and sexual expression indicate a deeper anxiety than a star being perceived as politically progressive—perhaps not a unanimously supported trait but definitely not a career-ruining foible. Stars like Pearl White, Shirley Manson, Olive Tell, and Mary Pickford, for instance, all spoke in favor of women's suffrage in the 1910s and their celebrity does not seem to have suffered much for it. The unerasable stigma of perversion seems a more plausible reason to orchestrate such a large-scale marketing operation. Without the added commentary by a star—her disavowal of anything but compliance to heteronormative femininity—cross-dressing could be taken by audiences at face value. That value seemed too rife with problematic interpretations for press agents to let it stand on its own. By itself, the fear of interpretative open-endedness connotes that press officials could not trust general audiences to be automatically unaware of queer readings conjured by movie actresses in drag.

In sum, Horak is correct in assuming that "newspapers and magazines brought lesbianism and inversion to the public eye, . . . [teaching] American readers the representational codes of lesbianism and provid[ing] a vocabulary to name it"; only the codification of such "public, accessible discourse about same-sex desire" took place between the 1890s and the late 1910s, nearly three decades earlier than Horak posits.[58] Under the stigma of criminality and deviance, early twentieth-century periodicals popularized clinical jargon and propagated a visual taxonomy of the female invert. They pathologized female same-sex desire and cross-dressing by tethering both to transgressive behavior. However, mass press exposure also "carved out critical space within these [criminal] narratives [for] . . . alternative readings." As Sears proposes, "Newspaper stories on cross-dressing offenses advertised the possibilities of doing gender differently, and some readers may have been inspired rather than repelled" by these news pieces.[59] Such self-reflexive identificatory response is what traditionalist film officials actively sought to forestall.

When put into a vaster cultural context it becomes evident that in the 1910s, female cross-dressing was a charged practice, laden with negative or, at the very least, dubious connotations. To collect and mimic images of actresses in drag in such a precarious social environment thus reveals a deliberate fan attachment, one powerful enough to override the alarmist messages publicly stitched to male impersonation. In their scrapbooks, movie-loving girls bypass the denigrating reportage on gender-crossing "Amazons," favoring the promotional stills of film actresses in drag. In dailies like Chicago's *Day Book,* news items of both kinds often shared the same page.

In fact, actresses in menswear make frequent appearances in movie-loving girls' private caches. The ambivalent, if prevalent, media coverage of female cross-dressing likely caught the attention of girl fans who scanned the movies for alternatives to conformist representations of young womanhood. The discursive and aesthetic androgyny inherent to images of actresses in masculine clothing replenished them with interpretative open-endedness. In their fetching tuxedos and jodhpurs, jockeying horses or racing behind the wheel, stars like Grace Cunard, Pearl White, and Mary Pickford could be momentarily read against the grain of presiding portrayals of compliant screen girlhood: the lovelorn ingenue, the dutiful daughter, the bride to be, the damsel in distress. Clad in symbols of masculinity that implicitly lent her power, the adolescent heroine in bespoke pants could be interpreted as a self-supporting businesswoman; with her long ringlets trapped under a cap and a whip at her hand, she could also embody sexual dominance and agency.

In the end, the ongoing public circulation of medical and legal discourses codifying the female invert introduced general audiences to a visual shorthand through which to recognize female nonnormativity. Movie-loving girls, active consumers of dailies due to their overabundance of film ephemera (e.g., novelizations of serials, star headshots, film listings, ads, reviews, etc.) would have crossed paths with illustrated crime reports itemizing the typical behavior and look of the troubling "she man." Fans also possibly noticed continuities between the "strange man woman" of sensational dailies and the boy-girl and serial queen of the screen, beloved archetypes at the time. A recognizable image of female deviance and defiance ultimately solidified in popular imagination at the same time that an operative language of filmdom emerged. Both would come to coalesce in the personal fan materials of early twentieth-century moviegoing girls.

CHAPTER 6

A Coding of Queer Delights

Gender Nonconformity in Girls' Movie
Scrapbooks

The silence of the dead is no obstacle to the exhumation of
their deepest desires.

—Benedict Anderson

Between 1914 and 1916—her fifteenth and seventeenth years—Edna
Garland Beverly Vercoe of Highland Park, Illinois (b. January 1, 1899),
crafted the "Motion Picture Pictorial," a multivolume scrapbook dedicated to her favorite picture players. Cherry-picking through a slew of
genres, the adolescent girl gathered over a dozen images of actresses in
male garb, including Norma Talmadge masquerading as a bellboy for
Vitagraph's short comedy *A Question of Clothes* (1914); Cleo Madison
in a workman's suit in Universal's *The Trey o' Hearts* (1914); Marie
Doro playing Oliver Twist in Lasky's film adaptation (1916) of Charles
Dickens's classic novel; and Grace Cunard with short hair and a three-
piece tuxedo, emulating her screen partner Francis Ford in Bison's *My
Lady Raffles* (1914), a series of short films chronicling the exploits of an
intrepid jewel thief.[1]

Across the country in Norfolk, Virginia, sixteen-year-old Katherine
(Kitty) Baker (b. February 6, 1900) engaged in a similar scavenger hunt.
In a scrapbook dated from 1916, the high schooler congregated ephemera
from local newspapers and film magazines next to handwritten captions
and snapshots of her friends.[2] Actresses in male attire once again grace the
fan's movie scrapbook. Among Baker's most striking promotional stills
are Lottie Pickford impersonating an eighteenth-century male aristocrat
in Biograph's lost short *The Prince's Portrayal* (1912) and Winifred
Greenwood, flirtatious in top hat and tails, in an unidentified film.[3]

These are only two examples of the many images girls collected of movie actresses in menswear during the 1910s. The pervasiveness of these clippings implies that a desire to play with gender conventions—already visible in male-voiced fan poems—spread to other forms of early female film reception. Experimentation with gender masquerade and feminine masculinity perfuses girls' fan artifacts, making appearances in handmade collages, in marginalia penned around star pictures, and in Kodaks movie-loving girls took of themselves wearing men's clothing.

That female cross-dressing—as an aesthetic motif, an embodied practice, and a narrative device—permeates girls' reception materials should not come as a surprise: "Cross-dressed women were a crucial part of American cinema" throughout the silent period, after all.[4] Defining what constitutes cross-dressing, in itself a performance on fluidity and polymorphism, nonetheless can be challenging. When analyzing fan materials, I apply the term to three types of images: production stills of female stars outfitted in menswear for a part (masculinity worn as a momentary disguise); published photos of actresses sporting male-coded items (such as ties, trousers, top hats, and tuxedoes) offscreen; and personal snapshots of girl fans donning similar apparel in everyday life. I pay close attention to actresses known for their girlish personas, whose cross-dressed images may include a caption highlighting their nonconforming fashion choices.

The presence of male drag in fan collections does not automatically signify homosexual investment. A recurrent gravitation towards female masculinity, however, does suggest a recognition of gender as play, as performance, to paraphrase Jack Halberstam. Masculinity is used as an ideogram and a lodestar in girls' scrapbooks, as on actresses' bodies. As a constructed cluster of symbols transited through legislation, social behavior, and biological essentialism, "masculinity conjures up notions of [white] power and legitimacy and privilege [that] extend outward into patriarchy and inward into the family; masculinity represents the power of inheritance, the consequences of the traffic in women, and the promise of social privilege"—all matters shaping girls' understanding of their place in US society, since that place was generally defined in opposition (and deference) to masculinity and manhood.[5] To borrow masculinity as a lens—no matter how briefly or makeshift—was thus to borrow power.

Like male-voiced poems to screen actresses, cross-dressed collages indicate that some female moviegoers derived pleasure from performances of girlhood divergent from the "curls and sunshine ingénues" populating US cinema during the 1910s.[6] These scrapbookers drifted to the in-between, the fraught potentialities signified by witnessing a known female player pass for a man in a film narrative and its adjunctive promotional ephemera. Such fictional passing was nurtured in freedom and physical ability—to fight, to escape, to seduce. Beyond questions of individual sexual proclivities, a prevalent fan interest in cross-dressed actresses complicates the theory that, in silent US cinema, temporary male drag succeeded in creating an "erotic female spectacle in service to a masculinized gaze."[7] Film manufacturers may have intended the intimacy between two female players—one dressed as a man, the other in feminine garb—to titillate a universal male spectator with the specter of lesbianism, but personal movie scrapbooks suggest that some female viewers latched on to those homoerotic images as evocative representation.

As discussed in previous chapters, figures of speech and visual clues exchanged between literate young women telegraphed a rich network of unspoken desire, eroticized devotion, and clandestine complicity. Apparel, and cross-dressing in particular, becomes another useful entryway to map early queer fan reception. Because clothing is deeply linked with social performances of gender, sexuality, and belonging, intentional attempts to move against the grain—to favor actresses in menswear, to clothe oneself in suits—connotes a deliberate act of divergence. It is well known that queer people have historically communicated their identities through fashion. Discussing cross-dressed heroines in US silent cinema, Laura Horak observes that "the reference to real-life lesbians via clothing, hairstyle, and posture was precisely the sort of code that could be picked up only by the 'wise.'"[8] On an actress's body, a tuxedo or a cigarette could signify nonnormativity to a kindred eye.

The recurrence of scrapbooked images depicting cross-dressed stars points to a number of adolescent moviegoers transferring these decoding strategies to their reception practices. Film stardom in the 1910s celebrated hyperfemininity. Newspapermen and directors declared that blonde or brunette, virginal or sensual, "All-American" or "exotic," "girlishness and youth [were] essential to the success of the moving picture actress."[9] Ephemera of actresses in menswear were not unavailable in the mid- to late 1910s, but they were certainly harder to find, being seldom used as stars' headshots or included in industry giveaways. Images of female masculinity must therefore have mattered to girls willing to wade through hundreds of moving pictures and print sources in search of these irregular representations.

By picking such occasional images from a deluge of stock photos presenting actresses as ringleted waifs and fashionable beauties, female fans also circumvented the conservative messages furthered by the "temporary transvestitism" narrative popularized on stage and screen, where a heroine shed masculine traits once settled into heterosexual romance.[10] In spite of their normative resolution, for a period of time cross-dressing screen heroines refused to embody hegemonic femininity. While passing as men, they experienced social activities denied to any respectable young lady had she appeared legible as such, including public smoking, drinking, gambling, traipsing through foreign lands, chasing criminals, and courting men and women. As seen in the pictures, adolescent cross-dressing thus provided a moratorium on the gendered constrictions imposed on female spectators coming of age during World War I.

Engaged as "intertext," the photo of a passing actress could also facilitate durable queer readings the film narrative evaded: not only did picture-going constitute a fleeting experience, but the redolent on-screen image of the cross-dressed heroine was always fated to vanish, to be replaced by heterosexual love and gender conformity. By preserving images of actresses in men's fashion, girl fans refused the ephemerality of the cross-dressing act as portrayed in cinematic time. Retained in paper, glue, ink, and memory, the male-clad heroine lived on forever inside the fan's scrapbook, her nonnormativity not a phase but a permanent identity marker. From this perspective the cross-dressed promotional still functions as an intertextual beacon for queer female audiences.[11] In fans' hands, gender disguise and its invitations to fantasy, transgression, and fluidity did not disappear but adhered to the page. Signposts of queer spectatorial self-fashionings facilitated by a rising star system, these cropped pieces of personalized ephemera continue to endure.

By preserving ephemera of film actresses in menswear, white schoolgirls left for posteriority a recorded affinity for gender play. On its own, a clipping of a minor actress gender-crossing may not seem significant, but that image accumulates queer density once it is stored in a movie scrapbook kept by a girl (Baker) who self-presented as a tomboy, identified as a suffragette, and documented herself kissing another girl; or once it is pasted next to other cross-dressed images by a high schooler who used male aliases and grew up never to marry or bear children (Vercoe). In short, hunting and gathering images of cross-dressed stars—images that often diverged from an actress's commercial picture personality and thus were less readily available in print sources—reflects intentional fan engagement. Read alongside biographical data, personal collages of cross-dressing screen actresses lend access to an unexplored history of queer fan investments that took kaleidoscopic shape: a distinct disinterest in motherhood and marriage, a proclivity for athletics, adventure and same-sex attraction, or a distaste for early twentieth-century ladies' fashion with its implied frivolousness and subservience. Rather than attempting to "reclaim" early twentieth-century moviegoers who favored cross-dressing as "proto-lesbians," I follow Horak's suggestion that these audience members belong "to a wide-ranging genealogy of gender non-conforming people," a significant but often overlooked constituency in LGBTQ+ history.[12]

" 'TWIXT JOSEPHINE AND JOE": THE QUEER PLEASURES OF THE "BOY-GIRL" FILM TYPE

By 1917, the practice of costuming a young beauty in male attire was so popular in US cinema that a *Photoplay* critic bemoaned: "Clothe the average actress in a suit of men's or boys' garments and one of two things invariably happens: she becomes a giggling, simpering ninny, or she becomes a struggling, brazen hussy."[13] Still, three years later, the profitability of the boy-girl showed no signs of waning: trade writers encouraged film exhibitors to keep "playing up the boy-girl . . . , backing it up with as liberal a display of stills and lithographs as you can command."[14]

Unlike the "female boy," a gender-crossing screen figure Horak describes as a fantasy of asexual boyhood played by female "performers between the ages of seven and twelve," the "boy-girl," as defined by journalists and screenwriters, was a female protagonist *in her teens,* whose distinct coming-of-age narrative revolved around a temporary gender masquerade.[15] In most cases, the adolescent heroine assumed a boy's identity to eke out a living or elude trouble.[16] Occasionally, she cross-dressed to escape seclusion and boredom (as at a repressive boarding school or in a restrictive household), and briefly indulge in a life of public amusements prohibited to proper young ladies.[17] Whatever her circumstances, by the last reel the boy-girl's ruse was unwittingly discovered or willingly abandoned and replaced by heterosexual coupling.

While the childish "female boy" faded during World War I, the teenage boy-girl flourished. The sheer number of productions with boy-girl leads places their apex of popularity between 1916 and 1918. The over-reliance on illustrated promotional materials mentioned above reveals that film impresarios knew audiences' interest in the boy-girl figure stemmed from her specific look. Though a few pundits deemed the boy-girl hokey and passé, moviegoers enjoyed the ambiguity of seeing a known actress cloaked in menswear. Some of those moviegoers were girls in their teens who combed the press for publicity "stills and lithographs" featuring the film type. Perhaps not surprisingly, the pleasures girl fans derived from contemplating cross-dressed actresses were more expansive than those imagined by newspapermen. For female viewers drawn to gender variance, the character of the boy-girl radiated exciting possibility. On the screen, she embodied a positive blend of characteristics linked with gender difference: male-coded strength and fearlessness coexisted with female-coded vulnerability and cunning. In a sea of ingenues and vamps—screen types generally defined by opposite modes of sexual experience—the nonbinary boy-girl proffered a benign ambivalence rarely found in commercial cinema but desired by many female moviegoers, especially those on the edge of adulthood.

Columnists described the boy-girl as "'twixt Josephine and Joe," a play on words that apprehends the key interstitiality of the film type.[18] Her gendered hybridism is shared with an earlier, equally beloved performance of female development: the tomboy. A marked difference between the tomboy and the boy-girl of early narrative cinema is that the latter was not bound by "spindly-legged, gawky kidhood."[19] Traditional tomboy narratives demanded that heroines outgrew their love of androgynous clothing and rough-and-tumble activities once their sexual awakening took hold. In Halberstam's words, "As soon as puberty begins, the full force of gender conformity descends on the girl. . . . Tomboyism is punished when it appears to be an extreme male identification (taking a boy's name or refusing girl clothing of any type) and when it threatens to extend beyond childhood and into adolescence."[20] The boy-girl, on the contrary, wore shapeless overalls and suits, frolicked, flirted, and chased rowdies in her late teens and well into her twenties. Zestfully inhabiting the limbo "'twixt Josephine and Joe," the boy-girl allowed affinities with masculinity, homoeroticism, and gender nonconformity to stretch beyond the bounds of female pubescence. That allowance conferred a certain legitimization to public performances of nonnormative female identity, affording uncoupled, gender-complicated, asexual, and/or nonheterosexual adolescent moviegoers a glimpse into alternative models of a gratifying adulthood that celebrated their "tomboyish instincts."[21]

A central feature of the boy-girl's narrative is the momentary refusal of ladylikeness, matrimony, and domesticity as the be-all and end-all of female identity. Though still upholding gender determinism through a binary dress code, the boy-girl's nonbinary gender performance could be acknowledged by film reviewers: "The boy-girl who plays boy [on screen] *is boy* . . . until she flashes back to skirts and tripled charm."[22]

This visual malleability, limited as it may have been, resonated with young fans who did not relate to or did not wish to grow into normative womanhood.

Reception of the boy-girl thus sets forward a case of localized fan response subverting industry expectations. Most movies depicting cross-dressed women did not aim to complicate governing models of gender, romance, or sociability—in fact, they frequently "worked to support white supremacist [and] heterosexual American national mythology," Horak notes. Yet for some female moviegoers, witnessing the mediated act of cross-dressing "offered a temporary freedom from the burdens of middle-class femininity" that overrode intended industry lessons on female submission and heteronormative compliance.[23] Individual fan records of female cross-dressing indicate that, for a number of adolescent girls, the movies provided a template for "temporary freedoms," catalyzing nonnormative spectatorial identifications that translated into lived behaviors.

Female cross-dressing and gender-nonconforming behavior might have been treated as garnish in most features and popular serials—including *The Trey o' Hearts* (1914), *The Master Key* (1914), and *The Perils of Pauline* (1914), and *The Hazards of Helen* (1914–17)—but for some girl fans these functioned as identarian indexes of aspiration and futurity. Take Miss Mary Florence Stott, a sophomore at Portsmouth High School, New Hampshire. Circa September 1917, the sixteen-year-old pasted a clipping of Mary Pickford on her self-titled "Movie Book." The image is from Paramount's *Poor Little Peppina* (1916), one of the first features where Pickford cross-dressed for a large portion of the narrative.[24] In *Peppina,* Pickford plays a runaway Italian girl who disguises herself as a street-smart messenger boy to elude an undesired match and earn a living in America. The role of the struggling immigrant who finds wealth possibly appealed to Stott, whose parents had immigrated from Ireland and whose livelihood depended on a small grocery store her father managed in town. Stott may have also felt an affinity for Peppina, since in the 1910s US nativist policies targeted Italian, Irish, and other non-Anglo-Saxon/non-Protestant Europeans as undesirable immigrants.[25] To see a young foreign-born protagonist succeed in the New World through her own means and ingenuity likely spoke to a working-class schoolgirl with middle-class aspirations (figure 20).

Stott was born on Valentine's Day 1901, the daughter of Washington Stott, a forty-five-year-old grocer, and Florence N. Mitchell Stott, a forty-year-old former widow. Named after her mother, Stott was the second offspring of the mature couple. Having survived the deaths of a

FIGURE 20. In ladylike company: Mary Pickford cross-dressing as Peppina in Mary Florence Stott's "Movie Book," 1917.

young husband and all three of her infant children, Mrs. Stott doted on her daughter. Born into a working-class family with a half-sister fifteen years her senior, Stott grew up with all the privileges of an only child, spending vacations away with her parents, going on shopping trips, and attending the pictures. The movie lover dreamed of traveling and seeing the world, so the complete absence of romantic pairings from her "Movie Book" is somewhat telling: the high-schooler prized female role models, style, and freedom over cinematic renditions of heteronormative romance. Repetition of sources suggests Stott preferred the Gish sisters, Anita Stewart, and Marguerite Clark, followed by serial queens Grace Cunard, Lillian Walker, and Pearl White.

It is also meaningful that in a sixty-two-page composition book crammed with studio portraits of film ingenues—looking their most feminine selves in soft curls, bashful smiles, and gossamer dresses—Stott highlighted a full-body clipping of Pickford as male-clad Peppina. Carefully scissored to encase only her figure, the shot portrays the actress in disheveled menswear, with capped curls and sneering face, traits departing from her trademark "soft, immature" feminine image.[26] In addition to atypical male clothing and sour expression, Pickford is seen in the act of stealing, hands and pockets overflowing with purloined fruit. Including this outlier image adjacent to Lillian Gish and Pearl White reads as deliberate evidence of the moviegoer's preference for strong female leads. However, despite sharing a page, Pickford's androgynous figure towers over Gish's and White's refined headshots. Such a visual choice implies that Stott found greater resonance in Peppina's gender nonconformity, poignantly on display in this promotional shot.

Kristen Hatch argues that perennial film juveniles like Pickford "helped to identify girls' rebelliousness with immature masculinity," while assuring audiences that such brash behaviors would in time "be exchanged by feminine decorum."[27] Though that may have been its intent, the reception of the boy-girl archetype propounds that some girls did not see it as a model of tradition. For moviegoers like Stott, the boy-girl conferred an avenue for female mobility and self-made independence. On the screen, the character introduced cross-dressing as a temporary tool that allowed girls from the underclass to experience pleasures (e.g., unchaperoned travel, ribaldry, nightlife) barred to them due to their assigned gender and station, and to do so without compromising their reputation. More importantly, Stott's singling out of the Italian Peppina demonstrates the impact diverse film representation had on minority audiences at a time when right-wing US pundits maligned working-class immigrants. Stott, like Peppina, would grow up to settle into respectable heteronormativity. Sometime in 1920, the nineteen-year-old moviegoer would marry Phillip Edward Marvin, an eminent Portsmouth resident, and produce at least one heir, Alexander. But as with Peppina, Stott's embrace of a well-off status quo came with self-awareness, the recognition of an inherent difference. Like Pickford's boy-girl, Stott parlayed heterosexual marriage and femininity as a stepping stone, enabling her transition from foreign-born worker to assimilated society lady. Finally able to concretize her adolescent wanderlust, Mrs. Marvin's travels often adorned the pages of her local paper.

If the boy-girl validated some fans' adolescent escapism and ambition, for others the androgynous film type tapped "inchoate and as yet inarticulable" homoerotic desires, providing an indirect means of enhanced self-acceptance through which young movie lovers could experiment with dissident models of female identity.[28] With sources dating as far back as 1911, Kitty Baker constructed a scrapbook that chronicles her middle-class adolescence in a waterfront city in southeastern Virginia. Assembled in a blank bound book manually titled "Norfolk Virginia 1916," Baker's hundred-plus-page scrapbook acts as a mixed and remediated media archive, a reception history pulsing with juvenile affect.

Cobbling together local news, candy wrappers, and school records, the gigantic scrapbook works primarily as a film archive, juxtaposing star headshots with snapshots of Baker and her coed peers. Handwritten questionnaires circulated among thirteen of Baker's moviegoing friends throughout 1916 contain personal data, such as addresses, birthdates, and preferred colors, players, and pastimes. Focused on the 1910s, the scrapbook also incorporates sources from later decades, often as counterpoint. For example, a picture of Charles Ray dated from 1914 is pasted next to a newspaper clipping from 1943 announcing that the "silent-screen star who wrung tears from early movie audiences with his portrayals of a bashful country bumpkin . . . [is] sick." Constitutionally queer, Baker's scrapbook is both immediate and retroactive, its temporality bent out of linearity, as some sources were created during the moviegoer's adolescence (the questionnaires, the photographs) while others were arranged in later years (the collaged juxtapositions).

In spite of its heterogeneity—including male and female performers, comedians and tragediennes, stage veterans and screen newcomers—a kinship with nonnormativity pervades Baker's ephemera collection. If understood as a visual resumé, Baker's scrapbook tells the story of a fun-loving tomboy and self-identified suffragette who followed the beat of her own drum and loved cinema because of the possibilities it begot. Most of her collages showcase an attraction to difference. Like Stott, Baker avoids conventional images of screen romance, instead privileging representations of male physicality: Charlie Chaplin sneezing, yawning, or laughing, Jack W. Kerrigan pouting and brooding, a headshot of Harold Lockwood scribbled with cursive. When movie couples do pop up, they are all flesh and motion, actors locking leading ladies in a passionate embrace or "a real kiss kiss."[29] Giving center-stage to these clippings, Baker manifests her spectatorial identification with male dynamism, with its socially accepted freedom of expression, desire, and unsanctioned energy. In family photos, Baker herself seems incapable of standing still, blurring the exposure with a turning head, a roving hand, a mouth moving against another girl's. When including images of female stars, they tend to be of stage-dancer-turned-film-star Irene Castle, capturing the lithe actress mid-twirl or waving her arms in spectacular pantsuits, her whole mobile body on display.

Male drag is present, but every chosen image features cross-dressing in its most fraught iterations: an anonymous woman on a horse so convincingly dressed in masculine garb it takes zooming in on her face to ascertain her sex; Winifred Greenwood masquerading as a dandy, seductively offering her cigarette to unseen company; a still from *The Prince's Portrait* (1912) depicting Lottie Pickford as a love-struck eighteenth-century male aristocrat staring up at Mary Pickford while painting her portrait. This last image in particular divulges much about the pointed attachment driving Baker's ephemera selection. The still comes from a piece *Photoplay* ran in 1916 entitled "Mary Pickford: Herself and Her Career." Illustrated with half a dozen "rare and authentic photographs" of Pickford in glossy studio portraits, Baker chose to pluck this image, small and low-quality, from a minor production in which Pickford shares the spotlight with her lesser-known sister. [30] Why would Baker select this one photo unless the presence of the cross-dressed actress and her adoring gaze spoke to the fan? And why place the Pickford picture across from the cutout of the female horse-rider in menswear, an aesthetic choice enacting a conversational exchange, a tonal affinity between the two gender-crossing women?

Queer desire and identification coalesce in Baker's film reception then, strengthened by additional paraphernalia such as a valentine card sent by a female friend in 1919. Illustrated with a hand-painted pouting girl, the card outs Baker as a suffragette:

I am a Little Suffragette
But oh! please tell me why
The boys just take a look at me
And then they pass me by?

Playfully, the poem engages prevalent associations of suffragettes with gender nonconformity, undesirability, and homosexuality. Many turn-of-the-century sexologists explicitly enjoined that "the female possessed of masculine ideas of independence" could not be distinguished from "that disgusting anti-social being, the female sexual invert. [They] are simply different degrees of the same class—degenerates."[31] Baker proudly identified as a suffragette from twelve years of age. Her scrapbook preserves a stamp from August 1912 annotated with "in memoriam of my first suffragette parade," implying that many others were yet to come. Further indicative of a queer subtext, Baker drew two red hearts pierced together by an arrow under the valentine, intimating a romantic attachment to the girl who sent the tongue-and-cheek card.

The presentation of self Baker secured in her personal scrapbook is everywhere defined by difference and rebellion: the suffragette stamp; a failing report card from Maury High School and another for truancy; photographic self-portraits eschewing conventional femininity; and her affinity with the boy-girl's main characteristics of unpolished self-reliance, physical assertiveness, and audacious fun. She also names athletic actors Wallace Reid, Lou Tellegen, and Douglas Fairbanks and young female prodigies Gladys Hulette, Norma Talmadge, and Mae Marsh as her favorite movie stars. Often Baker conveys her identarian divergence via stark contrast with her older sister. In one Kodak, the latter sits primly on a stoop in her white dress while a rumpled Baker hikes her hands up on her hips and thrusts out her chin, mugging a pantomime of tomboyish irreverence. In another family photograph, Baker stands at a seafront with her three siblings, arms crossed over chest, bare legs planted apart, plain clothes disheveled, a bow perched messily over her windswept face. The high schooler looks defiant, mouth caught midsentence, once again a striking contrast to her sister's polite smile, long lacy dress, folded hands, and tidy hair. While her sister performs the idealized model of ladylike white girlhood, Baker is flanked by her two brothers, visually aligning herself with tousled boyhood (figure 21). The aesthetic parallels between the cinematic boy-girl and the fan's everyday appearance insinuate spectatorial identification. That Baker states in her handwritten questionnaire that she prefers activities like "surf, swimming, riding, and motoring" reinforces a possible spectatorial identification with a gender-nonconforming model of female adolescence such as the one proffered by daring boy-girls and serial queens.

The image of the boy-girl may also have helped moviegoers negotiate sapphic yearnings. As recognized by press reviewers, the boy-girl invited homoerotic readings by positioning a cross-dressed woman in the guise of a male suitor romancing an unsuspecting female character. A surviving example can be found in Keystone's short *The Danger Girl* (1916), where, to make her gender masquerade more convincing, "madcap" Gloria Swanson is seen smoking, drinking, and publicly caressing a demimondaine. Aware of Swanson's temporary transvestism, the audience could choose to read the sensual exchange between the two women as homoerotic. That Baker kept a clipping of what resembles this common

FIGURE 21. A tomboy that can't stand still: movie fan Kitty Baker (second from right) in 1916.

seduction scene speaks of a spectatorial gravitation toward instances where female cross-dressing overlapped with same-sex flirtation.

The fact that the Norfolk moviegoer picked images of cross-dressed heroines in the act of wooing women, and combined them with a photograph where she passionately kisses another girl on the lips, pushes spectatorial identification with gender variance into the realm of queer desire. Supporting this claim, the kissing Kodak is glued next to a published drawing of a young heterosexual couple in the throes of a tiff. The print caption reads: "I want you to forget that I told you I didn't mean what I said about not taking back my refusal to change my mind. I've been thinking it over and I've decided that I was mistaken in the first place," to which her skeptical beau replies, "Do you really mean that, Isabel?" Through collage, Baker engenders an explicit analogy between opposite- and same-sex courtship. She juxtaposes the mechanical reproduction of two girls kissing captioned "too sweet" with a commercial cartoon portraying heterosexual desire as equally excessive. The female hand draws this libidinal charge to the visible surface, the illus-

FIGURE 22. Passionate lovemaking: Kitty Baker creates a collage on female excess that draws parallels between opposite- and same-sex intimacy.

trated girl's hand fluttering toward her lover as a friend's hand arches to caress Baker's mouth. Though informed by a view of female emotionality as superlative, Baker's collage presents same-sex physical intimacy on equal footing with heterosexual romance, ultimately confirming that a queer way of feeling shaped her gaze (figure 22).

In performing a masculinity separated from male biology, the boy-girl additionally afforded some gender-nonconforming female viewers access to a perceptual genderqueer experience. Vis-à-vis the character, moviegoing girls could step into a male suitor's perspective and—from that vantage point, from under that cover—look at other women with a desirous gaze. The film scrapbook becomes one venue where these queer fan responses can be rehearsed. Manipulating star ephemera aids girl fans in creating parallel narratives where same-sex attraction and cross-dressing are arranged as central instead of peripheral, permanent instead of temporary. For Baker, the very notion of gender seems to be understood as performance, pictures of hyperfeminine stars Billie Burke and Irene Castle tacked side-by-side one of famous female impersonator Julian Eltinge. There is something resonant about paper-based film ephemera—by definition disposable, marginal, transient—being the chosen material to preserve both the queer possibilities of screen cross-dressing and the queer imaginings of individual moviegoers.

A similarly significant clipping can be found in Vercoe's "Motion Picture Pictorial": a scissored full-body still of Marguerite Clark dressed in a three-piece evening suit and bow tie. Gamine and predatory, Clark is unrecognizable from her typical girlish persona. The cropped paper scrap actually originates from a larger publicity still from Famous Players–Lasky's 1917 adaptation of Arthur Pinero's play *The Amazons* (1893). The homonymous five-reel comedy tells the story of an eccentric marchioness who, disappointed with having produced female heirs, decides to raise her three daughters as boys. Sporting masculine names and finery, the three protagonists grow up in isolation believing to have a male identity until heterosexual romance reroutes them to conventional femininity. At the time the film came out, critics raved about Clark's performance as Lord Tommy, emphasizing that in a role that "should visualize the absurdity of trying to smother femininity with masculine attire," the actress embodied manhood effortlessly and believably: "In the knickers and sweaters and tuxedoes of Lord Tommy, Marguerite Clark is as supremely unconscious of her clothes as a Hottentot is of her absence of clothes."[32] Packaged as testimony to her acting talent, accolades for Clark's gender-crossing nonetheless strained to reconnect male drag with compulsory female heterosexuality, embodied here by the racist stereotype of the oversexed "Hottentot" woman.

In fact, by the late 1910s, both general audiences and reviewers were well aware that movies starring cross-dressed heroines invited homoerotic readings. Proof is found in trade journalists preemptively decrying cross-dressed scenes redolent with same-sex desire as "vulgar." Though "Miss Clark could not be vulgar," *Moving Picture World* says of *The Amazons,* "the flirtation of the girl usher with Miss Clark dressed as a boy is a trifle low. It is not up to the Pinero scene which it represents."[33] The imputation that injecting homoeroticism in the film adaptation betrayed the spirit of Pinero's farcical play clearly aims to delegitimize and discourage queer spectatorial affordances. Instead, the scathing observation confirms the ubiquitous accessibility of such audience response.

Riddled with anxiety, film reviews chiding onscreen allusions to female queerness confirm both that actresses in drag invited homoerotic readings and that by 1917 the social, moral, and clinical urgency to police female sexual agency had reached US cinema. This rapid escalation was made obvious when, in 1914, the *Chicago Daily Tribune* advertised Norma Talmadge's screen impersonation of a boy with the following droll anecdote: while filming Vitagraph's *A Question of Clothes* "in one of New York's busy stores, . . . Miss Talmadge, perfectly made up to represent a young man, had finished her work, when in a spirit of adventure, *she started a flirtation with a young woman* who happened to have an escort nearby. Only a hasty apology and hurried explanation saved Miss Talmadge from receiving a good trouncing."[34] An off-the-clock flirtation between an eighteen-year-old actress in male drag and an unsuspecting woman is passed off as entertaining, a girlish act of good-natured mischief. Less than three years later, Clark's scripted onscreen seduction would be deemed "vulgar" and "a trifle low."

In her personal collages, Vercoe circumvents press discourse chastising or heteronormalizing Clark's gender-crossing. Employing scavenged print ephemera, the fan teases out the queer subtext permeating the actress's performance. In the original publicity still, Clark stands in the privacy of an elegant boudoir, the middle point in a triangulation between her two girl "brothers," Noel (Helen Greene) and Willie (Eleanor Lawson). Clark's body language is masculinized, looking dominant and debonair: hands in pants pockets, shoulders squared, hair trimmed and slicked back, her spine slouched and her legs spread apart in a pugilistic stance. Her intense gaze appraises Lawson, who stands stiffly to the left, hands on hips, chest puffed, eyes chagrined and turned away, as if awkwardly on display. Over her shoulder, Greene lounges on a chair dressed in a sharp tuxedo, smoking and intently regarding Lawson over Clark's shoulder. As a whole, the image throbs with same-sex desire, while simultaneously undercutting it: despite the intimate setting and charged body language, the actresses' gazes never meet. Further, within the film narrative the three appeared as sisters, a familial bond that textually foreclosed the possibility of sexual attraction (figure 23).

Vercoe's scissoring changes this official script. Excerpted from the group photo, Clark's masculinized body regains a homoerotic potential otherwise annulled by the heteronormative narrative that bracketed her—after all, by the end of the movie the three boy-girls fall in love with men and conform as much to feminine fashion as to heterosexual norms. As an independent cutout figure, however, Clark's Lord Tommy is emancipated from the tomboy-to-bride teleology; she persists in androgynous abeyance.

Of greater import, in the fan-made cutout, the addressee of Clark's sensuous glare is left unknown. Released from sisterly unresponsiveness, the image's indeterminacy blossoms with queer potentialities. Fragmented from the linear film narrative and seamlessly transformed in male clothing, Clark's fan-doctored image holds screen transvestism in permanence, while inviting onlookers to slot themselves as the recipient of such a smoldering gaze. Vercoe's deliberate selection and manipulation of this promotional image can be construed as a "queer act" in José

FIGURE 23. Queering industry scripts: publicity shot for *The Amazons* (1917) and Edna Vercoe's scissoring of Marguerite Clark in drag.

Esteban Muñoz's terminology—an act that seeks to "contest and rewrite the protocols of critical writing," or in this case, film reception.[35] By selecting a shot of a cross-dressed actress whose reputation stood on her fairy-tale beauty and repertoire, Vercoe is already going against the grain—of Clark's hyperfeminine star text as of the standard press discourse introducing screen-struck girls as dominantly heteronormative and passively consumptive. Vercoe inserted herself in both the industry protocol and the film text, actively reworking the commercial image of Lord Tommy and consequently "rewriting" (i.e., dilating, densifying, queering) its narrative, aesthetic, and identificatory potential.

Stage stars turned movie queens, like Clark, and Broadway plays adapted into feature films, like *The Amazons*, bespeak a long traffic of influence between the two mediums. Since the stage established a reputable model of female cross-dressing and gender masquerade, such creative shuttling is fundamental to queer female film reception. According to Susan Glenn, from the 1880s to the 1910s, male and female impersonators took over the American footlights. Girls, however, garnered the higher recompense in this line of work due to the widespread belief that female adolescence was a naturally plastic and imitative life-stage.[36] Those three decades also encompassed, according to Sharon Marcus, "the golden age of theatrical scrapbooks [which] coincided with the heyday of US theatre."[37] The successful proliferation of commercialized stage celebrity is rendered visible in fan scrapbooks, a reception practice adopted by female theatergoers as a means to honor favorite actresses, many of whom built stage careers on cross-dressed performances (e.g., Maude Adams, Elsie Janis, and, later in life, a reinvented Sarah Bernhardt).

The cachet theater granted female thespians who cross-dressed likely held sway over movie-loving girls' investment in gender-crossing. However, I argue that such affective response had less to do with industry officials succeeding in legitimizing filmmaking by drawing on revered stage traditions, and more to do with a cohort of girl consumers being hungry for options to traditional femininity. Fourteen-year-old Margaret Harroun of Saint Joseph, Missouri, for example, elected to include in her movie-themed "Picture Book" a full-body photograph of Billie Burke costumed as Lord Tommy for the 1913 Broadway revival of *The Amazons*.[38] Dapper and confident, short-haired Burke stands with a hand on her waist and a cane behind her back. She is clad in a fitted tuxedo, buttoned vest, striped tie, and bowler hat, a light carnation on her lapel (coincidentally, since Oscar Wilde's late-nineteenth-century trials, wearing a green carnation boutonniere telegraphed homosexuality). Reinforcing her taste for androgynous screen girlhood, Harroun added a picture of Pickford in bulky overalls, men's work boots, and untucked undershirt, an outfit she wore in James Kirkwood's *Rags* (1915).

Stars like Clark, Burke, and Pickford did not trade primarily in gender masquerades. Burke, in particular, achieved screen fame playing spirited debutantes, film publications repeatedly applauding her social-butterfly roles and her "love of shopping [for] pretty clothes." "What woman's heart wouldn't melt towards Billie, after such humanizing statement?," *Motion Picture Magazine* inquired.[39] Harroun's did not, apparently. She, like Vercoe, Stott, and Baker, decided to safekeep images that were incongruent with actresses' feminine star personas. To forage for rarified representations of movie girlhood with such diligence ultimately implies a strong fan investment in representations of female masculinity.

In fact, collages dedicated to *The Amazons* evince that girls' attachment to boy-girl protagonists refused to be hemmed in by medium, leaping across assorted iterations: stage, film, print.[40] The positive valence the theater lent to male impersonation may account for film-loving girls recurrently including images of cross-dressed stage actresses in their otherwise movie-themed scrapbooks. In the second page of her scrapbook, for example, Baker affixed a large publicity shot of Lillian Russell dressed as a sailor, her young body filled with kinetic energy as she goes about pulling ropes and paddles. A print caption discloses that the image is from the 1881 production of *Pinafore,* when Russell was only twenty and a chorus girl. What other reason would a sixteen-year-old moviegoer and discriminating scrapbooker like Baker have to collect the photo of a stage diva from thirty-five years prior—an image from when said actress was an unknown, of all things—if not for being drawn to female bodies in menswear?

A similar phenomenon can be found in Vercoe's "Motion Picture Pictorial," by name a film-only repository. A full-page headshot of a young Ethel Barrymore stands out as a curious and anomalous addition, one that the methodical movie-fan girl probably collected out of sheer mesmeric attraction. First and foremost, it is one of very few photos of a stage actor included in Vercoe's six-volume movie scrapbook. Second, like Russell's, it is a promotional headshot that predates Barrymore's dalliances with the silver screen. It is, in fact, a publicity still from Barrymore's 1903 play *Carrots,* in which the then twenty-three year-old impersonated a lovelorn male painter. Third, the headshot is scuffed and untrimmed, pulled from an unknown publication and simply stuck to the page, unlike most of Vercoe's cleanly mounted and complexly composed film collages. The page containing the image is torn from the scrapbook as if Vercoe had ripped it away in a moment of anger or uncertainty, a physical separation that enhances the image's otherness. Last, the headshot is erroneously labelled "Margaret Barrymore," which suggests the picture was not gathered because it represented a familiar and beloved performer.[41] It is fair to assume, then, that Vercoe responded to the androgynous face framed by a short unkept bob, pale flesh subtly revealed under an unbuttoned man's undershirt, and the two piercing eyes staring straight at the camera, haunting in their provocative intensity and ambiguity (figure 24).

By including a picture of a stage actress in male drag in her film repository, Vercoe, much like Harroun and Baker, showcases an attraction not just to mediated male impersonation generally, but specifically to young actresses whose gender-crossing performance diverged from their well-established picture personality. That spectatorial penchant for gender nonconformity cannot be disarticulated from girl fans like Vercoe and Baker identifying with masculinity in their daily lives, either through attire, mannerisms, pastimes, or chosen aliases. According to Vercoe's 1917 yearbook, the senior went by "'Micky,' 'Edward,' and 'Eddie'" among her peers, and at least one personal postcard shows the high schooler signing off "Edward."[42] Selecting a male nickname was unusual among Vercoe's group of female moviegoers, her close

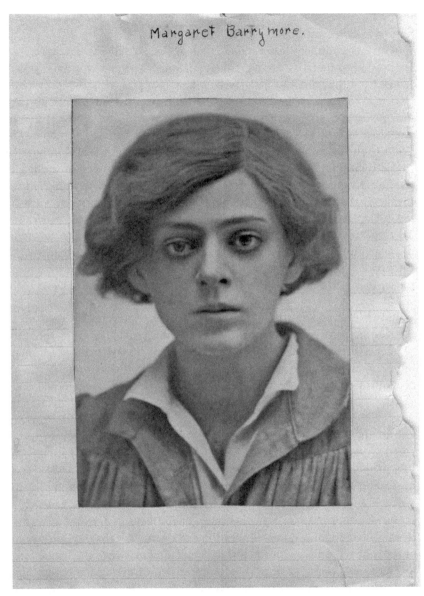

FIGURE 24. A cross-dressed Ethel Barrymore in Edna Vercoe's "Motion Picture Pictorial" scrapbook, 1914.

friend Florence Schreiber and younger sister Constance going by typical feminine abbreviations like "Flo" and "Connie."[43]

There is an inherent resistance, then—a queer self-identification—in fans safekeeping cross-dressed images of stars renowned for their hyperfeminine public image. This willingness to play with the polysemic potential of mass images, to move against the industrial grain and tease out possible counterpunching significations, would become a staple in twenty-first-century fan practices, particularly in female-led media fandoms of the last sixty years. These reception methods are also indicative of the relational dynamics the first generation of (white, educated) girl movie fans enacted with the first cohort of female movie stars. Horak mentions that silent film critics frequently expressed distaste at witnessing a recognizable actress like Pickford playing male roles, because her massive popularity made it impossible for viewers to suspend disbelief and see past the star's characteristic girlishness. In other words, the boy-girl never convincingly surfaced from beneath the movie trappings: Pickford remained Pickford whether in masculine frocks or frilly skirts.

However, for movie-loving girls like Vercoe, Stott, and Baker, the recognizability of a feminine star under male drag seems to be at the crux of spectatorial pleasure—a pleasure so dear it leaked from the limited moment of moviegoing into girls' leisure and self-documenting. Each cross-dressed image appears neatly labelled with the player's name, suggesting that movie scrapbookers enjoyed recognizing the actress underneath the gender masquerade. The queer pleasures of being "in the know" thus informed girls' fan collections of actresses in menswear.

To see male impersonation likely offered queer girls in their teens a two-pronged gratification: on the one hand, that of visual androgyny, of watching female bodies inhabit and negotiate male-assigned characteristics and experiences in everyday life; on the other, the reward of public legitimization, of seeing their unconventional traits validated through feted icons. After all, despite their gender transgressions, none of the male-clad protagonists girl fans collaged met with the tragic fates foretold in newspaper headlines. Aspirations of upward mobility also played a part in mobilizing girls' attachment to cross-dressed actresses. It is not without meaning that most heroines in drag, from *The Amazons* to sundry serials, concluded their journeys well-off and well-loved. With their tailored suits and workman boots, cross-dressed actresses like Burke and Clark made class and gender seem as changeable as a disguise, privilege as easy to achieve as a change of clothes.

Fan interest in mediated portrayals of masculine girlhood may not have always translated into same-sex desire, then, but it invariably indicated that some girl audiences found nonstandard representations of female identity enticing. Once again, it warrants remarking that, though the trope of girls passing as boys mushroomed on the US screen and stage during the early twentieth century, press images of film actresses in male drag did not: they came into view intermittently in periodical publications under the guise of behind-the-scene peeks, in low-resolution and at small scale, nearly illicit in their capturing of a temporary state, an identity held in abeyance and at the margins, waiting for the last reel to be corrected or elided. The effort to seek and seize so many of these infrequent images proves early girl fans' commitment to scavenge for gender-nonconforming renditions of female film celebrity.

STRONG, SINGLE, AND MOTORIZED: THE CROSS-DRESSED SERIAL QUEEN

The spectatorial pleasures afforded by the boy-girl intersected with those hosted by the serial queen, a physically dynamic screen protagonist. Like the former, the serial queen regularly wore gender-nonconforming clothing. However, while a gender masquerade defined the boy-girl's narrative arch, for the serial queen cross-dressing was usually a brief and ancillary act, a means to forward her crime-solving adventures or ostend her athletic prowess.[44] An archetype of self-sufficient young womanhood, the cross-dressed serial queen pervades movie scrapbooks assembled by girls during WWI. Vercoe, a self-confessed serial aficionada, amassed several transcripts and pictures of *The Perils of Pauline* (1914), *The Trey o' Hearts* (1914), *Lucille Love, Girl of Mystery* (1914), *The Master Key* (1914), *The Million Dollar Mystery* (1914), *My Lady Raffles* (1914), and *Pearl of the Army* (1916), to name a few. In many of these clippings, the young female stars appear in menswear: Grace Cunard in a fake mustache and a Mexican military uniform, Florence LaBadie in handsome equestrian garb, Pearl White in army fatigues, and Cleo Madison in a safari tuxedo, a pilot uniform, and a workman's suit.

Common in fan scrapbooks, cross-dressing occupied only passing moments in serial narratives. To hunt for such images in the press was thus nothing short of a labor of fan love and recovery. In 1914, Vercoe *twice* excepted a diminutive full-body image of White clad in a jockey costume, standing with feet apart in knee-high leather boots, face congealed in a stony expression, hair hidden under a helmet, whip taut behind her back, cigarette between her lips—the opposite of White's picture personality.[45] According to Charles Goddard's original *Pauline* novelization, this cross-dressing moment takes place in the eighteenth chapter of the twenty-part serial. Titled "A Hot Young Comet," the episode has Pauline transform from a long-haired girl into a manly horseback-rider in order to catch a criminal. "Pauline, in full jockey uniform, white and blue and yellow, was pirouetting on her gleaming black boots" when her fiancé, Harry Marvin, is perplexed at the gender-bending metamorphosis: "'Polly! Have you cut off your hair?' [Harry] added in alarm. 'No; here it is,' she laughed, snapping off her visored cap and revealing her masses of hair."[46] On screen, Pauline in male drag would have occupied only a few minutes, a few instants of comedic relief followed by a "steeple chase" at the races. Yet, amidst a slew of promotional images depicting White in the popular serial, Vercoe decided to find and keep *two copies* of this dissonant image. Other outré cross-dressed clippings collected by Vercoe include White writhing on the ground after being "thrown from the horse 'Firefly,'" and Cleo Madison in a rancher's suit, hogtied to the "rawhide" back of a mare.[47] Framed by horse-riding, both stills focus on the heroines' splayed body, their male attire adding to the voyeuristic frisson of female sexual objectification and eroticized helplessness.

Integral to serials' trademark stunts and plot-twists, cross-dressing and gender-bending always operated as a momentary veneer. Like Pauline's "visored cap" merely hiding "masses" of luscious curls, the transgressive appeal of cross-dressing never derailed a protagonist's heteronormative ending. As Shelley Stamp points out, no matter how much "they promoted a kind of modern femininity clearly tailored to appeal to their cadre of female fans, serials' woman-oriented plots [ultimately] offered alarmist tales in which independence is always circumscribed by the shadow of danger, the determinacy of familial ties, and the inevitability of marriage."[48]

This ongoing disavowal of women's progressiveness jumps out in several articles introducing female film stars as energetic, self-sufficient individuals while making a point of slotting them back into conservative feminine roles. For instance, in 1918 *Motion Picture Magazine* ran a photo of Louise Huff—then a known ingenue—with bobbed hair, dressed in white jodhpurs, a tucked-in man's shirt, black vest, and knee-high leather boots. In her masculine outfit, the actress looks confident and capable, her hands on her hips, her body slouched against an imposing motor car. A caption tells the story of how, when Huff "discovered that she was to have five days' rest . . . , she dressed in the most boyish of riding-togs, climbed into her little Paige race-about, and set off for Mount Baldy all alone, her first unescorted trip into the wilderness in a motor." Aware that "the accompanying picture" might imply "that Louise has about made up her mind that 'back to nature' stuff is all right," the journalist quickly dismissed any possibility of the actress embracing such "unfeminine" conduct permanently. The audiences could rest at ease— Huff's off-the-clock dalliance with masculinity was as short-lived as cross-dressing onscreen: "After this, she will continue to be what the public thinks of her: a fluffy, frilly, adorable little ingénue!"[49]

These press write-ups demonstrate that, by 1918, links between self-reliant womanhood and female deviance had begun to seep from medical discourse into film discourse on female stardom, subtly shaping it. Since the early 1910s, small-town clinicians like L. Pierce Clark of Ithaca, New York, had taught patients to differentiate "homosexual women" from their "normal" counterparts by gauging their physical stamina. Unlike heterosexual women, "the homosexual woman leads an active, energetic life, is enterprising, aggressive, adventurous, and at times brutal and regardless. In general she is cold-blooded."[50] A proclivity for physical activity suggested a girl who had not properly progressed from tomboy child into ladylike adult. Her biological arrest manifested in a surplus of strapping energy doctors understood as innately male-coded. A British physician best encapsulates this essentialist view of developmental determinism by proposing that a "normal transition to manhood and womanhood, respectively" rests on the "accruing of notable differences" in adolescence—most emphatically a girl's abandonment of all muscular endeavors: "From having been a strong, young, active, boy-like creature, [once entering adolescence] . . . the girl loses physical activity and strength. A phase of invalidation sets in. Instinctively, she no longer runs and romps. . . . She lounges and muses. . . . Nature suddenly locked the door upon her differentiating and escaping energies, in order that these might be conserved and knit into" marriage and childbearing.[51]

Serial actresses provided a positive counterpoint to this depowered view of white girlhood, reclaiming female physicality as necessary and heroic. As a genre, Nan Enstad claims that silent film serials tended to "emphasize adventure [and] suspense over romance."[52] Diverging from the norm also granted serial queens increased diegetic power and fan appeal. For gender-nonconforming girl spectators like Vercoe and Barker, who prided themselves on their ability to motor and play sports, the image of the adventurous serial heroine might have supplied a reaffirming model of able femininity that transformed difference into skill rather than handicap.

Although the press refused ascribing salutary nonnormativity to actresses who favored masculinity on or off the screen, fan scrapbooks suggest that moviegoing girls used the transitory images of actresses in male drag as aspirational models. Vercoe's painstaking efforts to stockpile representations of cinematic cross-dressing when cross-dressing itself existed primarily as a generic flourish, signals the fan's scrupulous dedication to screen portrayals of gender-nonconforming girlhood. Judging by the number of sources, Pearl White was Vercoe's favorite male-clad heroine, followed closely by Cleo Madison in *The Trey of Hearts.* In a handmade collage, White seems nearly unrecognizable behind a steering-wheel: her curly hair is completely covered by a dark hunt cap, body clad in a man's suit, and face stern and blank, evacuated of any emblematic dimples.[53] As if realizing the opacity of White's identity, the scrapbooker pasted a print caption, "Miss White as 'Pauline,'" under the scissored photo. Messaging that she especially enjoyed this iteration of female gender-crossing, Vercoe drew one of her customary ladybugs next to the collage (figure 25). Ladybugs make appearances in paper shrines honoring Vercoe's most beloved players, which include White and her screen partner Crane Wilbur.

The act of wearing male garments onscreen did not exhaust the queer potential of serial heroines but rather fostered plural exercises of queer reception. Take Marie Doro in *Oliver Twist* (1916), for instance. The multireeler included a sequence of Doro in an elegant gown sharing the screen with herself costumed as the bedraggled boy scamp. A technological trick aiming to showcase Doro's acting versatility, this superimposition appeared in myriad publications, including *Motion Picture Magazine,* one of Vercoe's prime sources. Refusing to uncritically follow industrial scripts on gender binarism, Vercoe chose to clip only the rendition of Doro as Oliver, telegraphing that her spectatorial attachment to gender-crossing actresses did not depend on their usual feminine presentations and might actually do without.

Personal identification with independent womanhood likely drew Vercoe to serial actresses, since fan magazines customarily marketed them as self-made and hardworking, with a real-life predilection for escapades and fast automobiles. In press interviews, White gleefully touted her love for car stunts and behind-the-scenes brushes with danger while driving.[54] *Motion Picture Magazine* regularly ran pieces lauding serial queens for their masculine talents, including one stating that "if

FIGURE 25. Edna Vercoe highlights her admiration for a cross-dressed Pearl White in the serial *The Perils of Pauline* (1914) by ladybugging her collage.

motoring is Helen Holmes' favorite and greatest amusement, then working on her car is her hobby. The engine of the racer runs as smoothly as a sewing-machine, and its rate of speed is positively vicious. All of which is due to Helen's tinkering."[55]

By mid-decade, driving had become a symbol of women's expanding mobility, benefiting in particular a new generation of well-off adolescent girls. In 1915, *Scribner's Magazine* admired the throngs of "young girls, most of them, hardly out of their teens [who] meet you everywhere, garbed in duster and gauntlets, manipulating gears and brakes with the assurance of veterans [and] not always in little ladylike cars."[56] Jennifer Parchesky adds that, "the woman motorist—typically young, affluent and attractive" was celebrated in early Hollywood. "Behind the wheel or behind the camera, women's mastery of exciting new technologies offered a spectacular image of New Womanhood as both practical power and thrilling adventure."[57] Modern and freeing, the experience of driving was not without its queer pleasures. Quoting silent movie actresses, Parchesky argues that "early women drivers described their experience in highly erotic terms, citing the 'thrills and excitement' of

speed and power as well as *the queer intimacy of body and machine.*"
Building upon Audre Lorde's view of "the erotic . . . [as] firmly rooted
in the power of [women's] unexpressed or unrecognized feeling,"
Parchesky proposes that "whole constellations of emotional and creative energies suffusing a woman's being" resulted from engaging with
new mechanical marvels, whether the car or the movies.[58]

Availing itself of the thrill of automotive autonomy as seen onscreen
and experienced in day-to-day life, Vercoe's ephemera collection deliv-
ers a compelling example of film reception combining the embodied
erotics of fan scrapbooking with the "auto-erotics" of female stardom.[59]
In the early 1920s, Vercoe would drive her illustrious father and family
friends around Chicago's affluent Highland Park suburb. Her love for
motoring must have been quite ardent for her father to have allowed his
young daughter to take the wheel. However, the twenty-four-year-old's
passion for speeding came to a halt on December 4, 1923, when her car
was "struck by a train north in Deerfield."[60] According to eyewitness
reports, Vercoe was behind the wheel when the crash took place. Her
father, two male friends, and one married lady were also in the car and
suffered "bad cuts" and bruises. As a result of injuries sustained, a Mr.
Greer died two days later, and Vercoe's father "attended the funeral
with bandaged head."[61] Jesse Lowe Smith, the superintendent of Highland Park school district and a close friend of the Vercoes, had to testify
in court to legitimize Mr. Greer's death as accidental. This biographical
anecdote puts into perspective Vercoe's juvenile penchant for serial
queens, lady motorists, and car stunts, intimating that the high-schooler
preserved images of actresses in masculine attire as a site of projected
futurity and aspirational womanhood.

Concurrently, serial queens endorsed an image of capable patriotism
that masked a yearning for increased female agency in the public sphere.
In chaptered film dramas, cross-dressing functioned as a temporary disguise that helped plucky girls chip in with the war effort in ways usually
cordoned off from them, such as by going undercover, fighting behind
enemy lines, or keeping families safe before joining their ranks and
becoming homebound mothers and wives themselves. World War I
momentarily troubled the teleological narrative of adolescent girlhood,
bequeathing young women with uncommon opportunities to participate in public life. Pearl White, like many other film players, took deliberate measures to connect her patriotic screen characterizations to her
offscreen actions. In 1916, as her latest serial heroine joined the army
and donned fatigues in *Pearl of the Army,* White became involved in

war-relief efforts, speaking in public venues and promoting liberty bonds. She also grew vocal about her wish to go overseas and join the war as "a nurse [or] an ambulance driver," plans that never materialized. In her 1919 autobiography, the actress would confess, "The only thing that I am thoroughly ashamed of concerning my life is that I didn't get over and help to do something toward winning 'the big fight.'"[62]

Such concerted synchronization between a player's screen persona and lived actions underpinned the early success of the star system by easing audience's affective identification with picture personalities. Vercoe's admiration for White's star text—evidenced by the amount of ephemera the fan collected—follows this pattern, while imparting the moviegoer's core ambition of having an atypical adult life. In 1914, in private correspondence with film director Romaine Fielding, Vercoe expressed a desire to avoid the traditional path of wifeliness and motherhood. Instead, like White, the fifteen-year-old wished to become a nurse and participate in the war relief effort, possibly overseas.[63]

Though that ambition never came to pass, Vercoe still did not follow a conventional trajectory. After graduating from coed Elm Place School in 1917, she attended a four-year training program at the Pestalozzi-Froebel College in downtown Chicago, only seven miles from her home. The fan would graduate in 1921 in the field of kindergarten and elementary-school education. Vercoe's interest in early childhood probably stemmed from her high school introducing kindergarten and primary-level education classes the year she was a sophomore. Her elaborate film collages seem to peter out after 1916, though occasional loose clippings date from late 1917. However, the teachings promoted by Pestalozzi-Froebel emphasized object-lessons and hands-on experimentation in early childhood development, pedagogical methods that intersected with Vercoe's fan love for handcrafts. Such professional training may have provided the young woman with a new outlet to express a creative temperament noticeable since adolescence: in 1917, Vercoe's senior class "prophecized" that the eighteen-year-old would become "a swell landscape designer."[64] Neither a field nurse nor a landscaper, after being certified as a school teacher Vercoe continued to live with her unmarried older sisters Winifred and Vivian at their childhood address of 860 Sheridan Road, until she passed away in 1984. Both her sisters and parents preceded her in death, leaving her in charge of the old family home for the last decade of her life. Continuing to embrace varied interests, she was a member of the American Rose Society, owned a car, and saw at least three nieces come of age. In the end, Vercoe never married,

FIGURE 26. A serial scrapbooker: Edna
Vercoe in her senior yearbook, 1917.

bore children, or relied on a husband to pay her bills, suggesting that
she fulfilled some fantasies of bachelor independence drafted in her teen
years (figure 26).

The creation of fan repositories dedicated to preserving screen
moments of female nonnormativity can thus be interpreted as a queer
act of female resistance. Lauren Berlant describes "the archive of wom-
en's culture" as comprised of sentimental narratives over-reliant on
monogamous heterosexual romance. For Berlant, those mainstream
novels, short stories, and films function as instruments of social control.
Often written by and targeting women, such fictions strive to reconcile
female consumers to the "emotional bargains" and "ordinary emotional labor" required to acquire "participation in the good life."[65]
Hetero-romantic "fantasies of love as reciprocity" are thus tantamount
to keeping women trapped in "an ongoing circuit of attachment" to
subservience and longing "that can . . . look like and feel like a zero."[66]
By turning their attentions to the cross-dressed heroine—the feisty,
untethered, in-flux boy-girl and serial queen—movie lovers like Baker,
Vercoe, Harroun, and Stott chased alternatives to the narrative of
"normative femininity" US cinema promoted through its heterosexual
"love plots." For girls who saw themselves as different from the norm,

heteronormative coupledom and ladylike womanhood were not the goal nor "the promise" driving their film consumption or coming of age. Female independence and dynamism eclipsed a normative happy ending, symbolized by the heroine in drag trading her masculine items and adventures for a bridal gown and a house to keep.

Ephemera of girlish picture personalities passing as men while engaging in daring activities ultimately appealed to girl fans who searched for alternatives to essentialist gender expectations. To select these intermittent images from among a barrage of other available options—the vast majority depicting actresses in luxurious gowns, shopping, introducing their homes and babies, or playing the desirable bride—was an act of queer resistance. If movie-loving girls simply favored risqué representations of heterosexual womanhood, they could have gravitated toward the vamp, a quite popular film archetype during WWI. That fans chose to collect cross-dressed clippings reveals that their interests lay elsewhere: with gender and sexual ambivalence, not disambiguated femininity. In the end, the rogue androgyny inherent to female cross-dressing contributed to the figure's spectatorial appeal. The temporary nature of actresses' gender-crossing likely provoked more pleasure than dismay in fans who identified as adolescent—by definition unfixed subjects, self-perceived and culturally imagined as being(s) in transition. Pain and frustration, however, do thread through queer fan reception, so the possibility cannot be ignored that safekeeping visual signifiers of nonnormativity may have made some girls feel their difference more keenly, their collages a sign of hope as much as of suffering.[67]

IN THE SCRAPBOOK AND ON THE STREETS: GIRLS CROSS-DRESSING IN EVERYDAY LIFE

Collecting print images of cross-dressed actresses allowed moviegoing girls to vicariously enjoy gender variance, to experience the world from a borrowed male-passing perspective without being encumbered by attendant social responsibilities. This shift in standpoint might have been presented as inconsequential or comedic onscreen, but its impact on certain female spectators seems meaningful and lasting. Kodaks stored in college memory books and personal scrapbooks confirm that, throughout the 1910s, working, middle-class, and moneyed moviegoing girls cross-dressed in their day-to-day, embracing it as a form of transformative play. Some did it publicly, in stage performances organized by schools and churches. Others did it privately, in dorm rooms

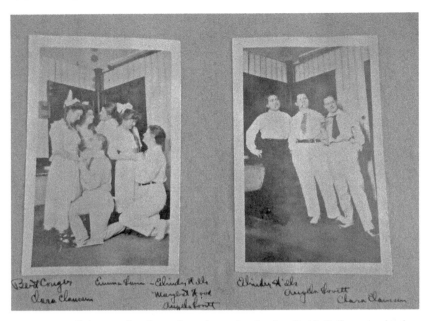

FIGURE 27. Girls cross-dressing and wooing each other in a Smith College scrapbook, Class of 1920.

and secluded backyards, in the company of their female-presenting peers. In either situation, wearing masculine attire elicited a smile from the photographed girls.[68]

"Dressing up," material culture scholar Beverly Gordon argues, "is a way of playing with ideas and identities through one's own body; it is an embodied way of relating to the world."[69] The scrapbook works as a handcrafted mediation where young female fans rehearsed fantasy and desire through images of their own dressed-up bodies in tandem with the bodies of favorite stars. In 1918, Henrietta Atwater—a self-declared fan of D. W. Griffith and Mack Sennett—preserved personal snapshots of anonymous girls in handsome suits and masculine riding habits that resemble the costumes worn onscreen by boy-girls and serial queens. Atwater's friends inhabit Smith College's grounds, sidewalks, and parks, posturing with other cross-dressed friends, laughing or dancing with a female-presenting partner.[70] Marian Hill's scrapbook records similar behavior, housing pictures of girls posing and kissing in male drag.[71] In these artifacts, college-goers' embodiment of a male persona does not seem secretive or shameful, but a component of their public presentation, a lubricator of their social belonging (figure 27).

Though it is not always possible to determine if the cross-dressing act was part of daily routine or staged for a special event (e.g., a local performance, a costume party), the repetition of male garb in some girls' personal photographs, as well as the colloquial location and manner in which they pose, insinuates that gender-crossing was integrated with their social identities and presentations of self. Furthermore, the telltale signs of theatricality are absent from these photos. Scrapbooks assembled by college girls overflow with candid shots from on-campus theatrical stagings, their makeup, outfits, and mannerisms deliberately exaggerated and clownish. That is lacking in many of these intimate cross-dressed portraits; tuxedos, vests, and ties tend to fit the wearer's body, no penciled-in mustaches or floppy wigs revealing the performative seams of male impersonation. The absence of spectacularized artifice suggests that, for these movie-loving girls, wearing menswear was a common and lived-in practice.

Other times, girls' masculine self-presentation mirrors that popularized by male film stars, pointing to a judicious playacting. With a shoe-polish mustache, slicked short hair, top hat, awkward stance, and dark tuxedo, a girl named Win resembles Charlie Chaplin's beloved "Tramp" (figure 28).[72] The visual homology between fan's masquerade and actor's alter ego was not accidental or unusual. Sometime in the late 1910s, Kitty Baker inked a quick drawing of Chaplin's stylistic trademarks in her scrapbook. Placed next to Chaplin's clipped headshot, the fan doodle supplies a visual index of how to cosplay as the notable picture personality. Win brings that to life through her embodied gender masquerade (figure 29).

Through the act of imitative cross-dressing, moviegoing girls brought their relationship with film celebrity to an enhanced level of intimacy. They brought Hollywood into their bodies, incorporating stars' aesthetic markers into themselves. This distillation of stardom into sartorial indexes, however, was not limited to fans. From the mid-1910s onward, newspapers, movie magazines, and women's periodicals popularized the mass accessibility of picture personalities by commercializing their paper dolls, with screen wardrobes being the heart of the toy. Unsurprisingly, Chaplin and Pickford were the stars who most recurrently had their likenesses turned into dolls, thus inviting audiences to think of their outfits and physiognomies as something that could be readily fragmented and manipulated.[73]

Last but of no less importance, the visual codes college girls employed in their self-portraits sometimes resemble the images of criminal male impersonators then reproduced in US newspapers. Such detail may signal

FIGURE 28. Win cross-dresses as
Charlie Chaplin's "the Tramp," Smith
College, Class of 1919.

a paradoxical traffic of influence: the characteristics differentiating and pathologizing nonnormative women in the public eye came to be adopted by that same minority as a means to make themselves recognizable to one another. Emerging at a time when queer legibility was being extensively redefined, film-inspired male drag became a double-edged practice. On the one hand, it allowed moviegoing girls to publicly express their gender-nonconforming and sapphic identities under the playful cover of imitative fandom and performance; on the other, it replicated heterosexist views on binary gender and sexual identification historically deployed to marginalize queer people.

If the reasons motivating everyday cross-dressing likely varied, the photographic results seem unanimously joyous. Studiously composed or shaky with motion, girls' cross-dressed snapshots are self-crafted attempts at engendering "a happy, conflict-free, rather magical world" where gender identity and sexual attraction appear effortlessly fluid and accepted.[74] Class did not limit their enjoyment, since amateur Kodaks of girl fans in male drag are found in scrapbooks compiled by blue-collar and clerical workers, middle-class college girls, and wealthy debutantes.

FIGURE 29. Charlie Chaplin's iconography, according to fans: Kitty Baker's drawing and collage, ca. 1916.

Society may have been intolerant of difference, but most of these vernacular artifacts exude a sense of belonging, of gregariousness and peer inclusion. The fabrication of a welcoming "magical world" through the manipulation of fashion, imagination, and visual technology is at the core of filmmaking as it is of fandom. Cross-dressing, playacting, and scrapbooking share related components and rewards: they are all subjective labors stemming from the marshaling of materiality, individual creativity, and embodied affect, and they are all a sort of voyeuristic performance of self, produced to be looked at, whether by an audience of one or of many.

In the late 1920s and early 1930s, the figure of the "lesbian chic" clothed in dapper male attire would rise to cultural prominence through the likes of Radcliffe Hall, Mercedes de Acosta, and Greta Garbo.[75] Predating them by over a decade, girl fans' cross-dressed photos aid in delineating a genealogy of queer desire and gender play before these became hotly debated in Hollywood filmdom. Imitative dress-up, in fact, occupied a salient role in female film reception since its formative days. Mary Pickford noticed schoolgirls mimicking Theda Bara's vampish style as early as 1915: "After Theda Bara appeared in *A Fool There Was*, a vampire wave surged over the country. . . . Young girls were attempting to change from frank, open-eyed ingenues to the almond-eyed, carmine-lipped woman of subtlety and mystery."[76] Correspondence exchanged between Vassar College girls in 1918 confirms that young moviegoers periodically threw "vampire parties [where] . . . the key . . . is to wear as little as possible and look your 'toughest.' The best part of the fun is the dressing up. We make good use of the ten-cent store jewellery."[77] By the following year, the film-specific colloquialisms "vamp" and "vamping" had entered the diaries of moviegoing girls to denote stylized young women who blatantly pursued male attention.[78] That educated white girls copied an eroticized and exoticized screen type complicates narratives of female film consumption disseminated during the 1910s.[79] "Good girls" like Pickford and Marguerite Clark may have led in box-office and popularity polls, but a number of girl fans from that decade chose to emulate the sybaritic vampire, whose self-assured demeanor conjured life-wrecking power over those around her, especially men. In popular consciousness, the cross-dressed dandy or butch Amazon traded on similar anxieties of male emasculation and female sexual deviance, while evoking unusual liberties and pleasures for the women who admired them.

Socially construed as a "female attitude," dressing up further pervaded many of women's early twentieth-century social practices, from private costume parties, to charity bazaars, to public reenactments, church gatherings, and school activities.[80] It was a normalized occupation and an accepted mode of female relationality and amusement. "Inversion costumes"—occasionally donned by prosperous women who derived satisfaction from "playing with gender, class and social roles"—however fell into disuse by the late 1900s, as associations between cross-dressing, homosexuality, and mannish suffragism began to infiltrate popular consciousness.[81] At the same time, amateur photography entered US life, with guests at fancy balls being prompted to bring portable cameras to record their temporary masquerades. Growing up in such a transitional period, the first generation of moviegoing girls found their reception practices informed by these two parallel occurrences: the widespread use of portable visual technologies and a souring towards gender-nonconforming presentation.

By the mid-1910s, occasions for women to freely dress in men's fashion were on the wane. Media-inspired dress-up remained one of the few venues where clothes socially attributed to the opposite sex could be safely appropriated by movie followers. Under the guise of a "put on" male persona, many of the photographed cross-dressed girls—like their fan-poet counterparts—elected to play the part of heterosexual male lover with all its tactile attributes. Vernacular snapshots preserved in college scrapbooks portray cross-dressed girls kissing, tenderly embracing a female partner, and reenacting iconic tableaus of heterosexual courtship, namely marriage proposals, wedding ceremonies, cheek-to-cheek dancing, close-mouthed kissing, and kneeling down to declare their love.

On the one hand, such preponderant adoption of traditionalist gender norms may seem to uphold a male-supremacist worldview, where "the presumption of male citizenship," "the worship of the penis," and "compulsory male heterosexuality" relegates women and femininity to second-class status.[82] On the other hand, as lesbian photographer Tessa Boffin alerts, given "the relative paucity of lesbian images, . . . one way we can move forward is by embracing the idealized fantasy figures, by placing ourselves into the great heterosexual narratives of courtly and romantic love."[83] Moviegoing girls' decisions to reenact tableaus of lovelorn knights and blushing brides in their private snapshots and fan writings announce, then, a willful self-insertion into the dominant archive of heterosexual storytelling long glorified by Hollywood cinema and US society at large. These fan-made artifacts, limited as they may seem in their eagerness to replicate standardized hallmarks of heteronormative romance, evidence that past queer desire refused to occupy the negative space around the opposite-sex "love plot." They prove that, in the early twentieth century, regular girls seized visual technology—photography, film, mass print—to claim *for themselves, by themselves* social rituals, roles, fantasies, and ensembles that had been interdicted for centuries.

Following the lead of picture actresses, some moviegoing girls chose menswear to undergo an array of embodied experiences otherwise barred to them, including openly romancing other women. This does not mean that girl fans invariably went against the grain of binary narratives on gender and sexual essentialism. The messages furthered by Hollywood's boy-girls (of romantic monogamy, of two opposite modes of sexual attraction and gender performance, of dresses coded as feminine and tuxedoes as masculine) persisted in girls' self-engineered play-acting. However, when histories of early Hollywood reception focus on compulsory heteronormativity, these "minor or inconsequential swerves from the usual" become essential to queering histories of women's culture—to bringing to the fore female audiences' past "episodes of refusal and creative contravention to heteronormativity, even as [they held] tightly to some versions of the imaginable conventional good life."[84] As "inconsequential," intermittent, or "minor" as these queer gestures may appear to twenty-first-century eyes, their very existence countermines homogenous modes of normative female identification and reception prescribed during the 1910s and still associated with silent moviegoing.

Dressing up as a screen vampire or a male tramp in daily life also unveils a larger interplay between female audiences and the film industry. In the mid-1910s, not only general-distribution fan magazines disseminated pictures of female stars in unconventional costumes; local movie theaters did too. By 1916, it had become a standard marketing ploy to fabricate elaborate lobby displays that promoted film premieres. Movie exhibitors across the country extended the "magical world" projected onscreen to foyers and ticket booths. Girls, then the primary demographic working as ushers and ticket sellers, were tasked to become part of the immersive filmgoing experience by dressing up in costumes inspired by the film releases and integrating the three-dimensional promotional displays set up in their place of employment. Trade magazines published amateur photographs of young female employees costumed as Japanese geishas for the Colonial Theatre's premiere of *The Dividend* (1916) in Sioux Falls, South Dakota. In Seattle, usherettes clad head-to-toe in Native American garb advertised the Liberty's showing of *The Dawnmaker* (1916).[85] Snapshots of female dress-up taken by local film managers document young employees being treated as commercial props. Othered in exotic garb, their bodies serve as dress-forms from which racist stereotypes could be easily distributed under the cover of longstanding feminized practices like fabulation, dressing-up, and playacting (figure 30).

Small-town exhibitors further advocated for using live female bodies to enhance regular film screenings. In 1919, the Fox Theater in Aurora, Illinois, reported placing a young actress in front of a pop-up painted backdrop and projecting Maurice Tourneur's *Woman* upon the three surfaces: screen, paper, skin. In creating movements onstage that duplicated those playing onscreen (especially that "in which Eve is shown reaching for the forbidden fruit"), the girl's live body was said to lend unusual immediacy, immersiveness, and emotion to the filmgoing experience. According to two exhibitors, inserting "a human agent" into movie screenings augmented revenues and generated "word-of mouth advertisement [of which] there is no better variety."[86] By dressing up in styles replicating those worn by the stars, movie-loving girls thus engaged in a practice industry officials had already assigned to young working women. In adopting gender masquerades outside the scope of professional obligation, however, female fans added a willful twist to their reception, not unlike those schoolgirls who elected to copy Bara's predatory look in their daily life.

As a side note, an interesting correlation may be drawn between this nationwide trend of costuming female film ushers and ticket sellers

FIGURE 30. Dressing up for work: usherettes and ticket sellers in "exotic" costume for film premieres.

in exotic fashions and the proliferation of World's Fairs in the United States in the early twentieth century. At least two of the moviegoing girls whose fan archives I located mention attending World's Fairs as teenagers: Constance Topping was at the 1915 Panama–Pacific International Exposition in San Francisco, and Helen Davis went to the 1918 Bronx International Exposition of Science, Arts and Industries in New York City.[87] Coming of age at a time when female bodies were treated as sites of performative display and exotic spectacle across so many public venues may have influenced some queer movie-loving girls to think of dress-up as a practical means to externalize an innate sense of otherness.

In the end, queerness punches through personal collages and snapshots of gender-crossing. And yet, what makes them particularly powerful is not a presumed ability to prove the existence of queer spectators at the time Hollywood's star system took root. Queer people have always existed, whether they wind up captured in amateur celluloid or not. What is remarkable about these vernacular photographs is how deliberate they are: that girls from all walks of life decided to pose and be immortalized in this manner—in male drag, being physically intimate with one another—at a historical moment when women's gender-crossing and same-sex attraction had begun to be flagrantly stigmatized in scientific and popular discourse. As Helen Davis's movie-illustrated diaries remind us, girls who did not cohere with the traditional paradigm of heteronormative womanhood suffered enormous familial, societal, and self-imposed pressures. Divergent behavior was tolerated only if temporary—part of the wages of female adolescence—and only if a girl's adult outcome complied with the norm. Movie magazines make this expectation clear, looking kindly on the new "miladies of the film and trousers," while "hop[ing] that when the wave of masculinity has passed, we will once again find the fair sex arrayed in all its frills."[88] Such regressive attitude toward gender and fashion should hardly come as a surprise. That gender variance must be replaced by heteronormative compliance is, after all, the serial queen's and the boy-girl's final lesson to their audience.

The permanent act of presenting oneself as gender nonconforming in personal photographs—portable visual documents that could easily fall in the hands of strangers, employers, and judgmental families—reaffirms the significance cross-dressing must have held for some college-age spectators. Not being deterred by newspapers welding gender-crossings to female criminality and perversion suggests that the pleasures of wearing menswear and adopting male-coded mannerisms outweighed the possible social backlash. Whether interpreted as manifestations of playful subversion or identarian actualization, these self-fashioned images introduce an audience who already questioned the artificiality of fixed gender, sex, and erotic binaries. Lastly, that so many girls chose to collect images of actresses in male drag indicates a type of queer spectatorship that derived pleasure from *insistently looking at* female masculinity.

If girl fans' vernacular photography can be helpful in excavating a far-reaching heritage of queer media reception, it may also be leveraged to challenge the teleological upholding of the present as a culminating moment in LGBTQ+ history. Although welcome and long overdue, the recent surge of gender-nonconforming visibility in mainstream entertainment and social media encourages a linear understanding of queer history that tends to erase the vital, variegated practices young nonnormative audiences have cultivated across time. Over a century ago, adolescent media consumers were already performing preferred gender identities and homoerotic/homosexual investments in their everyday lives—not only through chosen aliases and explicit androgynous vestiary choices, but also through an embodied relationship with the new motion pictures and their catalogue of versatile performers. Interspersed with film ephemera, girls' recreational snapshots propose that a number of young moviegoers regarded picture players as respected public figures who could be coopted as inspiration for atypical preferences and identities. For those female fans, dressing up in masculine clothing seemed to actuate a peer culture of belonging, freedom, and fun.

In conclusion, female audiences' attraction to movie actresses manifested in more assorted ways than credited by contemporaneous newspapermen and movie impresarios. During WWI—a period when women redrafted their roles in US public life through labor and legislation—girl audiences flocked to film actresses who performed hard-to-classify types of female identity, be they butch serial queens or gender-fluid boy-girls. By the end of the 1910s, modernity had wrought profound changes in the lives of working and middle-class girls. Unlike many of their predecessors, white girls coming of age in the war years could attain higher education, drive a car, earn their keep, migrate to urban spaces, travel, date, and frequent public entertainments unchaperoned, participate in social reform, and live outside the family home without devastating reprisals. By the end of the decade, most of them could vote. Screen heroines who projected themselves as mobile, entrepreneurial, and free-thinking hence mirrored more closely the generation of white girls growing up in the United States than did the demure, homebound "glad girls" upheld as the ideal of young womanhood only a decade before.

Defined by a fusion of imaginative life-writing and pragmatic record-keeping, movie scrapbooks and movie-illustrated diaries ultimately furnished some girl fans with a unique marquee for displaying consumer tastes while obliquely experimenting with marginal identities. The film press sought to capitalize on the former to discipline the latter, but many screen-struck girls called on picture heroines to validate divergent modes of being and feeling, so as to frame same-sex intimacies with stars and peers. The most compelling valence fan artifacts holds for film historians is exactly that versatility—the structural ability to straddle spheres of knowledge production, spectatorial response, and affective expenditure that have traditionally been theorized as invisible, nugatory, or impermeable to one another.

One of Us

*The Corporatization of Female Fan Love
and Labor*

I admit that I am of "the younger generation." . . . You see, I
am an ardent "movie fan" and defend it as a panther defends
its young!

—Sixteen-year-old Florence H. Fitch, 1927

When the US film industry first feminized and juvenated the archetypal
"screen-struck" fan in the 1910s, it sought to divest fandom of power
by associating it with a dependent social group: unmarried adolescent
girls who relied on parents and guardians for respectability, shelter, and
subsidy. However, in advancing the flourishing of a fledgling star system, girls' fan love and labor laid the ground for a women-centered
culture of kinship, desire, and consumption that would become central
to the continued profitability of Hollywood's star system. Industrial
attempts to harness and regulate young female fandom continued into
the post-World War I era, shifting to enlist female moviegoers into new
modes of film production and promotion.[1]

Throughout the 1920s, the film industry redoubled its address to
young women. Rather than a grassroots pastime or the fulfilment of an
innate calling, movie fandom and screen acting were now marketed as
disciplined corporate occupations. In an article published in 1926, *Photoplay* specified that the few actresses who still achieved lucrative con-
tracts had not serendipitously waltzed off the streets but been hard at
work, training in private acting academies like the Paramount Pictures
School. The article further stipulated that all girls were in their teens
and, before attending "the big Astoria schoolhouse," had been employed
as school teachers, fashion models, or store clerks.[2] By stressing the

prior work experience of aspiring actresses in tandem with their ongoing professionalization, the feature introduced screen performing as a job—encumbered by schedules, demands, hierarchies, and obligations—and hence not suitable for girls with self-indulgent natures. In this way, fan magazines tried to discourage untrained wayfarers from flooding the studio lots, while furthering the industry's longstanding goal of legitimizing movie acting. Repackaged as white-collar cogs in a corporate film factory, camera-struck girls of the 1920s appeared as dependable employees, not starry-eyed dreamers or inexperienced drifters.

Seeking to rebrand filmmaking as a serious occupation while keeping a handle on fervent female fan investment, early Hollywood also created girl-targeted associations that enforced institutional assimilation and supervision. Founded in the mid-1920s, both the Hollywood Studio Club (1925) and the Central Casting Bureau (1926) were instrumental in corporatizing female labor. Combined, the two associations offered shelter, training, and moral guidance to unemployed actresses, scouted and professionalized new young talent, and outsourced inexperienced female workers for "extra parts," which resultantly kept the studios "well served by the steady flow of unskilled [low-cost] workers who potentially could be trained to meet the specific requirements of a marketable product."[3] Though social efforts to aid and regulate female labor in the city of Los Angeles grew more visible in the 1920s, they built upon institutions created in the 1910s, such as the City Mother's Bureau, which opened in the fall of 1914 in Westwood's "old Normal School building" under the supervision of Mrs. Aletha Gilbert, "an appointed policeman [and] the daughter of the first police matron of Los Angeles." In Gilbert's own words, her bureau sought "to reduce the work of the juvenile court by saving girls after they have gone only short distance in the wrong direction."[4] This "wrong direction" included minor forms of delinquency such as running away from home, loitering, intoxication, petty theft, premarital sex, and prostitution—transgressions commonly linked with the transient and indigent movie-struck girl.

The push to corporatize female labor also extended to fan crafts. In the early 1920s, readymade film scrapbooks and instructional features on how to assemble your own movie album inundated the US marketplace. Companies such as the Motion Picture Directors Association and Universal Press Chicago commercialized blank books specifically for movie scrapbooking. Titled "My Scrapbook of Movie Stars" or "On the Screen: Motion Picture Memories," these notebooks evidence that by the mid-1920s, scrapbooking had developed from an informal fan practice into an industry-sanctioned commodity.

The popularity of movie scrapbooking kept rising through the decade. In 1927, *Photoplay* named scrapbook-making one of "the current vogues of the year" and praised its readers' "thousands of [movie] albums, all of them neat, all of them correct."[5] Fan magazines also promoted movie scrapbooking as a financially rewarding activity, running craft contests that granted individual moviegoers cash prizes ranging from 25 to 1,500 dollars (about 370 to 22,000 dollars in today's currency). Competitions helped institutionalize fan labor, funneling scattered craftwork fans had sent to stars, movie magazines, and studios' post-office boxes into centralized industry oversight. The most popular and well-remunerated of these competitions was *Photoplay*'s annual Cut Puzzle Contest.

First launched in 1923 and active until 1933, the Cut Puzzle Contest invited movie fans from all over the world to manipulate fragmented headshots of stars into elaborate collaged objects. For four months (June to September), the magazine published scrambled star photos accompanied by a printed alphabet. Movie-loving crafters had to cut and reorganize the slivered pieces of paper into a recognizable face, name the actor, and create lists with the offered paper alphabet. Cash prizes of over 5,000 dollars were distributed to the fifty fans who produced extensive lists and delivered the reassembled faces in the most original handcrafted vessels. Each year over thirty-five thousand submissions reportedly reached *Photoplay*'s headquarters. Published photographs attest to the abundance of fan craft production: a large-sized warehouse appears filled roof to ceiling with hundreds of hand-stitched dolls, puppets, scrapbooks, parasols, bridal veils, shawls, fans, and small decorative pieces (including jewelry boxes, lampshades, and miniature movie theaters), all incorporating the clipped images and collaged names of screen stars.

The decade-long success of *Photoplay*'s handcraft fan contest demonstrates that an industrial interest in fan handwork planted in the 1910s bore fruit in the 1920s. In the 1910s, movie magazines and newspapers solicited fan craft labor sporadically, and results were very seldom advertised with fanfare. By 1924, fan craft production was not only commonly requested by the film press, but rewarded with cash prizes and publication. Scrapbooks and home furnishings garnered the most top prizes. Like in the previous decade, single white girls and married women snatched the majority of awards, though as the decade progressed more male fans entered craft competitions and won cash prizes. Male submissions, however, tended to convey expertise in carpentry and electric engineering, while female fans continued to rely on needlework, doll making, and paper collage.

The managerial embrace of female fan craftwork resulted from an ongoing sprint to augment sales of ancillary trademarked ephemera, as well as capitalize on the free labor and publicity generated by film devotees. Competitions like *Photoplay*'s Cut Puzzle encouraged fans to "get [their] scissors out" and produce movie-themed artifacts studios could later co-opt as tie-in promotional items.[6] For example, although *Photoplay* vowed to donate all craft proceeds to children's charities in New York City (where the magazine was headquartered), the movie-fan artifacts were first exhibited in its pages, arranged like goods in a department store's shopwindow or mail-order catalogue. The publication of fans' handcrafts clearly aimed to incite other fans to assemble their own film-themed treasure chests, scrapbooks, and dolls, an endeavor that required the purchase of additional screen paraphernalia. It is telling that the instructional level of detail included in the descriptions of winning artifacts resembled easy-to-follow tutorials.

Though touted as a democratic venue for expertise and creativity, it must be noted that the contest only distributed cash prizes to its top fifty crafters, which means that less than 2 percent of the entrants were actually paid for their manual work. The money that the remaining participants put into their supplies and shipping fare—as well as the time invested in making their intricate handmade pieces—was never remunerated. Yet the magazine used their craftwork as promotional devices, cost-free tools that helped reaffirm the US film industry's worldwide reach and cultural significance. By exalting audiences' craft labor, industry officials also attempted to prolong the illusion that movie fandom remained an intimate and all-inclusive venture at the same time its sponsoring enterprise moved to adopt a vertically integrated corporate model.

In the 1930s, craft work lost prominence in the press discourse on film fandom. By 1931, the submissions to *Photoplay*'s Cut Puzzle had dropped by almost half. The prizes had also shrunken in value. Two years later, images of fans' handiwork no longer made it to the page. Married women and male fans participated more assiduously throughout the 1930s, but adolescent girls ceased sending contributions. The Wall Street crash of 1929 and its resulting economic depression likely affected fans' ability to invest resources in movie-themed crafts. However, that the competition folded as girl fans stopped showing public interest in movie-themed handcrafts also indicates that young female audiences played a vital part in making craftwork relevant as both a fan praxis and a profitable marketing strategy.

"I AM CRAZY ABOUT HER": MOVIE-FAN SCRAPBOOKING IN THE AGE OF INDUSTRIAL INTEGRATION

Despite its commercial massification, surviving movie scrapbooks from the 1920s attest that girls in their teens continued to be the main compilers of film ephemera, privately assembling interstitial movie repositories that eschewed and expanded industrial dictates. Helen Nagel from Chicago, for instance, assembled two film "volumes" between 1920 and 1923 by papering over a popular limerick book. Audrey Chamberlin began her multivolume movie scrapbook collection in the early 1920s, likely while living in New York City during her young adulthood. In 1924, thirteen-year-old Elanor Nuenthal, a working-class girl from Lake View, Illinois, crafted her "Movie Stars" scrapbook, while well-to-do Yvonne Blue jotted down reviews of photoplays, wrote letters to movie-loving female friends, and collected star pictures in bound books while attending the high school of the University of Chicago.[7] Lastly, from January 1927 to December 1929, Dorothy Blum, an affluent girl from Los Angeles, compiled twenty-six film scrapbooks tracking her coming of age through favorite players, pictures watched, and theaters visited.[8]

Illustrating experiential film reviews with movie ephemera, Blum's extensive scrapbook collection lends insight into the ways handcrafts and girl fandom changed with Hollywood's corporate consolidation. Unlike other movie scrapbookers from the 1910s and early 1920s, Blum did not recycle old books, instead purchasing the readymade blank scrapbook "On the Screen: Motion Picture Memories," manufactured by Universal Press Chicago and decorated by W. T. Hay. The journaling aspect of scrapbooking is still dominant in this decade, film ephemera framed by handwritten captions describing personal outings and spectatorial reactions. In her early teens, most of Blum's movie excursions were chaperoned by family members or house staff and were to local theaters like the Vista in Los Feliz or the Orpheum and the Tower in downtown Los Angeles. Earlier entries also capture a thirteen-year-old's slang and same-sex crushes, while evidencing consistency between Hollywood's narrowcasting and reception: as a pubescent girl, Blum loves "adorable" fifteen-year-old ingenue Lisa Moran, prefers "cute stories with beautiful clothes," like Billie Dove's *The American Beauty* (1927), and reveres "darling" Colleen Moore, ringleted in the romantic drama *Tinkletoes* (1926).[9]

As Blum wades into adolescence, "mamma and papa" are replaced with young suitors Danny and Franklin and girlfriends Augusta and Rosebud, attendants in a commercial youth culture blooming around filmgoing. Trips to the movies also double as tourist attractions. Blum makes note of frequenting the plush boardwalk theatre the Stanley in Atlantic City, New Jersey; the Roxy (a 5,920-seat picture palace off Times Square), the New Amsterdam's roof theatre the Folic, and the Picadilly, later known as Warner's Theatre, all in New York City. While in Chicago, Blum patronizes the Tivoli in Uptown, the Roosevelt on State Street, the Harper in Hyde Park, and the Alcyon in Highland Park.

The detailed recording of *where, when,* and *with whom* feature films were consumed indicates an essential change in movie scrapbooking. While many fans in the 1910s focused on pictorial accumulation, treating the local theatre as a simple means to an end, later fan scrapbookers seem more preoccupied with creating a three-dimensional record of moviegoing, possibly influenced by film magazines' address and the development of themed movie houses. A product of the flamboyant "picture palace" age, the venue where titles are consumed becomes relevant to a fan's moviegoing experience. Less of a photo album and more of an illustrated critical log, movie scrapbooks like Blum's hence reveal an ideological and behavioral reframing of fan identity and performance in the 1920s. For Blum, to be a movie fan and scrapbooker could not be decoupled from being an *experiential* connoisseur, a definition now fully expanded to include evaluation of movie theatres' architecture, comfort, and decor. A fan's critical eye continued to mirror that modeled by professional female film reviewers during the 1910s. Many of Blum's glossy photo collages appear underlined by handwritten captions, wittily indicting Clara Bow for being "too 'flappery'" and Mae Murray for "looking younger, and younger—any younger and the Children's Societies will begin investigations."[10]

The industrialization of fan-made artifacts seems to have also incited movie lovers to begin to perceive themselves not as passive aggregators but as discerning experts whose personal film knowledge bolstered the crystallization of a star- and genre-driven studio system. Once picture personalities solidified into full-fledged commodities, selling not just movie tickets but a cornucopia of supplemental goods, fans became pivotal for the profitability of an expanding film industry. As *Photoplay* stated in 1927, "The 'fan' letters accurately reflect the trend of public opinion. . . . If the 'fan' mail of a star registers disapproval of a certain type of story, the star usually sees fit to change his or her policy." Trade and popular periodicals trumpeted fans as both experts and surveyors of movie idols, their interest so influential that "a steady increase in 'fan' letters means a nice new contract for a star. A slight decrease is instantly noted by the producers."[11]

By designating fan investment as "the barometer of motion picture popularity," the film industry officially welcomed screen-struck girls into the fold. Where once lurked distrust and distance, now flourished respect and reciprocity. Acknowledging the economic contribution of fandom was both an inevitability and a clever marketing strategy seeking to neutralize damaging ties between movie fandom and deviance seeded the decade before. Rather than as deranged followers, movie magazines in the 1920s painted fans as a potentially productive part of Hollywood's well-oiled machine. "Letters containing sound, well-expressed criticism are sorted from others and read to the stars. An intelligent letter," *Photoplay* assured, "seldom fails to get a hearing, even if it doesn't get an answer."[12] A narrative of assimilation and supervision thus promised fans who avoided "gushing nonsense" direct access to the stars. From a managerial perspective, the incorporation of ardent fan attachment rendered it more manageable and rehabilitative: manageable in that industrial recognition allowed passionate consumers the illusion of holding power to make or break a star, a remote semblance of agency intended to satiate their presumed longing for movieland inclusion; and rehabilitative in positioning fans as invited contributors instead of disruptive interlopers.

Though affecting a model of cooperation, this press discourse deliberately calcified distinctions between insider and outsider, suggesting that "good fans" played by the rules, helping stars and producers succeed, while "bad fans" presumably went rogue, continuing to display attitudes condemned a decade prior, and evicting themselves from filmdom. What this means is that, though Hollywood cinema went on influencing adolescent girls through the 1920s, by mid-decade the star-making industry they adored had begun a steady march towards vertically integrated consolidation, a business trajectory that significantly altered the ways industry officials courted girl fans and conceived of movie fandom. Opportunities for expressing queer modes of looking and feeling, somewhat amorphous and unpoliced in the 1910s, grew narrower in the following decade. The industry now energetically shepherded girl fans to filter their attachment to movie actresses through heteronormative identification and product consumption, made express via cosmetics, accessories, pageants, and advice columns that directed fans to adopt actresses' feminine apparel and heterosexual appeal.

Blum's scrapbooks show these managerial commands in action: reining in gushy feelings, fans should assess cinema on its technological merits and stars on their performance of heteronormativity. In an entry from January 1927, Blum remarks that *The Third Degree* (1926), a romantic thriller starring Dolores Costello, "was very good even though it had German camera angles," demonstrating knowledge of transnational film editing and aesthetics, in this case German Expressionism.[13] In another comment, the teenage girl informally describes silent horror films *The Unknown* (1927) and *The Cat and the Canary* (1927) as "really spooky and breath taking [sic]," proving understanding of generic specificity.[14] Attesting to the increasing overlap of film criticism and fandom, Blum's responses are also often informed by evaluation of production values and acting quality. In 1928, the girl crowned the WWI melodrama *7th Heaven* (1927) "the greatest picture produced," because in addition to a compelling script, the "acting [is] superb—beautiful love scenes . . . [and] Charles Farrell and Janet Gaynor sure make a marv. team. . . . One of the best pictures I have ever seen!"[15] In this entry, juvenile slang and formal analysis blend to produce a hybrid of fan pleasure and criticality.

If a novel industry-sanctioned appraisal of filmmaking influenced girls' scrapbooking in the late 1920s, attraction to screen actresses remained ever-potent. In later entries, Blum liberally registers sensual admiration for young female stars, observing that "Joan Crawford [is] the most attractive person I have ever laid eyes on," and "Dolores Costello is marv. I am crazy about her. . . . I think she is gorgeous."[16] In commending Esther Ralston for her dual role in the comedy *The Spotlight* (1927), Blum again zeroes in on a star's physical attributes, observing that "Esther Ralston in a black wig [is] just as attractive if not more so" than with her usual blonde mane.[17] Foregrounding her viewer pleasure on actresses' bodies, Blum continued to embrace both homoerotic spectatorship and the effusive language of romantic friendship, linchpins of fandom devised by moviegoing girls over a decade before. She also melded the role of film reviewer with that of excited fan, fulfilling a marriage of emotionality and expertise foreclosed in 1910s press coverage of screen-struck girlhood.

The Roaring Twenties, in sum, witnessed the consolidation of a Hollywood-based film industry and its policing of girls' fan affect and participation. The institutionalization of fandom came as a bid to rectify the fairytale narrative of "anyone can become a star" that had mobilized enormous numbers of screen-struck girls during the 1910s. Fan competitions and movie scrapbooks issued by industry affiliates forcefully steered girl fans to take up the roles of movie critic and collector instead of those of aspiring actress and star inamorata. The creation of girl-oriented associations, advice columns, and studio acting schools likewise strove to keep young female audiences engaged with a corporate film industry while curtailing the degree of agency they could exert within these venues. As a result, moviegoing girls in the 1920s reworked the ways they interacted with a progressively corporate Hollywood film industry, without ceasing to personalize their fan responses.

FUTURE STAKES: PAIN IS YET TO COME

Blum's scrapbooks, as those of her predecessors, are just an example of the many shapes young female fandom took through Hollywood's century-long history. For the next decades, girl spectators continued to subsidize film publications, consume star-sponsored goods, cut-and-paste images of stars, pen fan letters, and author first-person narratives that poignantly articulated their formative engagement with a female- and youth-oriented commercial media culture. With the new millennium, their reception practices eventually moved into digital spaces, taking familiar shapes in image-heavy social media platforms like Pinterest, LiveJournal, Instagram, and Tumblr.

A question of genealogy is at stake then. Though culturally diminished as "adolescent" due to their age and dependent status, screen-struck girls from the 1910s devised modes of media engagement that remain integral to the functioning of online communities. Their penchant for handcrafts and confessional writing persists as a tenet of fan connection and self-expression, visible from peer-shared collages, scrapbooks, and mood boards curated on social networking websites to fan-made anthologies and artisanal items sold on e-commerce platforms.

If pleasure and affinity subtended silent movie fandom, so did pain and nonbelonging. In my forthcoming work, I examine diaries, collages, criminal statements, and suicide letters crafted by early movie-loving girls who chronicled their disappointment with heteronormative life and romance through their engagement with Hollywood cinema. Such autobiographical archives show female audiences employing film stardom to explore a spectrum of negative feelings in the wake of WWI and the

influenza pandemic.[18] From mourning and melancholia to failure and
loss, these reception objects capture a chafing against the trappings of
heteronormative femininity and its attendant notions of romance, self-
sacrifice, happiness, and well-being.[19] Sara Ahmed claims that "queer
feelings may embrace a sense of discomfort, a lack of ease with the available scripts for living and loving."[20] Building upon feminist scholarship
on queer negativity, I propose that a nuanced historicization of female
spectatorship must grapple with the discomfort and hardship heteronormativity activated in moviegoing girls who felt different from the norm,
while questioning the roles early Hollywood played in reinforcing such
sensations of exclusion, ill-being, and alienation.[21]

Excavations of early fan documents, in the end, function as a means
to interrogate political scripts etched in recurrent phenomena: the ebb
and flow of "new" and "old" delivery technologies, the gendering of
affect and labor in media theory, and the unchanging identarian investment media consumers imbue in their purchases, their idols, their personal archives—physical or digital, paper-based or software-operated.
In fact, movie scrapbooks from the 1910s function as unique vestibules:
in their pages, we see early Hollywood beginning to parlay viewers'
individual emotional attachment into sustainable mass revenue. Industry officials repackaged paper ephemera into an affective commodity
that allowed Hollywood cinema to spread its reach into fans' leisure
and domestic practices, to be present in their lives beyond the time-
bound act of movie-watching. Silent film scrapbooks can therefore be
interpreted as early markers of a mass medium's "presence bleed," as
digital media researcher Melissa Gregg terms the current inability to
draw clear borders between play and work, content consumer and
content producer, being "on" or "off" mediated engagement. Gregg
argues that presence bleed results from the spread of social media to all
aspects of human life.[22] Although the magnitude of such phenomena is
undeniably linked with the advent of Web 2.0, blurring the lines between
the mediated and the everyday, the personal and the publicized, the
mass-produced and the self-crafted, was already instrumental to the
early success of Hollywood's celebrity culture.

It is urgent, then, to reintegrate young female fans in our histories of
media technology, a male-dominated canon from which they have sys-
tematically been sidelined. Leading media scholar Henry Jenkins, for
example, speaks of white, male, middle-class youth as the "early settlers
and first inhabitants" of "convergence culture," a term defining the
intersection of traditional media technologies (film, television, radio,

the press) and the internet.[23] But as the materials in this book have attested, working and middle-class girls growing up during the early twentieth century were among the first media consumers to employ many of the reception practices Jenkins readily attributes to white men of privilege. Complex in their straining of heteronormative preconceptions, these reception practices remain paramount to the formation and affective maintenance of digital communities, so to have a correct understanding of their origins is critical to the equitable redistribution of power in popular consciousness, as in US public history.

Notes

INTRODUCTION

Epigraph: William Faulkner, *Absalom, Absalom!* (New York: Vintage, [1936] 1972), 100.

1. Kitty Baker Scrapbook, 1915–1916, Beinecke Rare Book and Manuscript Library, Jessica Helfand Collection, Yale University.

2. Elsie Clews Parsons, *Social Rule: A Study of the Will to Power* (New York: G. P. Putman's, 1916), 55–56.

3. Richard Abel, *Americanizing the Movies and "Movie-Mad" Audiences, 1910–1914* (Berkeley: Univ. of California Press, 2006), 245.

4. Parsons, *Social Rule,* 55

5. Jennifer Bean, "Introduction: Towards a Feminist Historiography of Early Cinema," in *A Feminist Reader in Early Cinema,* ed. Jennifer Bean and Diana Negra (Durham, NC: Duke Univ. Press, 2002), 1–26; 8.

6. See Shelley Stamp, *Movie-Struck Girls: Women and Motion Picture Culture after the Nickelodeon* (Princeton, NJ: Princeton Univ. Press, 2000); Moya Luckett, *Cinema and Community: Progressivism, Exhibition, and Film Culture in Chicago, 1907–1917* (Detroit: Wayne State Univ. Press, 2014); and Kristin Olsen, *Daily Life of Women in the Progressive Era* (Santa Barbara, CA: Greenwood Press, 2019).

7. "Cut Out the Sobs, Exhibitors Say," *Motography,* March 2, 1918, 394.

8. See works in anthologies such as Vicki Callahan, ed., *Reclaiming the Archive: Feminism and Film History* (Detroit: Wayne State Univ. Press, 2010); Sofia Bull and Astrid Söderbergh-Widding, eds., *Not So Silent: Women in Cinema Before Sound* (Stockholm: Acta Universitatis Stockholmiensis, 2010); and Monica Dall'Asta, Victoria Duckett, and Lucia Tralli, eds., *Researching Women in Silent Cinema: New Findings and Perspectives* (Bologna, Italy: Univ. of Bologna, 2013). Also relevant are journal special issues on feminist historiography and silent

cinema, including Amelie Hastie and Shelley Stamp, eds., "Women and Silent Screen," *Film History: An International Journal* 18.2 (2006); Christine Gledhill, ed., "Transnationalizing Women's Film History," *Framework: The Journal of Cinema and Media* 51.2 (2010); Victoria Duckett and Susan Potter, eds., "Women and the Silent Screen," *Screening the Past* 40 (2015); and Mark Lynn Anderson, ed., "Special Issue on 'Betterment,'" *Feminist Media Histories* 3.4 (2017).

9. Jane M. Gaines, "Film History and the Two Presents of Feminist Film Theory," *Cinema Journal* 44.1 (2004): 113–19; 117.

10. See, for example, Annette Kuhn, *An Everyday Magic: Cinema and Cultural Memory* (New York: I. B. Tauris, 2002); Jacqueline Stewart, *Migrating to the Movies: Cinema and Black Urban Modernity* (Berkeley: Univ. of California Press, 2005); Amelie Hastie, *Cupboards of Curiosity: Women, Recollection, and Film History* (Durham, NC: Duke Univ. Press, 2007); Kathy Fuller-Seeley, "Dish Night at the Movies: Exhibitors and Female Audiences during the Great Depression," *Looking Past the Screen: Case Studies in American Film History and Method,* ed. Jon Lewis and Eric Smoodin (Durham, NC: Duke Univ. Press, 2007), 246–75; Laura Isabel Serna, *Making Cinelandia: American Films and Mexican Film Culture before the Golden Age* (Durham, NC: Duke Univ. Press, 2014); Shelley Stamp, *Lois Weber in Early Hollywood* (Berkeley: Univ. of California Press, 2015); Anette Kuhn, Daniel Biltereys, and Phillippe Meers, "Memories of Cinemagoing and Film Experience: An Introduction," *Memory Studies* 10.1 (2017): 3–16; and Annie Fee, "Les Midinettes Révolutionnaires: The Activist Cinema Girl in 1920s Montmartre," *Feminist Media Histories* 3.4 (2017): 162–94. Also see Saidyia Hartman's work on the vernacular archive of Black girls living in early-twentieth-century America, *Wayward Lives, Beautiful Experiments: Intimate Histories of Riotous Black Girls, Troublesome Women, and Queer Radicals* (New York: W. W. Norton, 2019).

11. Amelie Hastie, "The Miscellany of Film History," *Film History: An International Journal* 18.2 (2006): 222–30; 222.

12. Historian Paul Magdalino theorizes that "the essence of prosopography is to establish identity; the identity of an individual within a group, and individual identity as part of group identity. The prosopographer's card index is like a police file in which the historian can search, not only for the usual suspects, but also for the highly unusual and unlikely ones—including . . . [who] remains yet unreported or undetected." "Prosopography and Byzantine Identity," in *Fifty Years of Prosopography: The Later Roman Empire, Byzantium and Beyond,* ed. Averil Cameron (Oxford: Oxford Univ. Press, 2003), 41–56; 46–47.

13. In *Cinema and Community,* Luckett puts forward a close reading of girl-only star contests that movie magazines created in collaboration with film studios during the WWI years. Luckett argues these corporate incentives sought to train young women into becoming loyal film consumers and self-styled commodities. See also Diana W. Anselmo, "Screen-Struck: The Invention of the Movie Girl Fan," *Cinema Journal* 55.1 (2015): 1–28.

14. "Answer Department," *Motion Picture Magazine,* August 1915, 148.

15. "Letters to the Editor," *Motion Picture Magazine,* August 1914, 170.

16. Although scholarship on silent film audiences sprawls widely, it seldom attends to the specificities of age, which is to say it elides female adolescence.

For instance, Richard deCordova's work on early children's matinees does not broach first-person fan testimonies nor attend to the specificities of moviegoing adolescence, a life-stage defined by key psychosexual and social developments and thus particularly significant for mapping the impact a new star-driven cinema had in shaping targeted promotional address, exhibition, and production. See "Ethnography and Exhibition: The Child Audience, the Hays Office, and Saturday Matinees," *Camera Obscura* 23 (1990): 91–106. Drawing on oral history, Gregg Bachman shares a wealth of first-hand recollections of moviegoing during the silent period, though no discrete analysis is produced distinguishing childhood and teenage memories, nor does he survey spectatorship along gender, class, or racial lines. See "Still in the Dark: Silent Film Audiences," *Film History: An International Journal* 9.1 (1997): 23–48.

17. "Nickel Theaters Crime Breeders," *Chicago Tribune*, April 1907, 3, 66.

18. See Richard Abel, "G. M. Anderson: 'Broncho Billy' among the Early 'Picture Personalities,'" in *Flickers of Desire: Movie Stars of the 1910s*, ed. Jennifer M. Bean (New Brunswick, NJ: Rutgers Univ. Press), 22–43.

19. Kathy Fuller-Seeley, *At the Picture Show: Small-Town Audiences and the Creation of Movie Fan Culture* (Washington, DC: Smithsonian, 1996), 124.

20. Trade publications, however, recognized "the film fan" as a separate demographic much earlier. In October 1911, *Motography* already argued that "one of the reasons why we put [the magazine] on the news stands . . . [though] originally designed for the trade [is] *the film fan*. He forced us to it by sheer persistence in asking for it all over the country, and with this assurance of a new market and a big one, we met the demand." According to the trade magazine, "almost ten percent of picture show attendance classifies under the fan type," an intellectualized male figure described as "the earnest devotee of the art, who tries hard to see every film, who knows every maker as soon as he sees the picture on the screen, and whose acquaintances with the actors and actresses of the film stock company is almost personal." "Motography on the News Stands," *Motography*, October 1911, 155.

21. "Answers to Inquiries," *Motion Picture Story Magazine*, December 1912, 150

22. Nesbit, "American Favorites," *Motion Picture Magazine*, July 1914, 133.

23. "The Answer Man," *Motion Picture Magazine*, December 1917, 153.

24. "Answer Department," *Motion Picture Magazine*, November 1916, 152; January 1917, 146.

25. John Jr. Jesco, "The Movie Dictionary," *Motion Picture Magazine*, February 1916, 117.

26. "The Answer Man," *Motion Picture Magazine*, December 1917, 153. For more on the genealogy of the term "fan" see Henry Jenkins, *Textual Poachers: Television Fans and Participatory Culture* (New York: Routledge, 1992).

27. Charles Keil and Ben Singer, "Introduction," *American Cinema of the 1910s: Themes and Variations* (New Brunswick, NJ: Rutgers Univ. Press, 2009), 16.

28. Genevieve Harris, "'Girls You Know,'" *Motography*, January 12, 1918, 87.

29. Gladys Hall, "A Girl's Folly," *Motion Picture Magazine*, April 1917, 49.

30. Gertrude M. Price, "'Screen Girl' Is The Latest Movie Idea," *Day Book* (Chicago), May 8, 1915, 1. For more on the moral panic surrounding unsolicited female labor in early Hollywood, see Shelley Stamp, "'It's a Long Way to Filmland': Starlets, Screen Hopefuls and Extras in Early Hollywood," in *American Cinema's Transitional Era: Audiences, Institutions, Practices*, ed. Charlie Keil and Shelley Stamp (Berkeley: Univ. of California Press, 2004), 332–52; and Denise McKenna, "The Photoplay or the Pickaxe: Extras, Gender and Labour in Early Hollywood," *Film History: An International Journal* 23.1 (2011): 5–19.

31. For a history of stage fandom and women, see Daniel Cavicchi, "Fandom Before 'Fan': Shaping the History of Enthusiastic Audiences," *Reception: Texts, Readers, Audiences, History* (2014): 52–72; Ann Folino White, "In Behalf of the Feminine Side of the Commercial Stage: The Institute of the Woman's Theatre and Stagestruck Girls," *Theatre Survey* 60.1 (2019): 35–66; and Desirée J. Garcia, "Toil Behind the Footlights: The Spectacle of Female Suffering and the Rise of Musical Comedy," *Frontiers: A Journal of Women Studies* 40.1 (2019): 122–45.

32. A contemporaneous definition can be found in "Stage-Struck Girls," *New York Times,* July 1, 1911, 10.

33. "The Stage-Struck Girl," *Medford (NY) Mail Tribune,* July 18, 1910, 4.

34. Robert Edeson, "Stage Needs Girls With Brains," *Los Angeles Herald,* February 20, 1910, 37.

35. "The Stage-Struck Girl," 4.

36. In her study of stage actresses, *Female Spectacle: The Theatrical Roots of Modern Feminism* (Cambridge, MA: Harvard Univ. Press, 2002), Susan A. Glenn argues that, at the turn of the twentieth century, US collective consciousness thought of young women and girls as ideal imitative performers due to a psychological malleability and emotional excess innate to their gender and tender age.

37. Gaylyn Studlar, *Precocious Charms: Stars Performing Girlhood in Classical Hollywood Cinema* (Berkeley: Univ. of California Press, 2013). For more on admen harnessing screen girlishness as a targeted commodity, see Leslie Midkiff DeBauche, "Testimonial Advertising Using Movie Stars in the 1910s: How Billie Burke Came to Sell Pond's Vanishing Cream in 1917" *CHARM* (2007): 146–56. In *Before Glamour: Fashion in American Silent Film* (New York: Palgrave, 2013), Michelle Finamore also shows that, by the late 1910s, movie studios toiled alongside the expanding cosmetic and fashion industries to seduce a specific female constituency. In fact, by 1916, screen queens Mary Fuller, Mary Pickford, Mabel Normand, and Pearl White, among others, all advertised face creams, corsets, and beauty soaps in the pages of *Photoplay.*

38. Several film historians have traced the dynamic address the early film industry established with female audiences, proving their significance to the successful implementation of the Hollywood star system. Shelley Stamp, for instance, examines the numerous tie-in promotions and giveaways exhibitors and admen deployed to lure the patronage of working and middle-class women, while Nan Enstad and Richard Abel look at the ways newspapers singled out young and working female moviegoers in the early 1910s. However, most scholars have not analyzed these marketing efforts within the context of female

adolescence. It is important to do so, because in the 1910s, US culture regarded girlhood as a life-stage distinct from childhood and womanhood, thus addressing girl patrons as a specific target market. Stamp, *Movie-Struck Girls;* Nan Enstad, *Ladies of Labor, Girls of Adventure: Working Women, Popular Culture, and Labor Politics at the Turn of the Twentieth Century* (New York: Columbia Univ. Press, 1999); and Richard Abel, *Menus for Movieland: Newspapers and the Emergence of American Film Culture 1913–1916* (Berkeley: Univ. of California Press, 2015).

39. Stamp, *Movie-Struck Girls*, 37.

40. Viviana A. Zelizer, *Pricing the Priceless Child: The Changing Social Value of Children* (Princeton, NJ: Princeton Univ. Press, 1994), 57.

41. See Karen Sánchez-Eppler, *Dependent States: The Child's Part in Nineteenth-Century American Culture* (Chicago: Univ. of Chicago Press, 2005); Sarah E. Chinn, *Inventing Modern Adolescence: The Children of Immigrants in Turn -of-the-Century America* (New Brunswick, NJ: Rutgers Univ. Press, 2008); and Beth Rodgers, *Adolescent Girlhood and Literary Culture at the Fin de Siècle: Daughters of Today* (New York: Palgrave Macmillan, 2016).

42. See Kimberly Hamlin, "What Raising the Age of Sexual Consent Taught Women About the Vote," *Smithsonian Magazine,* 26 August, 2020, accessed November 16, 2021, https://www.smithsonianmag.com/history/what-raising-age-sexual-consent-taught-women-about-vote-180975658/.

43. G. Stanley Hall, *Adolescence: Its Psychology and Its Relations to Physiology, Anthropology, Sociology, Sex, Crime, Religion and Education* (New York: Appleton, 1904).

44. Ibid., xii.

45. G. Stanley Hall, "The Budding Girl," in *Educational Problems*, vol. 2 (New York: D. Appleton, 1911), 16 (italics mine). This article was first published in 1909 in the collection *Addresses and Proceedings of the Annual Session of Southern California Teachers,* from a conference that took place in 1908.

46. Crista DeLuzio, *Female Adolescence in American Scientific Thought, 1830–1930* (Baltimore: Johns Hopkins Univ. Press, 2007), 112.

47. Hall, "Budding Girl," 8. For more on Hall's cultural impact on associating adolescence with early US spectatorship, see Christina Peterson, "'The Best Synonym of Youth': G. Stanley Hall, Mimetic Play, and Early Cinema's Embodied Youth Spectator," in *Corporeality in Early Cinema: Viscera, Skin, and Physical Form,* ed. Doron Galili, Jan Olsson, Marina Dahlquist, and Valentine Robert (Bloomington: Indiana Univ. Press, 2018), 231–39.

48. Helen Edna Davis, Diaries 1914–1928, November 13, 1919, New-York Historical Society, New York City.

49. Constance Severance, "Her New York," *Photoplay,* February 1917, 123.

50. "The Speed King," *Photoplay,* February 1915, 30.

51. Hall, "Budding Girl," 9 (italics mine).

52. After conducting a survey of 125 high-school girls in 1896, physician Helen P. Kennedy concluded that the average age for girl's first menstruation was 13 years and 7 months. "Effect of High School Work Upon Girls During Menstruation," *Pedagogical Seminary* 3 (June 1896): 470. Another physician, Charles Roberts, observed that 14 years and 8 months was "the average age of

puberty of 575 American girls" in his article "Physical Maturity of Women," *Lancet* 126 (25 July 1885): 149–50. E. G. Lancaster, a colleague of Hall at Clark University, cites these results in his own article published in 1897. He states that "the time of puberty [for girls] varies with races . . . and places, but the average is not far from 14." "The Psychology and Pedagogy of Adolescence," *Pedagogical Seminar* 5 (July 1897): 78.

53. Alice Sterling, "The Class of 1892," clipped from *Boston Herald*. Alice Sterling Cook Scrapbook, Schlesinger Library, Harvard University.

54. For an impressive study of Hall's work and its intersection with early twentieth-century prejudices, see Gail Bederman, *Manliness and Civilization: A Cultural History of Gender and Race in the United States, 1880–1917* (Chicago: Univ. of Chicago Press, 1995).

55. "The Answer Man," *Motion Picture Magazine*, June 1917, 142.

56. "Who's Who and Where," *Film Fun*, July 1916, no page.

57. See Marsha Orgeron, "'You Are Invited to Participate': Interactive Fandom in the Age of the Movie Magazine," *Journal of Film and Video* 61.3 (2009): 3–23.

58. Hester Blum, *The News at the Ends of the Earth: The Print Culture of Polar Exploration* (Durham, NC: Duke Univ. Press, 2019), 182.

59. For more on the number of US films from the silent period currently believed lost, see David Pierce, *The Survival of American Silent Feature Films: 1912–1929* (Washington, DC: Council on Library and Information Resources and The Library of Congress, 2013).

60. Hilary Hallett, *Go West, Young Women!: The Rise of Early Hollywood* (Berkeley: Univ. of California Press, 2013), 4, 9. Key works studying women and early US cinema include Kathy Peiss, *Cheap Amusements: Working Women and Leisure in Turn-of-the-Century New York* (Philadelphia: Temple Univ. Press, 1986); Jackie Stacey, *Star Gazing: Hollywood Cinema and Female Spectatorship* (New York: Routledge, 1994); Janet Staiger, *Bad Women: Regulating Sexuality in Early American Cinema* (Minneapolis: Univ. of Minnesota Press, 1995); Lauren Rabinovitz, *For the Love of Pleasure: Women, Movies, and Culture in Turn-of-the-Century Chicago* (New Brunswick, NJ: Rutgers Univ. Press, 1998); Jennifer Bean and Diana Negra, eds. *A Feminist Reader in Early Cinema* (Durham, NC: Duke Univ. Press, 2002); Karen Ward Mahar, *Women Filmmakers in Early Hollywood* (Baltimore: John Hopkins Univ. Press, 2006); Mark Garrett Cooper, *Universal Women: Filmmaking and Institutional Change in Early Hollywood* (Urbana: Univ. of Illinois Press, 2010); and Rosanne Welch, ed., *When Women Wrote Hollywood: Essays on Female Screenwriters in the Early Film Industry* (New York: MacFarland, 2018).

61. Hallett, *Go West, Young Woman!*, 4.

62. Lisa Lewis, for example, points out how "fandom is overwhelmingly associated with adolescence or childhood, that is, with a state of arrested development or youth-oriented nostalgia, not mature adulthood. Furthermore, the fan impulse is presented as feminine." Researching the scrapbooks moviegoing girls dedicated to teenaged star Deanna Durbin in post-WWII Britain, Georganne Scheiner pioneered the inclusion of "the cultural agency of girls" in academic film histories, arguing that "exploring the link between the adolescent female spectators in the audience and fandom is essential." Lisa A. Lewis,

"'Something More Than Love': Fan Stories on Film," *The Adoring Audience: Fan Culture and Popular Media*, ed. Lisa A. Lewis (New York: Routledge, 1992), 157; and Georganne Scheiner, *Signifying Female Adolescence: Film Representations and Fans, 1920–1950* (New York: Praeger, 2000), 117.

63. Stacey, *Star Gazing,* 64.

64. Miriam Hansen, *Babel and Babylon: Spectatorship in American Silent Film* (Cambridge, MA: Harvard Univ. Press, 1991), 246.

65. Deborah Gould, "On Affect and Protest," in *Political Emotions: New Agendas in Communication,* ed Janet Staiger, Ann Cvetkovich, and Ann Reynolds(New York: Rutledge, 2010), 18–44; 32, 26.

66. Jennifer Bean, "Affect: The Alchemy of the Contingent," *Feminist Media Histories* 7.2 (2021): 1–20; 1.

67. Gould, "On Affect and Protest," 26.

68. Rosanna Maule and Catherine Russell, "Another Cinephilia: Women's Cinema in the 1920s," *Framework: The Journal of Cinema and Media* 46.1 (2005): 51–55; 52.

69. Ibid., 54 (italics mine). For more on early cinema and embodied spectatorship see Tom Gunning, "The Cinema of Attraction[s]: Early Film, The Spectator, and the Avant Garde," *Wide Angle* 3.4 (1986): 63–70; Patrice Petro, *Joyless Streets: Women and Melodramatic Representation in Weimar Germany* (Princeton NJ: Princeton Univ. Press, 1989); Hansen, *Babel and Babylon;* and Antonia Lant, "Haptical Cinema," *October* 74 (Autumn 1995): 45–73. For more on the tactility of early film, see Doron Galili, Jan Olsson, Marina Dahlquist, and Valentine Rober, eds., *Corporeality in Early Cinema: Viscera, Skin, and Physical Form* (Bloomington: Indiana Univ. Press, 2018).

70. Constance M. Topping Diary, November 2, 1915, 2. Constance Topping Papers, Bancroft Library, University of California, Berkeley. Earlier that spring, Ferrar had famously sung *Carmen* in the Metropolitan Opera House in New York City "for the benefit of unemployed sewing girls in Paris." "Opera Here to Help Paris Sewing Girls," *The Sun* (New York), May 9, 1915, 10.

71. Susan Tucker, Katherine Ott, and Patricia P. Buckler, eds. *The Scrapbook in American Life* (Philadelphia: Temple Univ. Press, 2006); Jessica Helfand, *Scrapbooks: An American History* (New Haven: Yale Univ. Press, 2008); and Ellen Gruber Garvey, *Writing with Scissors: American Scrapbooks from the Civil War to the Harlem Renaissance* (New York: Oxford Univ. Press, 2012).

72. For a study of nineteenth-century theater scrapbooks assembled by female fans see Sharon Marcus, "The Theatrical Scrapbook," *Theatre Survey* 54.2 (2013): 283–307.

73. See Orgeron, "'You Are Invited to Participate.'" For more on girls' movie scrapbooks during WWI, see Diana W. Anselmo, "Bound by Paper: Girl Fans, Movie Scrapbooks and Hollywood Reception During World War I," *Film History: An International Journal* 31.3 (2019): 141–72.

74. Maule and Russell, "Another Cinephilia," 54.

75. Ara Wilson, "The Infrastructure of Intimacy," *Signs: Journal of Women in Culture and Society* 41.2 (2016): 247–80; 247–48.

76. José Esteban Muñoz, "Ephemera as Evidence: Introductory Notes to Queer Acts," *Women and Performance: A Journal of Feminist Theory* 8.2 (1996):

5–16; Alana Kumbier, *Ephemeral Material: Queering the Archive* (Sacramento, CA: Litwin, 2014); and Rebecka Sheffield, *Documenting Rebellions: A Study of Four Lesbian and Gay Archives in Queer Times* (Sacramento, CA: Litwin, 2020).

77. Ann Cvetkovich, *An Archive of Feelings: Trauma, Sexuality, and Lesbian Public Cultures* (Durham, NC: Duke Univ. Press, 2003); and Heather Love, *Feeling Backward: Loss and the Politics of Queer History* (Cambridge MA: Harvard Univ. Press, 2009).

78. Ann Cvetkovich, "In the Archives of Lesbian Feelings: Documentary and Popular Culture," *Camera Obscura* 49 17.1 (2002): 107–47; 111.

79. With the term "social biography," I am drawing on work developed by anthropologist Ruth Tringham and archeologists Chris Gosden and Yvonne Marshall arguing that "objects become invested with meaning through the social interactions they are caught up in. . . . As people and objects gather time, movement and change, they are constantly transformed, and these transformations of person and object are tied up with each other," producing dense palimpsests of autobiography and history that invite the scholar's scalpel. See Gosden and Marshall, "The Cultural Biography of Objects," *World Archaeology* 31.2 (1999): 169–78; 169–70; and Tringham, "Archaeological Houses, Households, Housework and the Home," in *The Home: Words, Interpretations, Meanings, and Environments,* ed. David Benjamin, David Stea, and Eje Aren (Brookfield, VT: Avebury, 1995): 79–107.

80. Mary Desjardins, "Ephemeral Culture/eBay Culture: Film Collectibles and Fan Investments," in *Everyday eBay: Culture, Collecting, and Desire,* ed. Ken Hillis, Michael Petit, and Nathan Scott Epley (New York: Routledge, 2006), 31–43; 33.

81. For more on the embattled history of institutional film preservation in the Anglo-American context, see Penelope Houston, *Keepers of the Frame: The Film Archives* (London: British Film Institute, 1994); Karen F. Gracy, *Film Preservation: Competing Definitions of Value, Use, and Practice* (Chicago: Society of American Archivists, 2007); Caroline Frick, *Saving Cinema: The Politics of Preservation* (New York: Oxford Univ. Press, 2010); and Brian Real, "From Colorization to Orphans: The Evolution of American Public Policy on Film Preservation," *Moving Image* 13.1 (2013): 129–50.

82. Examples include the detailed scrapbook collection devoted to Mary Pickford and Colleen Moore housed in the Margaret Herrick Library in Los Angeles. Donated by the actresses, these fan documents survive either as a byproduct of star labor (Moore gathered the scrapbooks herself) or anonymous gifts presented to a star (Pickford). The anonymity of these fan scrapbookers exemplifies how audience materials often lose their identity and provenance history when granted official shelter. Three exceptions, where a silent-film scrapbooker is given top-billing, are Richard Hoffman's Collection housed in the Museum of Moving Image, New York; Edna Vercoe's scrapbooks at the Margaret Herrick; and Cara Hartwell's collection. According to Kathy Fuller-Seely, Hartwell donated her film scrapbooks and clippings to the Toronto Public Library in 1983. For research on the biography of fan compilers see Richard Abel's chapter "Edna Vercoe's 'Romance with the Movies," *Menus for Movieland,* 257–73.

83. Hastie, *Cupboards of Curiosity*, 4.

84. Paula Amad, *Counter-Archive: Film, the Everyday, and Albert Kahn's Archives de la Planète* (New York: Columbia Univ. Press, 2010).

85. Cvetkovich, *Archive of Feelings*, 253.

86. Ibid., 254.

87. Jane M. Gaines, "Are They 'Just Like Us'?," in *Pink-Slipped: What Happened to Women in the Silent Film Industries?* (Champaign: Univ. of Illinois Press, 2018), 112–31.

88. Hansen, *Babel and Babylon*, 251.

89. See Judith Mayne, "Lesbian Looks: Dorothy Anner and Female Authorship," in *How Do I Look? Queer Film and Video,*. ed. Bad Object Choices (Seattle: Bay Press, 1991), 103–43; Terry Castle, *The Apparitional Lesbian: Female Homosexuality and Modern Culture* (New York: Columbia Univ. Press, 1993); and Susan Potter, *Queer Timing: The Emergence of Lesbian Sexuality in Early Cinema* (Urbana-Champaign: Univ. of Illinois Press, 2019).

90. Laura Horak, *Girls Will Be Boys: Cross-Dressed Women, Lesbians, and American Cinema* (New Brunswick, NJ: Rutgers Univ. Press, 2016).

91. "Girls Admire Girls," *Motography*, April 15, 1916, 855.

92. Patricia White, *Uninvited: Classical Hollywood Cinema and Lesbian Representability* (Indianapolis: Indiana Univ. Press, 1999), 32, 36.

93. Patricia White, "Nazimova's Veils," in *A Feminist Reader in Early Cinema*, ed. Jennifer Bean and Diana Negra (Durham, NC: Duke Univ. Press, 2002), 60–87.

94. Mark Lynn Anderson, *Twilight of the Idols: Hollywood and the Human Sciences in 1920s America* (Berkeley: Univ. of California Press, 2011); and Potter, *Queer Timing*.

95. Sharon Marcus, *Between Women: Friendship, Desire, and Marriage in Victorian England* (New York: Columbia Univ. Press, 2007), 113.

96. See, for instance, K. Austin Collins, "Are We Really Going to Pretend that Gay Kiss in 'The Rise of Skywalker' Matters?," *Vanity Fair,* December 20, 2019, https://www.vanityfair.com/hollywood/2019/12/are-we-really-going-to-pretend-the-gay-kiss-in-the-rise-of-skywalker-matters; and Devin Randall, "Did Marvel's Bucky Barnes Hint That He's Bisexual?," *Instinct Magazine,* March 29, 2021, https://instinctmagazine.com/did-marvels-bucky-barnes-hint-that-hes-bisexual/.

97. Castle, *Apparitional Lesbian*.

98. Jean Baudrillard, *The System of Objects*, trans. James Benedict (London: Verso, 1996), 88. See also Giuliana Bruno, *Streetwalking on a Ruined Map: Cultural Theory and the City Films of Elvira Notari* (Princeton, NJ: Princeton Univ. Press, 1993).

99. Barbara M. Benedict, *Curiosity: A Cultural History of Early Modern Inquiry* (Chicago: Univ. of Chicago Press, 2001), 2.

100. Ibid., 5.

101. Between 1900 and 1903, S.H. James's short story "A Queer Girl" was reprinted many times in local papers across the rural United States, including Idaho's *The Silver Messenger,* February 10, 1903, 5; North Dakota's *Griggs Courier,* April 5, 1900, 6; Montana's *The Western News,* June 3, 1903, 6; and Louisiana's *St. Landry Clarion,* May 5, 1900, 1, and *Bossier Banner,* May 19, 1900,1.

102. Gertrude Barnum, "Vacation Vagaries," *The Evening World Daily Magazine* (New York), July 17, 1908, no page.

103. James, "Queer Girl."

104. Barnum, "Vacation Vagaries"; and James, "Queer Girl."

105. See Bert Hansen, "American Physicians' Earliest Writings about Homosexuals, 1880–1900," *Milbank Quarterly* 67 (1989): 92–108.

106. "Confessions of a Wife," *Day Book* (Chicago), September 20, 1915, 29.

107. Phil Bryce, "Left in Charge," *Coeur D'Alene Press,* August 20, 1904, no page.

108. Douglas Crawford McMurtrie, "Principles of Homosexuality and Sexual Inversion in the Female," *American Journal of Urology and Sexology* 9 (1913): 144–53.

109. See George Chauncey Jr, "From Sexual Inversion to Homosexuality: The Changing Medical Conceptualization of Female 'Deviance,'" in *Passion and Power: Sexuality in History,* ed. Kathy Lee Peiss, Christina Simmons, and Robert A. Padgug (Philadelphia: Temple Univ. Press, 1989), 87–117.

110. Laurel Mae Davis, "The Story Teller: Melons and Cheese," *Minneapolis Journal,* October 26, 1901, 5.

111. Research on first-person fan materials complicating such industrial flattening typically relies on letters women submitted to film magazines, published documents subject to editorial manipulation, and thus more complicated to analyze as autobiographical sources. See Gaylyn Studlar, "The Perils of Pleasure? Fan Magazine Discourse as Woman's Commodified Culture in the 1920s in Silent Film," *Silent Film,* ed. Richard Abel (New Brunswick, NJ: Rutgers Univ. Press, 1996); Sumiko Higashi, "Vitagraph Stardom: Constructing Personalities for 'New' Middle-Class Consumption," *Reclaiming the Archive: Feminism and Film History,* ed. Vicki Callahan (Detroit: Wayne State Univ. Press, 2010), 264–88; Lisa Rose Stead, "'So Oft to the Movies They've Been': British Fan Writing and Female Audiences in the Silent Cinema," *Transformative Works and Cultures* 6 (2011), https://journal.transformativeworks.org/index.php/twc/article/view/224/210; and Tamar Jeffers McDonald, "Reviewing Reviewing the Fan Mags," *Film History: An International Journal* 28.4 (2016): 29–57. Further, examinations of fan mail sent directly to movie celebrities like those conducted by Eric Smoodin and Marsha Orgeron not only survey later decades but also are limited to individual celebrities (Frank Capra and Clara Bow, respectively). See Eric Smoodin, "'This Business of America': Fan Mail, Film Reception, and Meet John Doe," *Screen* 37.1 (1996): 111–28; and Marsha Orgeron, "Making 'It' in Hollywood: Clara Bow, Fandom, and Consumer Culture," *Cinema Journal* 42.4 (2003): 76–97. Likewise, most scholarship on moviegoing girls' private archives tends to focus on post-WWI and WWII rather than on historicizing the emergence of female adolescence in tandem with that of Hollywood's star system. See, for example, Kelly Schrum, *Some Wore Bobby Sox: The Emergence of Teenage Girls' Culture, 1920–1945* (New York: Palgrave, 2004); Jane Greer, "Remixing Educational History: Girls and Their Memory Albums, 1913–1929," in *Mediated Girlhoods: New Explorations of Girls' Media Culture,* ed. Mary Celeste Kearney (New York: Peter Lang, 2011), 221–42; and Leslie Midkiff DeBauche, "Memory Books, the Movies, and Aspiring Vamps," *Observation on Film*

Art (blog), February 8, 2015, http://www.davidbordwell.net/blog/2015/02/08
/memory-books-the-movies-and-aspiring-vamps/

112. Mary Blanchard, "Flickering from Filmdom," *Motion Picture Classic,*
August 1917, 66.

113. White, *Uninvited,* 15.

114. Susan M. Pearce, *On Collecting: An Investigation into Collecting in the
European Tradition* (London: Routledge,1995), 222.

115. "There there" is an expression lesbian novelist Gertrude Stein used to
convey an ineffable sense of recognition, urgency, and identification, a personal
site of affect. Gertrude Stein, *Everybody's Autobiography* (New York: Random
House, 1937), 289.

116. See Carroll Smith-Rosenberg, "The Female World of Love and Ritual:
Relationships Between Women in Nineteenth-Century America," *Signs* 1.1
(1975): 1–29; Nancy Sahli, "Smashing: Women's Relationships Before the Fall,"
Chrysalis 8 (Summer 1979): 17–27; White, *Uninvited*; Martha Vicinus, *Intimate
Friends: Women Who Loved Women, 1778–1928* (Chicago: Univ. of Chicago
Press, 2004); Marcus, *Between Women*; and Muñoz, "Ephemera as Evidence."

117. Faulkner, *Absalom, Absalom!,* 100–101.

CHAPTER 1

Epigraph: Nell Dorr to Lillian Gish, Lillian Gish Papers, Correspondence with
Nell Dorr, 1930s, Billy Rose Theatre Division, New York Public Library for the
Performing Arts.

1. Jackie Stacey, *Star Gazing: Hollywood Cinema and Female Spectatorship*
(New York: Routledge, 1994), 173.

2. See Nancy F. Cott, *The Bonds of Womanhood: "Woman's Sphere" in
New England, 1780–1835* (New Haven, CT: Yale Univ. Press, 1977).

3. Martha Vicinus, *Intimate Friends: Women Who Loved Women, 1778–
1928* (Chicago: Univ. of Chicago Press, 2004).

4. Sharon Marcus, *Between Women: Friendship, Desire, and Marriage in
Victorian England* (New York: Columbia Univ. Press, 2007).

5. Jean Baudrillard, *The System of Objects,* trans. James Benedict (London:
Verso, 1996), 6.

6. Lisa Duggan, *Sapphic Slashers: Sex, Violence and American Modernity*
(Durham NC: Duke Univ. Press, 2000), 793.

7. Ibid., 793.

8. Ibid., 791.

9. See Vicinus, *Intimate Friends*; and Lillian Faderman, *Odd Girls and Twilight Lovers: A History of Lesbian Life in Twentieth-Century America* (New
York: Columbia Univ. Press, 1991).

10. See Elaine Showalter, *The Female Malady: Women, Madness, and Eng-
lish Culture, 1830–1980* (New York: Pantheon, 1985); and Elizabeth Lunbeck,
"'A New Generation of Women': Progressive Psychiatrists and the Hypersexual
Female," *Feminist Studies* 13.3 (1987): 513–43.

11. Robert A. Padgug, "Sexual Matters: On Conceptualizing Sexuality in
History," in *Passion and Power: Sexuality in History,* ed. Kathy Lee Peiss,

Christina Simmons, and Robert A. Padgug (Philadelphia: Temple Univ. Press, 1989), 14–31, 21–22.

12. When tracing the emergence of gender variation and homosexual self-identification in US medical literature, Bert Hansen remarks that turn-of-the-century clinicians "came to focus less on particular sexual actions than on consistent impulses—one might today say 'orientation' or 'preference'—and, by implication, personality. In moving to a level of characterization that departed from gross sexual behavior, the doctors were not inventing a scheme *ex nihilo;* they were following the lead of their patients, most of whom felt that there was *some interior quality which made them 'different,'* whether it appeared in their behavior or not." Bert Hansen, "American Physicians' Earliest Writings about Homosexuals, 1880–1900," *Milbank Quarterly* 67 (1989): 92–108; 97 (italics mine).

13. Heather Love, *Feeling Backward: Loss and the Politics of Queer History* (Cambridge: Harvard Univ. Press, 2009), 31–32.

14. Ibid., 21.

15. Elizabeth French Papers, Class of 1912, September 24, 1912, Vassar College Special Collections.

16. Love, *Feeling Backward,* 77. See, among others, Lillian Faderman, "The Morbidification of Love Between Women by 19th Century Sexologists," *Journal of Homosexuality* 4 (1978): 73–90; Vicinus, *Intimate Friends;* Marcus, *Between Women;* and Lois W. Banner, *Intertwined Lives: Margaret Mead, Ruth Benedict, and Their Circle* (New York: Virago, 2004).

17. See Clemence Dane, *Regiment of Women* (New York: Macmillan, 1917); and Clemence Dane, "A Problem in Education," in *The Woman's Side* (London: Herbert Jenkins, 1926), 173.

18. Carol Lasser, "'Let Us Be Sisters Forever': The Sororal Model of Nineteenth-Century Female Friendship," *Signs* 14 (1988): 158–81; and Carroll Smith-Rosenberg, "The Female World of Love and Ritual: Relations Between Women in Nineteenth-Century America," *Signs* (Autumn 1975): 1–29.

19. Richard von Krafft-Ebing, *Psychopathia Sexualis*, trans. Charles Gilbert Chaddock (Philadelphia: F. J. Rebman, 1894), 283.

20. Irving King, *The High-School Age* (New York: Bobbs-Merrill Company, 1914), 118–19.

21. Krafft-Ebing, *Psychopathia Sexualis,* 283.

22. Vicinus, *Intimate Friends,* xviii.

23. "The School Girl 'Crush,'" *The Medical Standard,* 37.4 (April 1914): 71.

24. Samuel Caldwell (1885). Quoted in Banner, *Intertwined Lives,* 34.

25. Vicinus, *Intimate Friends,* xviii.

26. Havelock Ellis, *Studies in the Psychology of Sex: Sexual Inversion* (Philadelphia: F. A. Davis, 1902), 121.

27. August Forel, *The Sexual Question: A Scientific, Psychological, Hygienic and Sociological Study,* trans. C. F. Marshal (New York, Rebman, 1908), 251.

28. Eve K. Sedgwick, *Epistemology of the Closet* (Berkeley: Univ. of California Press, 1990), 8.

29. "School Girl 'Crush,'" 71.

30. Mabelle Smith Kent Scrapbook, Schlesinger Library, Radcliffe Institute, Harvard University.

31. "School Girl 'Crush,'" 71. See also Douglas C. McMurtrie, "Principles of Homosexuality and Sexual Inversion in the Female," *American Journal of Urology* 9 (1913): 147; and "Manifestations of Sexual Inversion in the Female," *Urologic and Cutaneous Review* 18 (1914): 444–46.

32. "School Girl 'Crush,'" 71 (italics mine).

33. Margaret Otis, "A Perversion Not Commonly Noted," *Journal of Abnormal Psychology* 8.2 (1913): 113–16.

34. G. Stanley Hall, "The Awkward Age," *Appleton's Magazine,* August 1908, 156.

35. McMurtrie, "Principles of Homosexuality," 144.

36. Ibid., 149 (italics mine). See also George Chauncey Jr, "From Sexual Inversion to Homosexuality: Medicine and the Changing Conceptualization of Female Deviance," *Salmagundi* (Fall 1982/Winter1983): 114–46.

37. Duggan, *Sapphic Slashers,* 2

38. "Friends Prefer End Lives to Parting," *Los Angeles Evening Herald,* 23 March 1917, 1. Other examples include "Girl Prisoners Starts Fire in Jail; One Dies," discussing the attempted double suicide of Stella Maxwell and Freda Kampka, two girls who, before being cellmates, lived together and been had arrested together on "charges of stealing furs." Maxwell died of injuries sustained in the fire while Kampka recuperated. *Los Angeles Herald,* 20 January 1911, 3.

39. "Mystical Love Impels Suicide," *Los Angeles Herald,* 23 March 1917, 1.

40. Ibid.

41. "Mystical Love Impels Suicide"; and "Girls Commit Suicide in Booth at a Restaurant," *Indianapolis News,* 23 March 1917,14

42. Monica Witting, "Introduction," in "Special Section: Lesbians and Film," ed. Edith Becker, Michelle Citron, Julia Lesage, and B. Ruby Rich, *Jump Cut: A Review of Contemporary Media* (March 1981): 17.

43. "What Happened to Mary: The Remarkable Story of a Remarkable Girl," *Ladies' World* 33.8 (August 1912): 3.

44. Love, *Feeling Backwards,* 77.

45. Katherine Bement Davis, *Factors in the Sex Life of Twenty-Two Hundred Women* (New York: Harper and Brothers, 1929), 391 (italics mine).

46. Medora Espy Papers, Washington State Historical Society, Research Center, Tacoma WA.

47. Ibid., January 27, 1915; February 6, 1915.

48. Ibid., March 15, 1915 (italics mine).

49. Ibid., March 21, 1915.

50. Vicinus, *Intimate Friends,* 200; and Davis, *Factors in Sex and Life,* 255. See also the case studies recorded by Chicago psychologist James G. Kiernan, in which one young women testifies to being "aware of the fact that while her lascivious dreams and thoughts are excited by females, those of her female friends are excited by males. *She regards her feeling as morbid.*" James G. Kiernan, "Perverted Sexual Instinct," *Chicago Medical Journal and Examiner* 48 (March 1884): 263–65; 264 (italics mine).

51. Kathy Peiss, *Cheap Amusements: Working Women and Leisure in Turn-of-the-Century New York City* (Philadelphia: Temple Univ. Press, 1986).

52. Katherine Synon, "The Unspoiled Mary Pickford," *Photoplay,* September 1914, 144.

53. Della McLeod, "Mae Murray's Love-Letters Are All From Little Girls," *Motion Picture Magazine,* January 1918, 43.

54. Ibid.

55. Emma E. Walker, M.D. "Pretty Girl Papers," *Ladies' Home Journal,* January 1914, 21 (italics mine).

56. Clara Ewing Espey, *Leaders of Girls* (New York: Abingdon Press, 1915), 169.

57. "Are You Movie Struck?," *Los Angeles Times,* April 22, 1917, 3.

58. "Answer Department," *Motion Picture Magazine,* August 1915, 136.

59. Both archived at Natural History Museum of Los Angeles County, Seaver Center, Los Angeles.

60. See Cott, *Bonds of Womanhood.*

61. Joanne Dobson, "Reclaiming Sentimental Literature," *American Literature* 69.2 (1997): 263–88; 268.

62. Jennifer A. Williamson, "Introduction: American Sentimentalism from the Nineteenth Century to the Present," in *Sentimental Mode: Essays in Literature, Film and Television,* ed. Jennifer A. Williamson, Jennifer Larson, and Ashley Reed (Jefferson, NC: McFarland, 2014), 11.

63. Dobson, "Reclaiming Sentimental Literature," 266.

64. Kathy Fuller-Seeley, *At the Picture Show: Small-Town Audiences and the Creation of Movie Fan Culture* (Washington, DC: Smithsonian, 1996); Samantha Barbas, *Movie Crazy: Stars, Fans and the Cult of Celebrity* (New York: Palgrave Macmillan, 2011); Richard Abel, *Americanizing the Movies and 'Movie-Mad' Audiences, 1910–1914* (Berkeley: Univ. of California Press, 2006); and Marsha Orgeron, "'You Are Invited to Participate': Interactive Fandom in the Age of the Movie Magazine," *Journal of Film and Video* 61.3 (2009), 3–23; 19.

65. Anke Brouwers, "If it Worked for Mary . . . : Mary Pickford's 'Daily Talks' with the Fans," in *Researching Women in Silent Cinema: New Findings and Perspectives,* ed. Monica Dall'Asta, Victoria Duckett, and Lucia Tralli, Women and Screen Cultures (Bologna, Italy: Univ. of Bologna, 2013), 197–219; 197–98, ebook. Importantly, Brouwers mentions that Frances Marion ghostwrote Pickford's column.

66. Ibid., 197, 204.

67. Mary Pickford, "Mary Pickford's Daily Talks: Memories from Yesterday," *The Sun* (New York), 18 October, 1916.

68. See Leslie Midkiff DeBauche, "Testimonial Advertising Using Movie Stars in the 1910s: How Billie Burke Came to Sell Pond's Vanishing Cream in 1917," in *Marketing History at the Center,* ed. Blaine J Branchik (Durham, NC: CHARM Association, 2007), 146–56, accessed March 18, 2021, https://ojs.library.carleton.ca/index.php/pcharm/issue/view/102.

69. Dobson, "Reclaiming Sentimental Literature," 266–67.

70. Susan K. Harris, *Nineteenth-Century American Women Novels: Interpretative Strategies* (New York: Cambridge Univ. Press, 1990).

71. Williamson, "Introduction," 6.

72. Faye Halpern, *Sentimental Readers: The Rise, Fall, and Revival of a Disparaged Rhetoric* (Iowa City: Univ. of Iowa Press, 2013), 140.

73. Vicinus, *Intimate Friends,* xix.

74. Margaret Louise Croft Memory Book, 1921–1922, Beinecke Rare Book and Manuscript Library, Yale University.

75. Terry Castle, *The Apparitional Lesbian: Female Homosexuality and Modern Culture* (New York: Columbia Univ. Press,1993); and Judith Butler, "Imitation and Gender Insubordination," in *The Lesbian and Gay Studies Reader,* ed. Henry Abelove, Michèle Aina Barale, and David M. Halperin (New York: Routledge, 1993), 307–20.

76. Teresa de Lauretis, "Sexual Indifference and Lesbian Representation," *Theatre Journal* 40.2 (1988):155–77, 160.

77. Peter Brooks, *The Melodramatic Imagination: Balzac, Henry James, Melodrama, and the Mode of Excess* (New Haven, CT: Yale Univ. Press, 1976), 3.

78. Williamson, "Introduction," 6.

79. Cott, *Bonds of Womanhood,* 190 (italics mine).

80. Duggan, *Sapphic Slashers,* 793.

CHAPTER 2

Epigraph: Dorothy Strachey to André Gide, December 5, 1933, *Selected Letters of André Gide and Dorothy Bussy,* ed. Richard Tedesch (New York: Oxford Univ. Press, 1983).

1. See Patricia White, *Uninvited: Classical Hollywood Cinema and Lesbian Representability* (Indianapolis: Indiana Univ. Press, 1999).

2. For an overview of the creation of film stars in early Hollywood, see Richard deCordova, *Picture Personalities: The Emergence of the Star System in America* (Chicago: Univ. of Illinois Press, 1990).

3. Patricia White, "Black and White: Mercedes de Acosta's Glorious Enthusiasms," in *Reclaiming the Archive: Feminism and Film History,* ed. Vicki Callahan (Detroit: Wayne State Univ. Press, 2010), 231–57; 253. Though illuminating, scholarship on queer female spectatorship and fan correspondence tends to focus on classical Hollywood and the star text of female icons. See Andrea Weiss, "'A Queer Feeling When I Look at You': Female Stars and Lesbian Spectatorship in the 1930s," in *Stardom: Industry of Desire,* ed. Christine Gledhill (London: Routledge, 1991), 283–99; White, "Black and White"; and Lisa Cohen, *All We Know: Three Lives* (New York: Macmillan, 2012).

4. Elsie Johnson, Chicago, March 8, 1912, Florence Lawrence Papers, Seaver Center, Natural History Museum of Los Angeles County (NHMLAC). All correspondence quoted in this chapter originates from this collection, unless otherwise noted.

5. J. Cecile Holmes, New York, July 1, 1912.

6. Sharon Marcus, *Between Women: Friendship, Desire, and Marriage in Victorian England* (New York: Columbia Univ. Press, 2007), 46.

7. Theodora Anthony, Bristol, RI, December 10, ca. 1919. There is no year stated on this letter, only a postmark of "December 10." The girl mentions writing on a Sunday morning, and there are no visible breaks in the prose. Since

most letters seem to have been posted a couple of days after being written, and taking into consideration Anthony's peter-pan collar and bobbed hair, this missive likely dates from 1918 or 1919. Sundays fell on December 8th and 7th, respectively. The "bobbed hair" style began to be popular in periodicals and on celebrities in 1918.

8. Marie B. Hiller, Minneapolis, August 14, 1910.

9. Virginia Kramer and Helen Wood, Elizabeth City, NC, August 31, 1911.

10. Isabel Rae, New York, NY, March 22, 1911.

11. Nicknames are associated with youth, since this is the time when most become attached to a person. Cultivating fan-coined star monikers was thus a concerted marketing ploy on the part of the film industry, aiming to further humanize and juvenate picture personalities by endearing audiences' affective investment.

12. Jessie Virginia Wakefield, Pittsburgh, PA, January 15, 1913.

13. Nance O'Neill, New Bedford, MA, no day, 1914.

14. Mabel Hilton, Hartford, CT, November 24, 1911.

15. Dorothy E. Swart, Saratoga Springs, NY, January 1916.

16. "Slanguage," *Chicago Tribune,* c.1921, Lolita Hattie Woodward Scrapbook, Beinecke Rare Book and Manuscript Library, Yale University.

17. Holmes, July 1, 1912.

18. Miss Anna Mae Oldham, Philadelphia, November 14, 1911.

19. Edith Crutcher, Dallas, April 14th, 1910.

20. Rose Sachmmellen, St. Louis, April 11, 1910.

21. Hilton, November 24, 1911.

22. Emma E. Walker, M.D. "Pretty Girl Papers," *Ladies' Home Journal,* January 1914, 21.

23. Ruth Ashmore, "The Intense Friendships of Girls," *Ladies' Home Journal,* July 1898, 20.

24. Walker, "Pretty Girl Papers," 21.

25. Ashmore, "Intense Friendships of Girls," 20.

26. See Cheryl D. Hicks, "'Bright and Good Looking Colored Girl': Black Women's Sexuality and 'Harmful Intimacy' in Early-Twentieth-Century New York," *Journal of the History of Sexuality* (2009): 418–56.

27. Walker, "Pretty Girl Papers," 78 (italics mine).

28. Ashmore, "Intense Friendships of Girls," 20 (italics mine).

29. Ibid.

30. Marcus, *Between Women,* 47.

31. Dorothy Strachey, *Olivia* (New York: Penguin Books, [1949] 2020), 43.

32. Ibid., 57 (italics mine).

33. Walker, "Pretty Girl Papers," 78.

34. Wakefield, January 15, 1913.

35. Ibid. (italics mine).

36. Charles Baxter, "Introduction," in Wright Morris, *Plains Song* (Lincoln: Univ. of Nebraska Press, [1980] 2000), xiv.

37. Wakefield, January 15, 1913.

38. Sigmund Freud, "The Psychogenesis of a Case of Homosexuality in a Woman," *International Journal of Psycho-Analysis* 1.2 (1920): 125–49; 125, 132.

39. Marcus, *Between Women,* 49.

40. Karen V. Hansen, "'No Kisses Is Like Youres': An Erotic Friendship Between Two African-American Women during the Mid-Nineteenth Century," *Gender and History* 7.2 (1995): 153–82; Annamarie Jagose, *Queer Theory: An Introduction* (New York: NYU Press, 1996); Estelle B. Freedman, "'The Burning of Letters Continues': Elusive Identities and the Historical Construction of Sexuality," *Journal of Women's History* (Winter 1998): 181–99; and Jacquelyn Down Hall, "'To Widen the Reach of Our Love': Autobiography, History, and Desire," *Feminist Studies* 26.1 (2000): 230–47.

41. Walker, "Pretty Girl Papers," 78.

42. Teresa de Lauretis, "Sexual Indifference and Lesbian Representation," *Theatre Journal* 40.2 (1988):155–77; 165.

43. See Sigmund Freud, "Three Essays on the Theory of Sexuality" (1905), *The Standard Edition of the Complete Psychological Works of Sigmund Freud,* vol. 7, trans. James Strachey (London: Hogarth Press, 1953): 123–246; and Asti Hustvedt, *Medical Muses: Hysteria in Nineteenth-Century Paris* (New York: W. W. Norton, 2011).

44. Miss Marie Benson, Houston, February 6, likely 1916. The letter says "1915" but the post-office stamp reads "1916."

45. Nance O'Neill, New Bedford, MA, April, no day, 1915.

46. Lillian Faderman, *Odd Girls and Twilight Lovers: A History of Lesbian Life in Twentieth-Century America* (New York: Columbia Univ. Press, 1991).

47. "Executor Paints Miss Carroll as Ideal Character," *News Scimitar* (Memphis, TN), February 7, 1919, 1.

48. In the late 1890s, "unnatural affection" became a code reporters used to describe same-sex relationships suspected of homosexual content. Examples include "Bodies Recovered," *Scranton (PA) Tribune,* August 10, 1898, 8; "Loved One of Her Own Sex," *Wichita (KS) Daily Eagle,* May 4, 1899, 2; "Sworn Statement Saved Slorah from Fearful Fate," *Alaska Citizen,* October 28, 1912, 5; "Executor Paints Miss Carroll as Ideal Character," *News Scimitar* (Memphis, TN), February 7, 1919, 1.

49. Marsha Orgeron, "'You Are Invited to Participate': Interactive Fandom in the Age of the Movie Magazine," *Journal of Film and Video* 61.3 (2009): 3–23; 18–19 (italics mine).

50. Anna Ford, Hanover, PA, June 15, 1912.

51. Crutcher, April 14, 1910.

52. Swart, January 1916 (italics mine).

53. Myrtle Bradshaw, Somerville, MA, February 18, 1916 (italics mine).

54. Wakefield, January 15, 1913.

55. Miss Edna J. Hall, Bath, ME, February 14, 1916 (all underlining is Hall's). Likely this resurgence of fan mail to Lawrence stemmed from major film magazines publishing retrospectives on the pioneer actress in the mid-1910s. See, for example, the series of articles by Florence Lawrence "in collaboration with Monte M. Katterjohn" that *Photoplay* ran in 1915: "Growing Up With the Movies," *Photoplay,* February 1915, 142–46.

56. For more on the speed of modern time and how it took shape in urban American cities and cinema, see Ben Singer, *Melodrama and Modernity:*

Early Sensational Cinema and Its Contexts (New York: Columbia Univ. Press, 2001).

57. Marcus, *Between Women,* 45.

58. Joanne Dobson, "Reclaiming Sentimental Literature," *American Literature* 69.2 (1997): 263–88; 273.

59. Anthony, December 10, ca. 1919 (all underlining is Anthony's).

60. Rose Horte, Baltimore, May 1911.

61. Laura Baillargeon, New Bedford, MA, February 1916.

62. Jean Wilson Martin, Oberlin, OH, November 13, 1911.

63. Ibid.

64. Orgeron, "'You Are Invited to Participate," 18.

65. F. C. Singleton, Dallas, August 19, 1910.

66. Oldham, November 14, 1911

67. Denise McKenna, "The Photoplay or the Pickaxe: Extras, Gender and Labour in Early Hollywood," *Film History: An International Journal* 23.1 (2011): 5–19.

68. Bradshaw, December 18, 1916.

69. Medora Espy Correspondence and Loose Clippings, 1915, Medora Espy Papers, Research Center, Washington State Historical Society, Tacoma.

70. Miss Eileen A. Smith, Buffalo, NY, March 13, 1911.

71. Walter Benjamin, "Little History of Photography" (1931), *Selected Writings,* vol. 2, *1927–1934,* trans. Rodney Livingston, ed. Michael W. Jennings, Howard Eiland, and Gary Smith (Cambridge, MA: Harvard Univ. Press, 1999), 507–30; 519.

72. Aaron Ritzenberg, *The Sentimental Touch: The Language of Feeling in the Age of Managerialism* (New York: Fordham Univ. Press, 2013), 37.

73. "Advertising Section," *Photoplay,* November 1920, 115. According to Nitrateville, the Emerson Phonograph Company manufactured the professional recordings that the Talking Photo Corporation then commercialized in record stores across the country. Each recording seems to have run for about two minutes and up to ninety different titles may have been planned, though only twelve are confirmed to have been released. See: Harold Aherne, "Talk-O-Photo Records (1920)," January 27, 2013, accessed August 13, 2020, https://www.nitrateville.com/viewtopic.php?t=14189.

74. Miss Elsie Shallaby, Pittsburgh, PA, February 16, 1915.

75. Mathilda Thompson, Trenton, NJ, February 19, 1915.

76. Constance M. Topping Diary, May 23, 1921. Bancroft Library, University of California, Berkeley.

77. "Beauty and Brains Contest," *Photoplay,* November 1915, 86.

78. The actress in question is Norma Talmadge, whose "summer home at Beechhurst, Long Island, N.Y." provided the backdrop to the 1917 film *The Moth,* produced by the star's own film company. "Green Room Jottings," *Motion Picture Classic,* August 1917, 71.

79. "Sherbet Quaffman's Weekly Page," *Sun-Dial* (Athens, OH), April 1916, 19.

80. Miss Malina Wanamaker, Salt Lake City, UT, March 4, 1916.

81. "Mary Pickford: All Dressed Up Coming To You," *Boston Herald–Providence News,* April 30, 1921, 17.

82. Ibid.

83. Francis X. Bushman, Douglas Fairbanks, Charlie Chaplin, and Roscoe Arbuckle are the only male actors I could find that had paper dolls made in their likeness during the 1910s. That only two of these players were considered heartthrobs (the first two) says much about how, at this time, the film industry not only saw female audiences as compulsorily heteronormative but also labored to curtail female erotic investment in picture stars.

84. See Jane Gaines, "Costume and Narrative: How Dress Tells the Women's Story," in *Fabrications: Costume and the Female Body,* ed. Jane Gaines and Charlotte Herzog (New York: Routledge, 1990), 180–211; Lucy Fischer, *Designing Women: Cinema, Art Deco, and the Female Form* (New York: Columbia Univ. Press, 2003); and Michelle Finamore, *Hollywood Before Glamour: Fashion in American Silent Film* (New York: Palgrave, 2013).

85. "Mary Pickford," *Boston Herald–Providence News,* 17.

86. For more on the gendered and racial scripts etched on turn-of-the-century paper dolls, see Robin Bernstein, *Racial Innocence: Performing American Childhood from Slavery to Civil Rights* (New York: New York Univ. Press, 2011).

87. Clara Moore, New York, September 25, 1914 (?) and November 16, 1914. These images also evidence the cult of Japonism that gripped US visual culture. Since the turn of the century, the romanticized sexualization of non-Western peoples, in particular Japanese girls, had percolated through US popular culture. Japonism in the performing arts crystalized around a spectatorial fascination with Giacomo Puccini's opera *Madame Butterfly* (1903), which Mary Pickford first embodied on the big screen in 1915.

88. Shelley Stamp, *Movie-Struck Girls: Women and Motion Picture Culture after the Nickelodeon* (Princeton, NJ: Princeton Univ. Press, 2000), 125.

89. Lucile Pervas, Portland, OR, December 7, 1911.

90. Krafft-Ebing, *Psychopathia Sexualis,* 279, 285.

91. Pervas, December 7, 1911.

92. Ibid.

93. Faye Halpern, *Sentimental Readers: The Rise, Fall, and Revival of a Disparaged Rhetoric* (Iowa City: Univ. of Iowa Press, 2013), 142.

94. Bert Hansen, "American Physicians' Earliest Writings about Homosexuals, 1880–1900," *Milbank Quarterly* 67 (1989): 92–108; 96.

95. Lisa Spiro, "Reading with a Tender Rapture: Reveries of a Bachelor and the Rhetoric of Detached Intimacy," *Book History* 6 (2003): 53–93; 67.

96. Nance O'Neill, New Bedford, MA, December 5, 1914.

97. Ibid., May 4, 1915.

98. Ibid., no day, October 1914.

99. Ibid., May 4, 1915.

100. Ibid., no day, October 1914.

101. Marcus, *Between Women,* 47.

102. Peter Brooks, *The Melodramatic Imagination: Balzac, Henry James, Melodrama, and the Mode of Excess* (New Haven, CT: Yale Univ. Press, 1976), 9, 11.

103. Marcus, *Between Women,* 47.

104. Brooks, *Melodramatic Imagination,* 5.

105. Martha Vicinus, "Distance and Desire: English Boarding-School Friendships," *Signs: Journal of Women in Culture and Society* 9.4 (Summer 1984): 600–22; 607–8.

106. Ritzenberg, *Sentimental Touch*, 17.

107. Baldassare Castiglione, *The Book of the Courtier* (1528), trans. Leonard E. Opdyce (New York: Scribner's Sons, 1902), 232.

108. O'Neill, November 16, 1914.

109. For example, the term "queer" features repeatedly in a series of articles that ran in the *Los Angeles Times* throughout November 1914. The articles describe the uncovering by Long Beach police of a "social vagrant" club. "Degenerate" men would congregate to dress up in feminine garb, including "kimonos, silk underwear and hosiery, and some wore women's wigs." According to a witness, "at these 'drags' the 'queer' people have a good time," while preying on "young boys—chickens they call them." See, *Los Angeles Times,* November 14, 1914, 8; November 19, 1914, 10; November 26, 1914, 8; and November 21, 1914, 4. Also see Peter Boag, *Re-Dressing America's Frontier Past* (Berkeley: Univ. of California Press, 2011), 209.

110. O'Neill, December 19, 1917.

111. Pervas, December 7, 1911.

112. O'Neill, May 4, 1915 (italics mine).

113. For a history of nineteenth-century stage fandom, see Daniel Cavicchi, "Fandom Before 'Fan': Shaping the History of Enthusiastic Audiences," *Reception: Texts, Readers, Audiences, History* 6.1 (2014): 52–72.

114. Warren I. Susman, "'Personality' and the Making of Twentieth-Century Culture," in *Culture as History: The Transformation of American Society in the Twentieth Century* (New York: Pantheon, 1973), 277. For more on the centrality of "personality" to the promotion of early US film stars, see Richard Abel, *Americanizing the Movies and 'Movie-Mad' Audiences, 1910–1914* (Berkeley: Univ. of California Press, 2006).

115. Susman, "Personality," 277.

116. Lisa Duggan, *Sapphic Slashers: Sex, Violence and American Modernity* (Durham NC: Duke Univ. Press, 2000), 799–800.

117. Louise Johnson, Washington, DC, June 3, 1911.

118. Anthony, December 10, ca. 1919.

119. See Karen Sanchez-Eppler, *Dependent States: The Child's Part in Nineteenth-Century American Culture* (Chicago: Univ. of Chicago Press), 2005.

120. Angelina Mary Kovez, Regina, SK, Canada, February 14, 1916.

121. Francesca M. Cancian, *Love in America: Gender and Self-Development* (New York: Cambridge Univ. Press, 1987).

122. Ibid., 3.

123. Paul F. Lazarsfeld and Robert K. Merton, "Friendship as a Social Process: A Substantive and Methodological Analysis," in *Freedom and Control in Modern Society,* ed. Morroe Berger, Theodore Abel, and Charles Page (New York: Wiley, 1954), 18–66.

124. Wanamaker, March 4, 1916.

125. Florence Turner, in an interview with *The Daily Mirror,* July 12, 1924, cutout, NHMLAC.

CHAPTER 3

Epigraph: Helen Hartley Pease, Diary, 1915–1919, Class of 1918, Vassar College Special Collections, College Women, https://www.collegewomen.org /node/13671, Accessed May 30, 2021.

1. Mabel Hilton, Hartford, CT, November 24, 1911, Florence Lawrence Papers, Natural History Museum of Los Angeles County (NHMLAC) (italics mine).

2. Blondina, "Just a Little Advice," *Motion Picture Magazine,* June 1914, 122.

3. Betty Ethridge, "Of All the Maids Who Are So Sweet," *Motion Picture Magazine,* June 1914, 122.

4. Ernesta Hoawald, "To Edith Storey," *Motion Picture Magazine,* June 1914, 123. Her surname suggests German origins, which may explain the fan's confessed anxiety about not yet mastering the English language.

5. Mary Ann Doane, "Film and the Masquerade: Theorising the Female Spectator," *Screen* 23.3–4 (1982): 74–88; 81.

6. Emma Stewart Card, "A Film Fan's Favorites," *Motion Picture Classic,* April 1917, 34 (italics mine).

7. See Samuel Otter, *Melville's Anatomies* (Berkeley: Univ. of California Press, 1999).

8. Marianne Nobel, "'Weird Curves': Masochism and Feminism," *The Masochistic Pleasure of Sentimental Literature* (Princeton, NJ: Princeton Univ. Press, 2000), 6.

9. Sigmund Freud, "The Psychogenesis of a Case of Female Homosexuality," *International Journal of Psycho-Analysis* 1.2 (1920): 125–49, 132 (italics mine).

10. Ibid., 138.

11. Dorothy Strachey, *Olivia* (New York: Penguin Books, [1949] 2020), 56–57.

12. Luce Irigaray, *This Sex Which Is Not One,* trans. Catherine Porter (Ithaca, NY: Cornell Univ. Press, 1985), 172.

13. Lisa Spiro, "Reading with a Tender Rapture: Reveries of a Bachelor and the Rhetoric of Detached Intimacy," *Book History* 6 (2003): 53–93; 61.

14. Laura Horak, *Girls Will Be Boys: Cross-Dressed Women, Lesbians, and American Cinema* (New Brunswick, NJ: Rutgers Univ. Press, 2016), 52.

15. Minna Irving, "Reel Romance," *Motion Picture Classic,* March 1920, 70.

16. Florence Gertrude Ruthven, "Only a Face on the Screen," *Motion Picture Magazine,* February 1917, 35.

17. Terry Castle, *The Apparitional Lesbian: Female Homosexuality and Modern Culture* (New York: Columbia Univ. Press, 1993).

18. Constance Only, "The Voice of the Movie Fan," *Chicago Daily Tribune,* November 8, 1914, 9 (italics mine).

19. Susan Potter, *Queer Timing: The Emergence of Lesbian Sexuality in Early Cinema* (Urbana-Champaign: Univ. of Illinois Press, 2019).

20. Mabel W. Burleson, "Her Smacks Are All Certified and Screened," *Motion Picture Magazine,* November 1916, 130.

21. Patricia White, *Uninvited: Classical Hollywood Cinema and Lesbian Representability* (Indianapolis: Indiana Univ. Press, 1999), xi.

22. Dorothy M. Hills, *Motion Picture Magazine,* March 1915, 121.

23. Martha Vicinus, *Intimate Friends: Women Who Loved Women, 1778–1928* (Chicago: Univ. of Chicago Press, 2004), xxv.

24. Pearl White, *Just Me* (New York: George H. Doran, 1919), viii.

25. Ibid., ix.

26. See Melody Bridges and Cheryl Robson, eds., *Silent Women: Pioneers of Cinema* (Twickenham, UK: Supernova, 2016).

27. See Richard Abel, ed., *Movie Mavens: US Newspaper Women Take On the Movies, 1914–1923* (Champaign: Univ. of Illinois Press, 2021); and Roseanne Welch, ed., *When Women Wrote Hollywood: Essays on Female Screenwriters in the Early Film Industry* (New York: McFarland, 2018).

28. White, *Uninvited*, 36.

29. Miriam Hansen, "Pleasure, Ambivalence, Identification: Valentino and Female Spectatorship," *Cinema Journal* 25.4 (1986): 6–32.

30. Ibid., 18.

31. Janice Radway, *Reading the Romance: Women, Patriarchy, and Popular Literature* (Chapel Hill: Univ. of North Carolina Press, 1984).

32. Marilyn Frye, "Lesbian Feminism and the Gay Rights Movement: Another View of Male Supremacy, Another Separatism," in *Politics of Reality: Essays in Feminist Theory* (Berkeley, CA: Crossing Press, 1983), 129.

33. Jean Wilson Martin, Oberlin, OH, November 16, 1911, Florence Lawrence Papers, NHMLAC.

34. Jessie Virginia Wakefield, Pittsburgh, PA, January 15, 1913, Florence Lawrence Papers, NHMLAC.

35. Linda Williams, "'Personal Best': Women in Love," *Jump Cut: A Review of Contemporary Media* 27 (July 1982): 1, 11–12.

36. Chris Straayer, *Deviant Eyes, Deviant Bodies: Sexual Re-orientations in Film and Video* (New York: Columbia Univ. Press, 1996).

37. See Laura Mulvey's groundbreaking article "Visual Pleasure and Narrative Cinema," *Screen* 16.3 (1975): 6–18.

CHAPTER 4

Epigraph: Richard Hugo, *The Triggering Town: Lectures and Essays on Poetry and Writing* (New York: W. W. Norton, 1979), 15.

1. Deborah Gould, "On Affect and Protest," in *Political Emotions: New Agendas in Communication,* ed Janet Staiger, Ann Cvetkovich, and Ann Reynolds (New York: Routledge, 2010), 18–44; 26.

2. José Esteban Muñoz, "Ephemera as Evidence: Introductory Notes to Queer Acts," *Women and Performance: A Journal of Feminist Theory* 8.2 (1996): 5–16; 7.

3. Neil Bartlett, *Who Was That Man? A Present for Mr. Oscar Wilde* (London: Serpent's Tail, 1988), 99.

4. Barbara M. Benedict, *Curiosity: A Cultural History of Early Modern Inquiry* (Chicago: Univ. of Chicago Press, 2001), 16.

5. Muñoz, "Ephemera as Evidence," 6.

6. Richard deCordova, *Picture Personalities: The Emergence of the Star System in America* (Chicago: Univ. of Illinois Press, 1990), 140 (italics mine).

7. Linus W. Kline and C.J. France, "The Psychology of Ownership," in *Aspects of Child's Life and Education*, ed. G. Stanley Hall (Boston: Ginn and Company, 1907), 241–87. For a history of scrapbooking in the United States with careful readings of race and class, see Ellen Gruber Garvey, *Writing with Scissors: American Scrapbooks from the Civil War to the Harlem Renaissance* (New York: Oxford Univ. Press, 2012).

8. Kelly Schrum, *Some Wore Bobby Sox: The Emergence of Teenage Girls' Culture, 1920–1945* (New York: Palgrave, 2004); Jane Greer, "Remixing Educational History: Girls and Their Memory Albums, 1913–1929," in *Mediated Girlhoods: New Explorations of Girls' Media Culture*, ed. Mary Celeste Kearney (New York: Peter Lang, 2011), 221–42; and Leslie Midkiff DeBauche, "Memory Books, the Movies, and Aspiring Vamps," *Observation on Film Art* (blog), February 8, 2015, http://www.davidbordwell.net/blog/2015/02/08/memory-books-the-movies-and-aspiring-vamps/.

9. See Garvey, *Writing with Scissors.*

10. "Movy album" is a term used by teenaged Florence Schreiber in a letter to Edna Vercoe. Edna G. Vercoe Collection, December 1914, Margaret Herrick Library, The Academy of Motion Picture Arts and Sciences, Los Angeles (AMPAS). The hybridity of the fan-coined term "movy album," much like its purposeful misspelling, holds considerable meaning. Both instances gesture toward youth culture's appropriation of mainstream objects and to the scrapbook's own constitutional ambivalence. Editors Susan Tucker, Katherine Ott, and Patricia P. Buckler note that "from the beginning the scrapbook and the [photograph] album were interchangeable in function," that being to preserve cherished memories and broadcast intimacy through "domestic display." *The Scrapbook in American Life* (Philadelphia: Temple Univ. Press, 2006), 12.

11. Georganne Scheiner, *Signifying Female Adolescence: Film Representations and Fans, 1920–1950* (New York: Praeger, 2000), 130.

12. I found only two movie scrapbooks crafted by boy fans: one is by Richard Hoffman, a thirteen-year-old schoolboy from Staten Island, New York, who amassed an extensive collection of film ephemera between 1913 and 1916, now held at the Museum of the Moving Image in Astoria, New York. I own the other scrapbook. See Richard Koszarski, "Richard Hoffman: A Collector's Archive," in *A Companion to Early Cinema*, ed. André Gaudreault, Nicolas Dulac, and Santiago Hidalgo (Chichester, UK: Wiley-Blackwell, 2012), 498–523.

13. Esther Hoffman, "My Movie Scrap Book," *Tacoma (WA) Times,* April 19, 1915, 5. See also "Beautiful Foreign Actress Seen in Films," *Reading (PA) Times*, March 7, 1914, 3; and *Day Book* (Chicago), April 6, 1914, 23.

14. Esther Hoffman's "My Movie Scrap Book" write-up seems to have first appeared in the *Evening Republican* (PA), April 7, 1915, 9, and subsequently in the *Tacoma Times*, April 15, 1915, 5; the *Wilkes-Barre (PA) Times Leader*, April 21, 1915, 2; the *Wichita (KS) Beacon*, April 22, 1915, 8; the *Courier-Gazette* (McKinney, TX), April 27, 1915, 2; *Vicksburg (MS) Evening Post*, May 1, 1915, 3; and the *Day Book* (Chicago), May 7, 1915, 4, among others. Fans' movie scrapbooks continued to be of interest to US newspapers in the 1920s. For example, the illustrated feature For the Film Fan's Scrapbook supplied readers of the

New York Evening Public Ledger with cuttable star headshots throughout 1921 and 1922. All the headshots I could locate are of female stars.

15. "Patriotic 'War Tea,'" *El Paso (TX) Herald*, March 9, 1918, 11.

16. "Notes and Activities in the World of Society," *New York Sun*, April 20, 1919, 7.

17. "More Scrapbooks Needed to Cheer Wounded Soldiers," *New York Tribune*, March 23, 1919, 3.

18. "Film-Land Features," *Washington (DC) Herald*, May 5, 1918, 2 (italics mine).

19. Marguerite Eldenburg to actress Florence Lawrence, 24 October 1924, Florence Lawrence Papers, Natural History Museum of Los Angeles County, Seaver Center, Los Angeles.

20. *New York Harlem Home News,* March 23, 1921, no page; and *Bronx Home News,* March 22, 1921, no page.

21. Examples include passage of the 1906 Act for the Preservation of American Antiquities, formation of the United States Forest Service, and legislation to expand the National Parks system and protect native wildlife.

22. Jackson Lears's *Fables of Abundance: A Cultural History of Advertising in America* (New York: Basic Books, 1995) does a remarkable job of tracing how US advertisements captured the passage from a nineteenth-century ethos of natural abundance to a more ambiguous depiction of resource contention during World War I.

23. The cultural phenomenon of having young movie-loving girls contribute to the war effort via unpaid handcraft labor importantly happens at the same time as the Girl Scouts of the United States were being established. Formed in 1912, this girls-only organization trained members between ten and eighteen years old in useful manual labor, including knot-tying, clothes-making, first aid, and sewing. These were called "scout crafts." For more about lessons on patriotism, crafts, charity, and community work taught by the Girl Scouts, see W.J. Hoxie, *How Girls Can Help Their Country* (Bedford, MA: Applewood, 1913), and B.P. Scout, *Scoutcraft* (New York: Gale and Polden, 1910).

24. "The Very Latest Handicraft Fad Is Here!," *Motion Picture Magazine,* July 1917, 58.

25. Tapley picked up her big-sister sobriquet acting at Vitagraph. In addition to a staff position in *Motion Picture Magazine,* she conducted itinerant screenings of the behind-the-scenes documentary *From Script to Screen* (1916). A trade journal suggests that Tapley directed the one-reeler in response to letters from curious fans. Tapley was also one of the first women to tour the country lecturing general audiences on film manufacturing. "Star Tours Country," *Motography,* December 2, 1916, 1232.

26. "Very Latest Handicraft," 58.

27. Lyman Horace Weeks, *A History of Paper-Manufacturing in the United States, 1690–1916* (New York: Lockwood Trade Journal Company, 1916), 319.

28. "Answer Department: To Marcia," *Motion Picture Magazine,* December 1916, 156. The other answer, this time to Mary P., admonishes: "You want more Gallery in the Classic. Alas, alack, paper is so high!" *Motion Picture Magazine,* December 1916, 137.

29. "My Movie Scrap Book," *Day Book* (Chicago), May 7, 1915, 4.

30. Theda Bara, "Why Do People Hate Me and Attack Me," *Tacoma (WA) Times,* April 20, 1916, 1.

31. Harry R. Ravel, "An Appeal for Specialization," *Motography,* January 15, 1916, 123.

32. "Making Films Is a Publishing Business," *Motography,* January 22, 1916, 187.

33. "Beauty and Brains Contest," *Photoplay,* January 1916, 48–49; and "Beauty and Brains Contest," *Photoplay,* February 1916, 46–47.

34. See Buckler, Ott, and Tucker, *Scrapbook in American Life;* Jessica Helfand, *Scrapbooks: An American History* (New Haven, CT: Yale Univ. Press, 2008); and Garvey, *Writing with Scissors.*

35. DeBauche, "Memory Books, the Movies, and Aspiring Vamps."

36. Richard Abel, *Menus for Movieland: Newspapers and the Emergence of American Film Culture 1913–1916* (Berkeley: Univ. of California Press, 2015), 221.

37. "Seen on the Screen by The Film Girl," *Syracuse (NY) Herald,* December 28,1915, 5 (italics mine).

38. Marilyn Frye, "Lesbian Feminism and the Gay Rights Movement: Another View of Male Supremacy, Another Separatism," in *Politics of Reality: Essays in Feminist Theory* (Berkeley, CA: Crossing Press, 1983), 147.

39. Christina Michelon, "Touching Sentiment: The Tactility of Nineteenth-Century Valentines," *Commonplace: The Journal of Early American Life,* 6.2 (2016) (italics mine), accessed August 24, 2020, http://commonplace.online/article/touching-sentiment/.

40. DeCordova, *Picture Personalities,* 140–41.

41. Ibid., 14.

42. Schreiber to Vercoe, December 1914, AMPAS.

43. Tucker, Ott, and Buckler, *Scrapbook in American Life,* 12–13.

44. Betty Ross, Silent Film Actresses Scrapbook, AMPAS.

45. Margaret Harroun, "Picture Book: Scrapbook of Early Hollywood Movie Stars," Bancroft Library, University of California, Berkeley.

46. For more on the history of negative stereotypes associated with female stage performers in turn-of-the-century United States, see Susan E. Glenn, *Female Spectacle: The Theatrical Roots of Modern Feminism* (Cambridge, MA: Harvard Univ. Press, 2000).

47. Lea Stans, "Silent Film Makeup: What Was It Really Like?," *Silent-ology* (blog), February 22, 2016, https://silentology.wordpress.com/2016/02/22/silent-film-makeup-what-was-it-really-like/.

48. Quoted in James Bennett, "Early Movie Make-Up," *Cosmetics and Skin* (blog), October 9, 2018, https://www.cosmeticsandskin.com/cdc/early-movie.php.

49. Thelma Laird Lauer Majors, Scrapbooks of Magazine Pictures of Lillian and Dorothy Gish, Billy Rose Collection, New York Public Library for the Performing Arts.

50. See Joshua Yumibe, "French Film Colorists," in *Women Film Pioneers Project,* ed. Jane Gaines, Radha Vatsal, and Monica Dall'Asta (New York: Center for Digital Research and Scholarship, Columbia Univ. Libraries, 2013);

Federico Pierotti, "Coloring the Figures: Women's Labor in the Early Italian Film Industry," in *Researching Women in Silent Cinema: New Findings and Perspectives,* ed. Monica Dall'Asta, Victoria Duckett, and Lucia Tralli (Bologna, Italy: Studiorum Università di Bologna, 2013), 106–19; and Tom Gunning, Joshua Yumibe, Giovanna Fossati, and Jonathon Rose, eds., *Fantasia of Color in Early Cinema* (Amsterdam, Netherlands: Amsterdam Univ. Press, 2015).

51. DeCordova, *Picture Personalities;* Danae Clark, *Negotiating Hollywood: The Cultural Politics of Actors' Labor* (Minneapolis: Univ. of Minnesota Press, 1995).

52. Author's personal collection.

53. Sourced from "Questions and Answers," *Photoplay,* December 1915, 154.

54. Roland Barthes, *Camera Lucida: Reflections on Photography,* trans. Richard Howard (New York: Hill and Wang, 1980), 27.

55. Jennifer Bean, "Affect: The Alchemy of the Contingent," *Feminist Media Histories* 7.2 (2021): 1–20; 14.

56. Roberta Courtlandt, "Tom Forman, Huntsman and Dog-Fancier," *Motion Picture Magazine,* February 1916, 71; collected in Shefler's scrapbook.

57. Clipped from *Photoplay,* December 1916, 46. For more on the possibilities of queer reception being instantiated by male-male intimacy in silent film, especially in US war dramas, see Shane Brown, *Queer Sexualities in Early Film: Cinema and Male-Male Intimacy* (New York: I.B. Tauris, 2016).

58. Laura Horak, *Girls Will Be Boys: Cross-Dressed Women, Lesbians, and American Cinema* (New Brunswick, NJ: Rutgers Univ. Press, 2016), 47–48.

59. Susan Potter, "Valentino's Lesbianism: Stardom, Spectatorship, and Sexuality in 1920s Hollywood Cinema," *Framework: The Journal of Cinema and Media* 56.2 (2015): 288–89.

60. "John Addision Fulton, '71c," *Michigan Alumnus,* April 11, 1936, 331.

61. *The Motion Picture Blue Book*, May 1914, page unknown.

62. See William J. Mann, *Behind the Screen: How Gays and Lesbians Shaped Hollywood, 1910–1969* (New York: Viking, 2001).

63. Edward A. Lifka, "I'll Think of You," *Motion Picture Magazine,* March 1914, 111.

64. William De Ryee, "Sovereign of the Screen," *Motion Picture Magazine,* May 1916, 120.

65. Christian Metz, "Photography and Fetish," *October* 34 (Autumn, 1985): 81–90; 81.

66. Ibid., 84.

67. The wide streets and architecture also suggest a well-to-do Southern California location.

68. There is also a poetry to the fact of the scene captured in this film strip being that of a galloping horse rider, as if proving the point that a silent-film lover had to turn to photography in order to rein in the cinematic "stream of temporality where nothing can be *kept,* nothing can be stopped." Metz, "Photography and Fetish," 83.

69. Michelon, "Touching Sentiment."

70. Ibid.

71. "Rotogravure," *Photoplay,* July 1920, 61.

72. Potter, "Valentino's Lesbianism," 272.

73. See Miriam Hansen, *Babel and Babylon: Spectatorship in American Silent Film* (Cambridge MA: Harvard Univ. Press, 1991); and Kiki Loveday, "Sister Acts: Victorian Porn, Lesbian Drag, and Queer Reproduction," *Framework: The Journal of Cinema and Media* 60.2 (2019): 201–26.

74. Jackie Stacey, *Star Gazing: Hollywood Cinema and Female Spectatorship* (New York: Routledge, 1994),126.

75. Horak, *Girls Will Be Boys*, 39.

76. Biddy Martin, "Lesbian Identity and Autobiographical Difference[s]," in *Life/Lines: Theorizing Women's Autobiography,* ed. Bella Brodzki and Celeste Schenck (Ithaca, NY: Cornell Univ. Press, 1989), 380–92; 385.

77. Alexis Lothian, "Archival Anarchies: Online Fandom, Subcultural Conservation, and the Transformative Work of Digital Ephemera," *International Journal of Cultural Studies* 16.6 (2012): 541–56; 544.

78. Sara Ahmed, "A Wilfulness Archive," *Theory and Event* 15.3 (2012), muse.jhu.edu/article/484421.

CHAPTER 5

Epigraph: Sylvia Plath, "Poppies in October" [1962], in *Ariel* (New York: Harper Collins, 1999), 20.

1. Helen Edna Davis Papers, Sophia Smith Special Collections, Smith College, Northampton, MA (hereafter SCSC).

2. Born on July 4, 1898, Helen Davis attended the Rhodean School in Johannesburg from 1908 to 1913, followed by the wealthy finishing school Frl. Kollmorgen's Hohere Tochter Schule and the women-only Willard School, both in Berlin. Once WWI broke out, Davis's family seems to have moved from Germany to New York City. From 1914 to 1915, Davis frequented Miss McClintock's School in Boston. In 1915, the seventeen-year-old began her undergraduate studies at Smith College. The constant shuffling between schools symptomizes the turmoil of the times the immigrant girl grew up in.

3. August 27, 1917, Davis Papers, SCSC.

4. Ibid., February 10, 1917.

5. Ibid., August 24, 1917.

6. Ibid., December 19, 1916; August 24, 1917.

7. Ibid., August 24, 1917.

8. Ibid., December 30, 1916; July 18, 1917.

9. In both films and many others, including Fox's *Queen of the Sea* (1918), Kellerman either appears nude—her tall, svelte body strategically covered by masses of hair and nature—or clad in sparse gauzy outfits. The actress's "natural" approach to screen nudeness generated as much polemic as it bolstered her box-office appeal.

10. Julie Inness, *Privacy, Intimacy, and Isolation* (New York: Oxford Univ. Press, 1992), 82.

11. September, no day, 1917, Davis Papers, SCSC.

12. Ibid.

13. "Vassar College: President's Taylor's Report," newspaper clipping, 1912, Dorothy Whitman Scrapbook, Class of 1914, Vassar College Special Collections (hereafter VCSC).

14. Charlotte R. Peet (Smith) Scrapbook, Class of 1914, VCSC.

15. "Abnormal Psychology Exam," Vassar College, January 1918, Marie-Luise Binder Scrapbook, Class of 1918, VCSC.

16. Constance M. Topping Diary, January 14, 1920. Bancroft Library, University of California, Berkeley.

17. Laura Horak, *Girls Will Be Boys: Cross-Dressed Women, Lesbians, and American Cinema* (New Brunswick, NJ: Rutgers Univ. Press, 2016).

18. George M. Beard, *Sexual Neurasthenia,* ed. A. D. Rockwell (New York, 1884), 106.

19. Richard von Krafft-Ebing, *Psychopathia Sexualis*, trans. Charles Gilbert Chaddock (Philadelphia: F. J. Rebman, 1894), 398–99.

20. August Forel, *The Sexual Question: A Scientific, Psychological, Hygienic and Sociological Study*, trans. C. F. Marshal (New York: Rebman, 1908),

21. Havelock Ellis, *Studies in the Psychology of Sex,* vol. 2 (Philadelphia: F. A. Davis, 1905), 250.

22. Arabella Kenealy, *Feminism and Sex-Extinction* (London: T. Fisher Unwin, 1920), 110–11. For more on how, at the turn of the century, the American tomboy rendered visible "a doorway between normal and deviant," see Renée M. Sentilles, *American Tomboys, 1850–1915* (Amherst: Univ. of Massachusetts Press, 2018), 16.

23. See Jack Halberstam, *Female Masculinity* (Durham, NC: Duke Univ. Press, 1998), for a history of female masculinity as embodied by the nineteenth-century "androgyne, the tribade, and the female husband."

24. "Radcliffe Girls Can No Longer Wear Pants," *Boston Herald,* day unknown, 1905, 7, Mabelle Smith Kent Scrapbook, Schlesinger Library, Radcliffe College, Cambridge, MA (hereafter SL).

25. Ibid.

26. The author does note that, at the time, some states legally penalized women for "wearing any but the customary dress and that a lady who takes a fancy to masculine habiliments on an excursion may find it terminate in the station house." Robert De Valcourt, *The Illustrated Book of Manners: A Manual of Good Behavior and Polite Accomplishments* (New York: Lelan, Clay, 1855), 33.

27. Peter Boag, *Re-Dressing America's Frontier Past* (Berkeley: Univ. of California Press, 2012), 47.

28. Ibid., see pages 1–20.

29. "Works as Shop Girl and Urges Suffrage," newspaper unknown, 1905, Ruth Lansing Scrapbook, SL.

30. "Trousers are Barred," 1905, Ruth Lansing Scrapbook, SL.

31. Mabelle Smith Kent Scrapbook, SL.

32. "Memorabilia 1914," Jeanette Miller Scrapbook, Class of 1917, VCSC.

33. Clare Sears, *Arresting Dress: Cross-Dressing, Law, and Fascination in Nineteenth-Century San Francisco* (Durham, NC: Duke Univ. Press, 2015), 133.

34. Madiha Khayatt, *Lesbian Teachers: An Invisible Presence* (New York: SUNY Univ. Press, 1992), 18. Kiki Loveday similarly remarks that early twentieth-century visual culture was saturated with more-or-less explicit images of lesbian sexuality that troubled Victorian notions of female asexuality and pure sisterhood. See "Sister Acts: Victorian Porn, Lesbian Drag, and Queer Reproduction," *Framework: The Journal of Cinema and Media* 60.2 (2019): 201–26.

35. See Sears, *Arresting Dress*.

36. Lisa Duggan, *Sapphic Slashers: Sex, Violence, and American Modernity* (Durham, NC: Duke Univ. Press, 2001).

37. "Women in Men's Attire," *Duluth (MN) Evening Herald*, April 22, 1907, 12.

38. "Girl Dressed as Man," *Evening Statesman* (Walla Walla, WA), January 21, 1910, no page. A close reading of Nell Pickerell's life can be found in Boag, *Re-Dressing the Frontier*.

39. "How Catherine Madden Fell Victim to Strong Drinking & Why Nell Pickerell Will Not Wear Women's Clothing," *Spokesman-Review* (Spokane, WA), October 22, 1911, 2; "Girl Tries to End Her Life: Pearl Waldron Falls in Love with Notorious Nell Pickerell," *Seattle Daily Times*, November 4, 1903, 3; and "Shoots Herself in The Chest: Pretty Young Woman of Seattle Attempts Suicide," *San Francisco Call*, November 5, 1903, no page.

40. "This Girl Is a 'Bad Man' from the Coast," *Day Book* (Chicago), March 27, 1912, 20.

41. See "Girl's Strange Career," *Birmingham (AL) Age-Herald*, January 21, 1908, 4; and "Girl in Man's Clothing Goes A-Wooing Women," *Washington (DC) Times*, February 23, 1908, 7. Most papers attributed Quappe's death to drinking carbolic acid. See "Girl Loved a Girl," *Minneapolis Journal*, December 30, 1901, 3; and "Knew She Was Dying," *Seattle Star*, December 27, 1901, 4. Other conflicting reports suggest Waters died of self-poisoning instead of self-inflicted gunshot wounds. In 1902, the *Daily Alaskan* speculated both girls were one and the same: "the erring daughter of Rev. J.J. Waters," a Portland runaway living a "low career" in Seattle under multiple aliases. "Who Was Dolly Quappe?," January 8, 1902, 1.

42. Sears, *Arresting Dress*, 13 (italics mine).

43. Havelock Ellis, *Studies in the Psychology of Sex*, vol. 1 (Philadelphia: F.A. Davis, 1905), 201.

44. George Chauncey Jr, "From Sexual Inversion to Homosexuality: The Changing Medical Conceptualization of Female 'Deviance,'" in *Passion and Power: Sexuality in History*, ed. Kathy Lee Peiss, Christina Simmons, and Robert A. Padgug (Philadelphia: Temple Univ. Press, 1989),109.

45. Khayatt, *Lesbian Teachers*,18.

46. Jane Gaines, "Costume and Narrative: How Dress Tells the Women's Story," in *Fabrications: Costume and the Female Body*, ed. Jane Gaines and Charlotte Herzog (New York: Routledge, 1990), 180–211; 181.

47. Ibid., 188.

48. "The Movie Gossip-Shop," *Motion Picture Magazine*, January 1918, 168.

49. Roberta Courtland, "The Girl and the Habit," *Motion Picture Magazine*, January 1918, 37.

50. Ibid., 35, 38.

51. Ibid., 36.

52. Mary Pickford, "Daily Talks with Mary Pickford: My New Friend," *The Day* (New London, CT), September 26, 1916, no page. See also "Dressing for the Movies," *Photoplay*, January 1915, 117–20.

53. Lillian Faderman, *Odd Girls and Twilight Lovers: A History of Lesbian Life in Twentieth-Century America* (New York: Columbia Univ. Press, 1991), 57.

54. See Richard deCordova, *Picture Personalities: The Emergence of the Star System in America* (Urbana: Univ. of Illinois Press, 1990).

55. "Correspondence," *San Francisco Dramatic Review,* May 31, 1913, 6.

56. "Correspondence," *San Francisco Dramatic Review,* June 7, 1913, 6. Hilary Hallett argues that demarcations between a stage actress's "gender-bending" performances and an everyday feminine self hark back to the 1830s, when "the first female stars like [Charlotte] Cushman required modern methods of publicity to convey information about their private lives that helped to smooth the flouting of respectability that their melodramatic performances entailed." "Melodrama and the Making of Hollywood," in *Melodrama Unbound: Across History, Media, and National Cultures,* ed. Christine Gledhill and Linda Williams (New York: Columbia Univ. Press, 2018), 115–33; 119.

57. Sears, *Arresting Dress,* 100.

58. Horak, *Girls Will Be Boys,* 194.

59. Sears, *Arresting Dress,* 96.

CHAPTER 6

Epigraph: Benedict Anderson, *Imagined Communities* (London: Verso, [1983] 2006), 202.

1. Edna G. Vercoe Papers, vol. 5, 121; vol. 1, 116; and vol. 5, 102; Margaret Herrick Library, Academy of Motion Picture Arts and Sciences, Los Angeles. Thank you to Kathy Fuller-Seeley for information regarding Cunard and Ford's screen work during this period.

2. Kitty Baker, Norfolk Scrapbook 1916, Jessica Helfand Scrapbook Collection, Beinecke Rare Book and Manuscript Library, Yale University, New Haven, CT.

3. The film starring Winifred Greenwood may be either *Alice of Hudson's Bay* (1915), an American Film Manufacturing's short filmed on location in which Greenwood appears in masculine garb, or American's *Her Brother's Debt* (1915), since promotional ads for the latter film also show Greenwood in menswear.

4. Laura Horak, *Girls Will Be Boys: Cross-Dressed Women, Lesbians, and American Cinema* (New Brunswick, NJ: Rutgers Univ. Press, 2016), 17.

5. Jack Halberstam theorizes that female masculinity—including cross-dressing, boyishness, and butchness—has historically allowed for expressions of same-sex desire and gender play that throw light on the socially constructed nature of gender binarisms. *Female Masculinity* (Durham, NC: Duke Univ. Press, 1998), 2.

6. I am aware that in early silent cinema many leading ladies cross-dressed, including Pickford in *Wilful Peggy* (1910), *Rags* (1915), and *Little Lord Fauntleroy* (1921), among others. When I refer to "girlish" screen personae, I am thus referring to an archetype of virginal and youthful femininity audiences in the 1910s associated with certain picture actresses, regardless of their actual age. See Gaylyn Studlar, *Precocious Charms: Stars Performing Girlhood in Classical Hollywood Cinema* (Berkeley: Univ. of California Press, 2013); and Diana W. Anselmo, "Betwixt and Between, Forever Sixteen: American Silent Cinema and the Emergence of Female Adolescence," *Screen Journal* 58.3 (2017): 251–84.

7. Susan Potter, *Queer Timing: The Emergence of Lesbian Sexuality in Early Cinema* (Urbana-Champaign: Univ. of Illinois Press, 2019), 42.

8. Horak, *Girls Will Be Boys,* 77.

9. "'Girl With the Curl!'—Movie Directors Are Clamoring For More of Her Kind," *Day Book* (Chicago), September 14, 1914, 14.

10. In "Redressing the 'Natural': The Temporary Transvestite Film," Chris Straayer defines "temporary transvestism" as a narratively coherent gender reversal (often presented as a necessary disguise) that puts audiences at ease when seeing a character wearing clothes socially assigned to the opposite sex. *Wide Angle* 14.1 (1992): 36–55.

11. Patricia White argues that during the Hays Code, "homosexual content that was prohibited on-screen [could be] available to audiences through publicity or other intertexts." The cross-dressed clippings fans preserved in their movie scrapbooks support this claim. *Uninvited: Classical Hollywood Cinema and Lesbian Representability* (Indianapolis: Indiana Univ. Press, 1999), xviii.

12. Horak, *Girls Will Be Boys,* 70.

13. Randolph Bartlett, "Shadow Stage," *Photoplay,* November 1917, 127.

14. Edward Weitzel, "Latest Reviews and Comments," *Moving Picture World,* August 28, 1920, 1212.

15. Horak, *Girls Will be Boys,* 32.

16. Examples include *Are You a Crook?* (1913), *Peppina* (1916), *The Ragged Princess* (1917), *Little Brother* (1917), and *The Little Wanderer* (1920).

17. Examples of what are often comedies or lighthearted romances include *The Danger Girl* (1916) and *The Boy-Girl* (1917).

18. Jay Cole, "'Twixt Josephine and Joe," *Photoplay,* August 1918, 42.

19. Arabella Kenealy, *Feminism and Sex-Extinction* (London: T. Fisher Unwin, 1920), 110.

20. Halberstam, *Female Masculinity,* 6. For a discussion on Hollywood's tomboy figure, see "Looking Butch: A Rough Guide to Butches on Film," in *Female Masculinity,* 175–230; Kristen Hatch, "Little Butches: Tomboys in Hollywood Film," in *Mediated Girlhoods: New Explorations of Girls' Media Culture,* ed. Mary Celeste Kearney (New York: Peter Lang, 2011), 75–92; and Renée M. Sentilles, *American Tomboys, 1850–1915* (Amherst: Univ. of Massachusetts Press, 2018).

21. Halberstam, *Female Masculinity,* 6.

22. Julian Johnson, "The Shadow Stage," *Photoplay,* May 1917, 618.

23. Horak, *Girls Will Be Boys,* 58.

24. Mary Florence Stott, "Movie Book," 1917; author's personal collection.

25. See Matthew Frye Jacobson, *Whiteness of a Different Color: European Immigrants and the Alchemy of Race* (Cambridge, MA: Harvard Univ. Press, 1998); and Jacqueline Battalora, *Birth of a White Nation: The Invention of White People and Its Relevance Today* (New York: Routledge, 2021). See also Siobhan B. Somerville, *Queering the Color Line: Race and the Invention of Homosexuality in American Culture* (Durham, NC: Duke Univ. Press, 2000).

26. The image is clipped from Dorothy Donnell, "Poor Little Peppina," *Motion Picture Magazine,* 1916, 65.

27. Kristen Hatch, *Shirley Temple and the Performance of Girlhood* (New Brunswick, NJ: Rutgers Univ. Press, 2015), 40.

28. Deborah Gould, "On Affect and Protest," in *Political Emotions: New Agendas in Communication*, ed. Janet Staiger, Ann Cvetkovich, and Ann Reynolds (New York: Routledge, 2010), 18–44; 26.

29. Baker's term, inked on a film clipping.

30. Julian Johnson, "Mary Pickford: Herself and Her Career" *Photoplay*, January 1916, 43.

31. William Lee Howard, "Effeminate Men and Masculine Women," *New York Medical Journal*, May 5, 1900, 687.

32. Randolph Bartlett, "Shadow Stage," *Photoplay*, November 1917, 127.

33. Arthur W. Courtney, "The Amazons," *Moving Picture World*, August 18, 1917, 1084.

34. "In Movieland," *Chicago Daily Tribune*, November 15, 1914, no page (italics mine).

35. José Esteban Muñoz, "Ephemera as Evidence: Introductory Notes to Queer Acts," *Women and Performance: A Journal of Feminist Theory* 8.2 (1996): 5–16; 10.

36. Susan A. Glenn, *Female Spectacle: The Theatrical Roots of Modern Feminism* (Cambridge, MA: Harvard Univ. Press, 2000).

37. Sharon Marcus, "The Theatrical Scrapbook," *Theatre Survey* 54.2 (2013): 283–307; 287.

38. Margaret Harroun, "Picture Book: Scrapbook of Early Hollywood Movie Stars," Bancroft Library, University of California, Berkeley (BL).

39. Roberta Courtlandt, "Feminine Fads and Fancies," *Motion Picture Magazine*, January 1917, 40.

40. *The Amazons*' multimediated success amplified its signifiers of queerness. Not only did the narrative supply an eroticized gender masquerade, but its title also offered a brazen double-entendre. Since the late 1800s, popular and scientific writers had deployed the term "Amazon" as synonymous with athletic, cross-dressed, independent, professional, vindicative, threatening, and/or homosexual women. Examples of the term being widely associated with deviant femininity are found not just in press coverage sensationalizing gender-nonconforming women—they also permeate film parlance. For instance, in 1913, *Moving Picture World* highlighted "a Militant Suffragette" and "a Business Woman" as "representatives of the 'Amazon' type." "Mrs. Marston is a Regular Lamb," *Moving Picture World*, July 5, 1913, 56.

41. Vercoe Papers, vol. 1, July 22, 1914, 116.

42. *The Deerfield*, no. 5 (1917): 15; Highland Park History, Illinois Digital Archives, accessed March 20, 2021, http://www.idaillinois.org/digital/collection/highland003/id/38652.

43. Patricia White remarks that male appellations played a central role in the lesbian modes of engagement cultivated by classical film icons like Greta Garbo and Marlene Dietrich. "Black and White: Mercedes de Acosta's Glorious Enthusiasms," in *Reclaiming the Archive: Feminism and Film History*, ed. Vicki Callahan (Detroit: Wayne State Univ. Press, 2010), 231–57.

44. Many film scholars have theorized the feminist possibilities of the early serial queen. See, for instance, Shelley Stamp, *Movie-Struck Girls: Women and Motion Picture Culture after the Nickelodeon* (Princeton, NJ: Princeton Univ.

Press, 2000); Ben Singer, *Melodrama and Modernity: Early Sensational Cinema and its Contexts* (New York: Columbia Univ. Press, 2001); Jennifer Bean, "Technologies of Early Stardom and the Extraordinary Body," *Camera Obscura* 16.3 (2001): 8–57; and Mark Garrett Cooper, "Pearl White and Grace Cunard: The Serial Queen's Volatile Present," in *Flickers of Desire: Movie Stars of the 1910s,* ed. Jennifer Bean (New Brunswick, NJ: Rutgers Univ. Press, 2011), 174–95.

45. Vercoe Papers, vol. 2, September 2, 1914, 53. Both of White's images were sourced from Mabel Condon, "The Real Perils of Pauline," *Photoplay,* October 1914, 63.

46. Charles Goddard, *The Perils of Pauline: A Motion Picture Novel* (New York: Hearst's International Library, 1915), no page.

47. Vercoe Papers, vol. 4, 89; vol. 1, 53.

48. Stamp, *Movie-Struck Girls,*126.

49. "The Movie Gossip-Shop," *Motion Picture Magazine,* January 1918, 168.

50. L. Pierce Clark, *A Critical Digest of Some of the Newer Work Upon Homosexuality in Man and Woman,* reprinted from *State Hospital Bulletin for November 1914* (Utica, NY: State Hospital Press, 1914).

51. Kenealy, *Feminism,* 110–11.

52. Nan Enstad, *Ladies of Labor, Girls of Adventure: Working Women, Popular Culture, and Labor Politics at the Turn of the Twentieth Century* (New York: Columbia Univ. Press, 1999), 193.

53. Vercoe Papers, vol. 2, 53.

54. Condon, "The Real Perils of Pauline," 61–65.

55. Roberta Courtlandt, "Feminine Fancies & Fads," *Motion Picture Magazine,* January 1917, 39–40.

56. Herbert Ladd Towle, "The Woman at the Wheel," *Scribner's Magazine,* February 1915, 214.

57. Jennifer Parchesky, "Women in the Driver's Seat: The Auto-Erotics of Early Women's Films," *Film History* 18.2 (2006): 174–84; 174.

58. Audre Lorde, "Uses of the Erotic: The Erotic as Power," in *Sister Outsider: Essays and Speeches* (Berkeley, CA: Crossing Press, 1984), 41–48; 41. Parchesky, "Women in the Driver's Seat," 175 (italics mine).

59. Parchesky, "Women in the Driver's Seat," 175.

60. Jesse Lowe Smith, 1923 Diary, Highland Park Library, IL, no page.

61. Ibid.

62. Pearl White, *Just Me* (New York: George H. Doran, 1919), 50.

63. Romaine Field to Edna Vercoe, October 8, 1914, Vercoe Papers, vol. 1, correspondence.

64. *The Deerfield,* no. 5 (1917): 26.

65. Lauren Berlant, *The Female Complaint: The Unfinished Business of Sentimentality in American Culture* (Durham, NC: Duke Univ. Press, 2008), 19.

66. Ibid., 20.

67. In an article in *JCMS,* I survey the roles queer negativity played in female film fandom of the silent era. See Diana W. Anselmo "Picture Hurt: Anti-Heteronormative Female Reception in Early Hollywood," *JCMS: Journal of Cinema and Media Studies* 62.1 (Fall 2022): 7–35.

68. See, for example, Dorothy C. Putnam and Lois Mercer Papers 1914–1988, ONE National Gay and Lesbian Archives, USC Libraries, University of Southern California, Los Angeles; Regina Soreson, 1910s, Sacred Heart Photograph Collection, Minnesota Historical Society, Saint Paul; Mabelle Smith Kent, Scrapbook, Class 1904, Schlesinger Library on the History of Women in America. Radcliffe Institute, Cambridge, MA (SL); Mary Etta Turner Scrapbook 1902–1920, SL; Gertrude Barry, Memory Book, Class 1910, Smith College Special Collections. Smith College, Northampton, MA (SCSC); Emma D. Roth, Memory Book, Class 1918, SCSC; Doris Kendrick, Memory Book, Class 1918, SCSC; and Mariam Hill, Memory Book, Class 1919, SCSC (most images from 1917–18). These are only a few examples of personal records produced by working-class, middle-class, and well-to-do girls from rural and urban areas during the 1910s.

69. Beverly Gordon, *The Saturated World: Aesthetic Meaning, Intimate Objects, Women's Lives, 1890–1940* (Knoxville: Univ. of Tennessee Press, 2006), 109.

70. Henrietta Atwater, Memory Book, Class of 1919, SCSC.

71. Marian S. Hill, Scrapbook, Class of 1920, SCSC.

72. Marjorie R. Hopper, Memory Book, Class of 1919, SCSC.

73. See the "Who are They?" column in *The Delineator* from 1916 to 1918; "Paper Cut-Outs of Popular Players for the Players," *Motion Picture Magazine*, 1917; and "Movy-Dolls," *Photoplay*, 1919.

74. Gordon, *Saturated World*, 110.

75. See White, "Black and White," 231–57.

76. Mary Pickford, "Daily Chats with Mary Pickford: To Be or Not to Be a Vampire," *The Day* (New London, CT), May 16, 1916, no page.

77. Elsie [no last name], November 26, 1918, Syracuse, New York. Alice McBride Scrapbook, Vassar College Archives and Special Collections. Vassar College, Poughkeepsie, NY .

78. Constance M. Topping, Diaries 1913–1935, BL.

79. For more on girls' copying female stars, see Leslie Midkiff DeBauche, "Memory Books, the Movies, and Aspiring Vamps," *Observation on Film Art* (blog), February 8, 2015, http://www.davidbordwell.net/blog/2015/02/08/memory-books-the-movies-and-aspiring-vamps/; and Diana W. Anselmo, "Made in Movieland: Imitation, Agency, and Girl Movie Fandom in the 1910s," *Camera Obscura: Feminism, Culture and Media Studies* 32.1 (2017): 129–65.

80. Gordon, *Saturated World*, 116.

81. Ibid., 119.

82. Marilyn Frye, "Lesbian Feminism and the Gay Rights Movement: Another View of Male Supremacy, Another Separatism," in *Politics of Reality: Essays in Feminist Theory* (Berkeley, CA: Crossing Press, 1983), 130.

83. Jean Fraser and Tessa Boffin, "Tantalizing Glimpses of Stolen Glances: Lesbians Take Photographs," *Feminist Review* 38 (Summer 1991): 23.

84. Berlant, *Female Complaint*, 4.

85. "What Theatre Men Are Doing," *Motography*, August 26, 1916, 477; "What Theatre Men Are Doing," *Motography*, October 21, 1916, 911.

86. "How to Advertise," *Exhibitors Herald and Motography,* May 1919, 49–50.

87. Constance M. Topping, Diaries and Scrapbooks, 1913–1935, BL; and Helen E. Davis, Diaries 1914–1928, New-York Historical Society, New York City. Notice of World's Fair raised by M.M. Chandler. For insightful readings of the sexist and racist ways female bodies were instrumentalized in turn-of-the-century Western art and at World Fairs, see Fatimah Tobing Roby, *How Do We Look?: Resisting Visual Biopolitics* (Durham, NC: Duke Univ. Press, 2022); and T. J. Boisseau and Abigail M. Markwyn, eds., *Gendering the Fair: Histories of Women and Gender at World's Fairs* (Champaign: Univ. of Illinois Press, 2010).

88. Lloyd Robinson, "Milady of the Film and Trousers," *The Photo-Play Journal,* September 1917, 51.

EPILOGUE

Epigraph: "The Younger Generation Speaks," *Photoplay,* March 1927, 114.

1. See Marsha Orgeron, "Making It in Hollywood: Clara Bow, Fandom, and Consumer Culture," *Cinema Journal* 42.4 (2003): 76–97.

2. "Three Little Girls," *Photoplay,* June 1926, 86.

3. Heidi Kenaga, "Making the 'Studio Girl': The Hollywood Studio Club and Industry Regulation of Female Labour," *Film History* 18.2 (2006): 129–39; 130.

4. "Her Ears Hear Women's Woes," *Los Angeles Times,* October 4, 1914, 10. For more on the links between the City Mother's Bureau and early Hollywood, see Denise McKenna, "The Photoplay or the Pickaxe: Extras, Gender and Labour in Early Hollywood," *Film History: An International Journal* 23.1 (2011): 5–19.

5. "Here are the Winners," *Photoplay,* January 1927, 34.

6. "Get Your Scissors Out," *Photoplay,* April 1927, 58.

7. Kelly Schrum produces a helpful overview of Blue's personal movie fan collection. See *Some Wore Bobby Sox: The Emergence of Teenage Girls' Culture, 1920–1945* (New York: Palgrave, 2004).

8. Dorothy Blum's scrapbooks, On the Screen—Motion Picture Memories, are housed in the Library of Congress Moving Image Research Center, boxes A-0188 to A-0191, Washington, DC. The Library of Congress holds nineteen of the original twenty-six scrapbooks, in addition to Blum's nine star-specific movie albums. Audrey Chamberlin's and Helen Nagel's movie scrapbooks are held at the Margaret Herrick Library in Los Angeles, CA; Yvonne Blue Skinner's at the Schlesinger Library in Cambridge, MA; and Eleanor Neunthal's in the author's collection.

9. Dorothy Blum Scrapbook, On the Screen—Motion Picture Memories, Box I, no day, January 1927, Library of Congress Moving Image Research Center, Washington, DC. All of Blum's citations hereafter belong to this collection.

10. Blum, Book II, March 30, 1927; and March 2, 1927. For more on the writing style cultivated by pioneer women film critics, see Richard Abel, ed., *Movie Mavens: US Newspaper Women Take On the Movies, 1914–1923* (Champaign: Univ. of Illinois Press, 2021).

11. Frances Clark, "Their Funniest Fan Letters," *Photoplay,* April 1927, 63.

12. Ibid.

13. Blum, Book I, January 30, 1927.

14. Ibid., Book XI, November 28, 1927.

15. Ibid, Book III, January 12, 1928.

16. Ibid., Book XVI, September 6, 1928.

17. Ibid., December 30, 1927.

18. See Diana W. Anselmo, "Picture Hurt: Anti-Heteronormative Female Reception in Early Hollywood," *JCMS: Journal of Cinema and Media Studies* 62.1 (Fall 2022): 7–35.

19. See Diana W. Anselmo, "The 'Girl Suicide Epidemic' of the 1910s: Pain and Prejudice in US Newspapers," *Journal of Women's History* 34.3 (Fall 2022): 34–58.

20. Sara Ahmed, *The Cultural Politics of Emotion* (New York: Routledge, 2004), 155.

21. In addition to Ahmed's scholarship, see Ann Cvetkovich, *An Archive of Feelings: Trauma, Sexuality, and Lesbian Public Cultures* (Durham, NC: Duke Univ. Press, 2003); Lee Edelman, *No Future: Queer Theory and the Death Drive* (Durham, NC: Duke Univ. Press, 2004); Heather Love, *Feeling Backward: Loss and the Politics of Queer History* (Cambridge, MA: Harvard Univ. Press, 2009); Lauren Berlant, *The Female Complaint: The Unfinished Business of Sentimentality in American Culture* (Durham, NC: Duke Univ. Press, 2008) and *Cruel Optimism* (Durham, NC: Duke Univ. Press, 2011); J. Halberstam, *The Queer Art of Failure* (Durham, NC: Duke Univ. Press, 2011); and Jane Ward, *The Tragedy of Heterosexuality* (New York: New York Univ. Press, 2020).

22. Melissa Gregg, "Adultery Technologies," in *Identity Technologies: Constructing the Self Online,* ed. Anna Poletti and Julie Rak (Milwaukee: Univ. of Wisconsin Press, 2013), 99–111.

23. Henry Jenkins, *Convergence Culture: Where Old and New Media Collide* (New York: New York Univ. Press, 2006), 23.

Illustration Credits

1. Courtesy of Beinecke Rare Book and Manuscript Library, Yale University.
2. Courtesy of Beinecke Rare Book and Manuscript Library, Yale University.
3. Courtesy of Sidney Stevens.
4. Seaver Center for Western History Research, Los Angeles County Museum of Natural History.
5. *Photoplay,* November 1915.
6. *Photoplay,* 1919.
7. Seaver Center for Western History Research, Los Angeles County Museum of Natural History.
8. Seaver Center for Western History Research, Los Angeles County Museum of Natural History.
10. *Photoplay,* January 1916.
11. Courtesy of Margaret Herrick Library, Los Angeles.
12. Author's personal collection.
13. Author's personal collection.
14. Author's personal collection.
15. Author's personal collection.
16. Author's personal collection.
17. Author's personal collection.
18. Courtesy of Smith College Special Collections.
19. *Tacoma Times,* April 8, 1912.
20. Author's personal collection.
21. Courtesy of Beinecke Rare Book and Manuscript Library, Yale University.
22. Courtesy of Beinecke Rare Book and Manuscript Library, Yale University.

23. Courtesy of Margaret Herrick Library, Los Angeles.
24. Courtesy of Margaret Herrick Library, Los Angeles.
25. Courtesy of Margaret Herrick Library, Los Angeles.
26. Courtesy of Highland Park Public Library.
27. Courtesy of Smith College Special Collections.
28. Courtesy of Smith College Special Collections.
29. Courtesy of Beinecke Rare Book and Manuscript Library, Yale University.
30. Published in *Motography,* August 26, 1916, and October 21, 1916.

Index